TV SNAPSHOTS

TV SNAPSHOTS

AN ARCHIVE OF EVERYDAY LIFE

LYNN SPIGEL

DUKE UNIVERSITY PRESS   Durham and London   2022

Printed in the United States of America on acid-free paper ∞
Designed by Aimee C. Harrison
Typeset in Minion Pro by Copperline Book Services

Library of Congress Cataloging-in-Publication Data
Names: Spigel, Lynn, author.
Title: TV snapshots : an archive of everyday life / Lynn Spigel.
Description: Durham : Duke University Press, 2022. |
Includes bibliographical references and index.
Identifiers: LCCN 2021037395 (print)
LCCN 2021037396 (ebook)
ISBN 9781478015642 (hardcover)
ISBN 9781478018285 (paperback)
ISBN 9781478022893 (ebook)
Subjects: LCSH: Television—Social aspects—United States. |
Photography—Social aspects—United States. |
Television viewers—United States—Attitudes. | Popular
culture—United States—History—20th century. | BISAC:
PERFORMING ARTS / Television / History & Criticism
Classification: LCC PN1992.6.S6627 2022 (print) |
LCC PN1992.6 (ebook) | DDC 302.23/45—dc23/eng/20211118
LC record available at https://lccn.loc.gov/2021037395
LC ebook record available at https://lccn.loc.gov/2021037396

Cover art: Photograph circa 1962. From the author's collection.

FOR JEFF

CONTENTS

ACKNOWLEDGMENTS

I've been collecting TV snapshots for almost a decade, and I'm deeply grateful to those who supported me along the way. I especially want to thank Ken Wissoker, whose editorial wisdom and enthusiasm have been immeasurably important.

My initial research began as part of my ongoing project on media homes supported by a fellowship from the John Simon Guggenheim Memorial Foundation. I'm greatly indebted to that generosity.

Numerous people contributed to this book by extending invitations to their universities or conferences. Thank you to the Internationales Kolleg für Kulturtechnikforschung und Medienphilosophie, Bauhaus University, Weimar, Germany, and Professor Lorenz Engell, who supported me with a residential fellowship. Thank you as well to Jan Olson, Angela Koch, Helen Wheatley, Rachel Moseley, Lisa Parks, Janet Wasko, Matthew Bernstein, Randall Halle, Keith Eggener, Sonja de Leeuw, Timothy Havens, Kembrew McLeod, Loren P. Q. Baybrook, Gal Nadler, Ariel Avissar, Itay Harlap, Helen Thornham, David Hesmondhalgh, Patrick Jagoda, Peter McDonald, Judith Keilbach, William Uricchio, Sara Hall, Yeidy Rivero, and Dan Morgan. The opportunity these colleagues gave me to present my work in earlier stages of development was invaluable.

Many thanks to colleagues at Northwestern University who took an interest in this book or helped in various ways: Eric Patrick, Hamid Naficy,

Ariel Rogers, Scott Curtis, Neil Kanwar Harish Verma, the late Chuck Kleinhans, and especially Jacob Smith, who read several chapters and offered great advice. Thank you to Dean E. Patrick Johnson and Associate Dean Bonnie Martin-Harris for their support. For assistance with research, thank you to Hannah Spaulding, Karly-Lynne Scott, Madison Brown, Julia Peres Guimaraes, and Myrna Moretti.

I'm especially grateful to friends, colleagues, and family who sent me their TV snapshots or related visual materials: Marcia Untracht, Margie Solovay, Elizabeth Friedman, Tania Modleski, Angelo Restivo, Kathleen McHugh, Darrell Newton, Marsha Cassidy, Pamela Wojcik, Quinlan Miller, Mark Lynn Anderson, Jon Inge Faldalen, Jedd Hakimi, Yiyang Hou, Yael Levy, and Sébastien Girard. For various contributions, thank you to the late Jane Feuer and to Fred Turner and Dana Polan (who each generously read the manuscript), William Boddy, Matt Wolf, Allyson Nadia Field, Charlotte Brunsdon, Thomas Waugh, and James Toftness.

This book has benefited from the expertise and generosity of archivists and librarians. Thanks to Corinne Granof at Northwestern's Block Museum; the Kinsey Institute for Research in Sex, Gender, and Reproduction; Mark Quigley at the UCLA Film and Television Archive; the Eastman Kodak Museum; Ryerson University's Special Collection Library; the Hagley Museum and Library; and the Paley Center for Media. Several private collectors, galleries, and photographers were very generous with their materials and time. Thank you to Peter and Yael Cohen for inviting me to browse through their amazing snapshot collection; to David Chapman, who offered advice and supplied examples from his collections; and to the Grapefruit Gallery and Fraenkel Gallery for their assistance. Thank you to the photographers, artists, curators, and dealers on Flickr and eBay who provided their work and assistance: John Atherton, Darko Photography, Kelly McCarthy, Chrissie White, Chip York, Riddim Ryder, John Gonzales, Jordan Smith, and Stacey Waldman. I am also grateful to Robert Barnes for his generous legal advice with copyright law.

Jeffrey Sconce has supported this book in so many ways. In addition to his intellectual contributions, I especially appreciate his thrifting talents and his love of found things. Toward the end of this project, he was still jazzed enough to sort through thrift bins and give me some snapshots for Christmas. His continued faith in this book was really the best gift I could have received.

Most of all, thanks to the many people who posed for, shot, and saved these snapshots.

INTRODUCTION

COMPANION TECHNOLOGIES

Back in the 1980s, when I first started writing about television, I came across a photo of myself as a little girl posing in front of my TV set. Standing in my red, white, and blue party dress, attempting to curtsy, I was the subject of a snapshot that curiously depicted TV not as a mass-entertainment medium but as a backdrop for a social performance in an intimate family scene (see figure I.1). Struck by the snapshot, I wondered if there were others like it. But despite periodic searches at flea markets and thrift stores over the past thirty years, I could never find examples. My luck suddenly changed in the spring of 2011, when I discovered a proliferating set of similar TV snapshots. I found them in vintage stores and especially on eBay, blogs, and share sites like Pinterest and Flickr. And even while my own photo continues to be meaningful to me, I realize, too, that the snapshots have larger historical significance.

FIGURE I.1 Snapshot of author, circa 1963.

This book explores historical snapshots of people posing at home with television sets (primarily photographs taken in the 1950s through the early 1970s). Based on more than five thousand snapshots, the book examines a prevalent but virtually overlooked photographic practice that took place at a time when television secured its role as the dominant medium in US life and culture. During these years, people used snapshot cameras to take pictures of their TV sets, and they photographed themselves posing in front of TV sets on myriad occasions. Snapshots provide clues into the ways people arranged rooms for television and how they incorporated it into the daily rhythms of work and play. In this respect, TV snapshots provide a new sort of evidence for histories of media and everyday life. Cultural histories of media innovation typically use corporate records, government documents, trade journals, and related sources that shed light on technical design and industry practices. Historians also analyze promotional rhetoric (for example, at world fairs or in advertising), and they explore popular discourses and texts (movies, novels, short stories, jokes, or magazine articles about new or imagined media). A less typical but important strain of historical research uses methods of oral history to understand people's memories of media and (through the circuit of memory) tracks clues to the media past.[1] Building on this scholarship, but also rethinking its archival parameters, TV Snapshots uses what I call an "archive of everyday life"—my collection of images made by everyday people with ordinary snapshot cameras.

To be sure, snapshots are not a transparent window into the past. They are textual forms and highly conventionalized modes of representation. At first glance, they often look exactly alike, particularly if you or your loved ones are not in the photo. Snapshot cameras (especially the low-end cameras most people used) had a limited repertoire of image-making possibilities so that the film stock, framing, focus, lighting, distance, and even the development process for images were standardized before anyone shot a picture. Camera manuals recommended the sorts of pictures one would take (birthday parties, weddings, proms, new babies), and even if people did not always read or follow instructions, they usually adhered to a set of informal rules that were part of the social conventions of picture taking. Yet, despite their generic nature, snapshots provide an alternative framework through which to account for television and everyday life. They offer ways to think about how media consumers (as opposed to corporations or inventors) visualized and imagined their own relations to TV. Moreover, *snapping* pictures was a social and cultural practice in its own right. Therefore, this book examines TV snapshots as an activity, a hobby art, an expressive medium, and something people *did* with TV other than watch it.

TV Snapshots is in many ways a call back to my first book, *Make Room for TV*, which examined TV's arrival in the 1950s in the context of suburban domesticity.[2] That book explored how advertisements, women's home magazines, films, and other mass media depicted, promoted, and debated TV's effects on family life, and it demonstrated how television networks appealed to housewives and family viewers with programs that meshed with the rhythms of daily routines. TV Snapshots presents an alternate view from the images of television in mass-market magazines and ads for TV sets in the postwar period. While 1950s home magazines and advertisements typically depicted TV in rooms that spoke to prevailing middle-class decorative ideals, the snapshots show a much broader range of tastes and sensibilities. Moreover, as opposed to the focus on middle-class whiteness in ads for TV sets and in network programs, snapshots present a range of class, ethnic, and racial identities. TV snapshots also appeared in numerous national contexts. I have found examples from the Soviet Union, Sweden, Hungary, France, Israel, England, Canada, Argentina, China, Belgium, Germany, Bulgaria, Egypt, and other places around the globe.

TV snapshots call attention to the ways in which people used TV for purposes unintended by the television industry. While ads for television sets usually showed families circled around it (figure I.2), glued to the images on-screen, snapshots rarely show people watching TV. Instead, when pictured in snapshots, TV is typically a prop or backdrop for the presentation of self, family, and gender (figure I.3). People used cameras to make personally meaningful images and artistic renderings in which television played a central role. In addition to family portraits, there are TV trick shots, still lifes, glamour poses, and even TV pinups and nudes. Way before the advent of home video, people took "screenshots" off TV, documenting, but also interpreting, the images transmitted on television through their own camera lens.

Like contemporary selfies, TV snapshots were a quotidian form of self-display, a popular pastime, a mode of communication, and a way to craft images through mass-market media devices. Unlike selfies, however, TV snapshots were an analog mode of combining two devices—the camera and the TV set—in ways not predicted or even imagined by the industries that sold them. While histories of media technologies typically focus on one medium, in this book, I argue that we should also consider how people use media

technologies in connection with each other. This pertains not just to media devices that the industry markets as *component* parts (for example, the DVR is a component meant to be wired to a TV set). People also pair technologies on their own. In the postwar decades, people used the TV set and snapshot camera as *companion technologies*. As more and more people installed TVs in their homes, they also used snapshot cameras to picture themselves with the new medium. Even as TV became routine (by 1960, roughly 90 percent of US households had one or more sets), people continued to pose with television and use it as a subject of photos.

TV Snapshots tracks this parallel and intertwined history of media devices. The images I explore in this book were the product of the convergence between the two major domestic visual technologies in midcentury America. Together, TV and snapshot cameras afforded people opportunities to form a unique cultural practice. Armed with snapshot cameras, people reenvisioned the dominant (industry-prescribed) spectator uses of television and made themselves the stars of their own TV scenes.

KODAK FAMILIES

This book is primarily concerned with photographs of television rather than the history or theory of family photography. That said, as a photographic type, the family snapshot has a history of its own, and it has been the subject

FIGURE I.2 (*opposite*) Advertisement for RCA television, circa 1949.

FIGURE I.3 (*left*) Family snapshot, circa 1949–55.

of numerous theoretical explorations. By the time of television, snapshots were a major industry and cultural practice that engaged people around the globe. According to a Bell and Howell report on the leisure market, by 1959, US households were spending almost $300 million per year on photography compared to $313 million on concerts, opera, and theater combined. One year later, another Bell and Howell study claimed that photography was the most popular hobby in America.[3] By far, Kodak was the reigning corporate brand, and therefore not surprisingly, most TV snapshots in my collection were taken with Kodak cameras and developed as Kodak prints.

The Eastman Kodak Company marketed its first snapshot camera in 1888. One year later it adopted the slogan, "You Push the Button, We Do the Rest," a catchphrase that captured the minimal amount of technical skill the device required and the maximum amount of pleasure it promised. As Nancy West explains in her history of Kodak's marketing campaigns, Kodak's appeal to women was especially important to the company's rise and sustained success. In 1893, Kodak introduced its fashionable Kodak Girl, who appeared in advertisements and in women's magazines like *Ladies' Home Journal*. In her early incarnation, the Kodak Girl resonated with "new woman" discourses of leisure and mobility; she was often pictured with a camera around her neck or snapping pictures of outdoor scenes. In the 1930s and especially during World War II, Kodak still targeted female consumers, but its ads focused mainly on sentimental family iconography, promising women that snapshots would strengthen family ties and create instant memories in material form.[4] In the 1950s, in the context of the baby boom and the postwar emphasis on domesticity, Kodak ads often showed women as camera operators eagerly snapping images of children, pets, and household scenes. Nevertheless, in most TV snapshots I have found, women and children are the subject of the photo, and it therefore seems reasonable to assume that fathers often operated the cameras. Still, it's likely that women preserved the snapshots. Throughout the twentieth century, Kodak told women to "Make Kodak your family historian" and promoted the family album as a woman's concern, showing them how to create exciting books to share with family and friends.[5]

Family snapshots present idealized pictures of how people wish it were or how they want to be regarded and remembered. Posers typically smile and look happy, and they perform socially sanctioned gender roles as family members. In his 1965 book *Photography: A Middlebrow Art* (the first sustained sociological study of the form), Pierre Bourdieu argued that snapshots are foremost a "ritual domestic cult" that "expresses the celebratory sense which the [family] group gives to itself." Snapshots don't just represent the family; as a practice, taking pictures functions as a means "of reinforcing the integration of the family group by reasserting the sense that it has both of itself and of its unity."[6]

Like family snapshots in general, TV snapshots often reify the family as an ideological unit by showing people who look happy, and they often take place on ritual occasions. They employ what Richard Chalfen calls "home-mode" aesthetics, "a pattern of interpersonal and small group communication centered around the home."[7] Although I've found candid shots featuring TV sets, as Chalfen argues of snapshots in general, most TV snapshots are deliberately staged.[8] In the contemporary context of digital cameras, it's easy to forget that most analog cameras came with film rolls (or by 1963, Kodak's Instamatic cartridges) that took a finite number of pictures. The price of film and the fact that camera operators could run out of it meant that people often calculated shot choices without the luxury of digital deletion. Although there are many "bad" snapshots (blurry, crooked, overexposed), and while it's difficult to ascribe personal intentions, the general goal of getting things picture perfect was at least an aspiration for many families at the time. Yet, despite snapshots' veneer of family bliss, they are more than just glorified images of an idealized past.

Writing against the sociological view of photography as a means of family integration—or at least seeing that view as reductive—in *Camera Lucida* (1981), Roland Barthes calls attention to the textual and psychical dimensions of photographs and insists on their performative dimension (he speaks of the theatricality of the pose).[9] Rather than Kodak's version of sentimental nostalgia, Barthes considers the photograph's relation to melancholy, mourning, trauma, and the passing of time. In his oft-cited analysis of his mother's *Winter Garden* photo, Barthes recounts his search for a photograph that captures her essence, but the search also leads to his sense of his own ephemerality and impending death. The photograph records the "that-has-been" of the image.[10] It marks a place and moment in time. It assures us that this place and moment occurred, but in so doing, the photograph also records that which will not be again.

Capturing this doubleness (the positive registration of life in the past, and yet a sense of loss and negation), Barthes formulates the twin and related concepts of the *studium* and *punctum*. Derived from the Latin (a language that Barthes feels approximates his meaning more than any term in French), the *studium* refers to the habits of life presented in an image that can be easily recognized by other people (at least those familiar with the culture) and is therefore "ultimately always coded."[11] While the studium is present in all photos, only some elicit the *punctum*, that aspect of the image "which will disturb the studium," that "shoots out like an arrow and pierces me." The punctum "pricks me (but also bruises me, is poignant to me)," and it is often created through unintended, even "accidental" details in the frame.[12] In this regard, photographs are not just records of the past or emblems of family integration; they also belie the wounds of affective response. Although Barthes speaks of photography in general (using art photography, personal photos, portraits, and photojournalism as examples), his framework has become central to scholarship on family photography, and I refer to his concepts throughout this book.

As part of their affective range and textual complexity, family photos orchestrate identity and identification regarding sexuality, race, gender, and class. Feminist historians and critics such as Jo Spence, Patricia Holland, Annette Kuhn, and Marianne Hirsch consider how family photographs, and historical portraits of women and girls in particular, express reigning ideologies and sentimental notions of middle-class heterosexual white domesticity, and at times evoke family and sexual trauma.[13] Nevertheless, these and other feminist scholars also provide ways of thinking about family photos in relation to role playing and (following Judith Butler) conceptualize gender and sexuality as performances (as opposed to essential or natural forms of embodiment).[14] As with family snapshots more generally, TV snapshots reveal the modes of gender embodiment and pretense involved in midcentury family life, and in some cases people strike poses that appear self-consciously to play with (and perhaps defy) normative gender roles. Observing this "gender trouble" in photos, Elspeth Brown and Sara Davidmann explore the act of "queering the trans* family album." This is in part accomplished by LGBTQ art photographers. But Brown and Davidmann also consider how the ordinary family album might be reclaimed for affective memories and affiliations among LGBTQ publics, and for radical histories and present-day uses.[15] More generally, as artists, historians, and cultural theorists have increasingly come to view vernacular photography as worthy of study, scholarship and museum/gallery exhibitions explore family photos in relation to alternative histories and counter-hegemonic practices of everyday life.[16] While the people in TV snapshots often perform roles of nuclear family life, I also show how snapshots offer alternative ways of seeing the family and practices of looking (or not looking) at TV.

In her pathbreaking work on family photography, Hirsch discusses the visual complexities of what she calls the "familial gaze." For Hirsch, the dynamics of looking are an overlooked but important component of how family relations are worked out and worked through. "The photograph," Hirsch argues, "is the site at which numerous looks and gazes intersect," including the looks between the camera operator and the subject; the exchange of looks among people in the photo; and the gaze of the viewer looking at the photo. The familial gaze also includes "external institutional and ideological gazes" outside the frame of the picture, and in this respect, Hirsch sees family photos in the context of family imagery more generally: "When we photograph ourselves in a familial setting, we do not do so in a vacuum; we respond to dominant mythologies of family life, to conceptions we have inherited, to images we see on television, in advertising, in film."[17]

TV snapshots engage the "familial gaze" in particularly interesting ways. As a piece of furniture in the home, the TV set is often a site of visual pleasure. Yet, unlike other objects, television can be "turned on," and the ethereal images and performers on-screen often seem to look back at people in their homes and even become "actors" in the family pose, making TV photos especially uncanny. More generally, as a screen for attracting spectators, television provided a focal point through which camera operators framed family members (or guests) as visual attractions. But the familial gaze was not just a form of objectification. As I argue in chapter 3, women often delighted in using television as a backdrop against which to display their fashions in ways that often spoke to women's visual pleasure and relationships with one another, and not just to the voyeuristic pleasure of men.

Throughout, I analyze TV snapshots as a social practice. In her ethnographic work on British women's snapshot cultures (conducted in the 2000s), Gillian Rose calls attention to how women used analog snapshots to sustain family and friendship networks by, for example, enclosing them in letters or looking at them with guests. "Women's photographic practices suggest that photographing family and friends, and doing things with those photos like making albums, does in fact represent at least some aspects of women's domestic lives extraordinarily well, and indeed far from naively reproducing dominant ideologies of domestic femininity, family albums often negotiate such ideologies with remarkable skill."[18] Similarly, in the US context, family snapshots were an analog means of creating and sustaining social networks. In the late nineteenth century and through the midcentury period, photography was a popular activity at women's luncheons, children's birthday parties, and other domestic gatherings.

Kodak's major postwar competitor, Polaroid Land, carved out a niche for its products by marketing them as social media. When it first appeared in 1948, the Polaroid was the first snapshot camera to take photos that materialized in a minute, without the need to send film to development labs. Polaroid promoted the camera not only as a novel attraction, but also as a means for photographers to attract people to themselves. Unlike Kodak's focus on female consumers, Polaroid often advertised its camera as a boy's toy that dazzled friends, family, and strangers with the awesome technical trick of portraits on demand. As one ad put it, "You're the Life of the Party with a Polaroid Land Camera."[19] Considering the larger significance of Polaroid in the history of photography, Peter Buse argues that by focusing almost exclusively on family and memory, scholars have often overlooked the snapshot camera's relation to fun, play, and sociality.[20]

Regardless of camera brand or film stock, TV snapshots capture the fun people had by pairing TV and cameras. Some photos show family members and friends involved in ludic activities or performing before the TV screen (a subject I take up in chapter 2); others are modes of TV hobby art (as with still lifes, trick shots, and screenshots, which I discuss in chapters 1 and 2). Still others show people engaged in sexual playfulness (as with the dress-up photos and homemade pinups I consider in chapters 3 and 4).

While most snapshots appear to be taken with low-end cameras and developed in company labs, the postwar decades witnessed increased enthusiasm for amateur photography. Although *amateur* is a loaded term (implying lower skills or "not quite art"), and while it is a slippery category (many so-called amateurs aspired to—and sometimes did—exhibit their work and earn income for it), I use the term here as it was deployed by midcentury camera companies, photography magazines, and photographers themselves. At midcentury the term generally implied a hobby rather than a vocation. Like weekend painters who dabbled in the arts, *shutterbugs* proliferated in the 1950s and 1960s. Many amateurs—especially those striving toward professional status—used high-end equipment and set up dark rooms (often in their basements or garages—in other words, men's spaces). Notably, the advice discourses aimed at amateurs were highly gendered. The Kodak manual showed men manhandling photos (for example, men appear in darkrooms processing negatives or scaling up photos on the Kodak Hobbyist Enlarger), while women place photos in albums, arrange them on walls, or engage in the "pleasant habit" of putting snapshots into letters.[21] Despite growing numbers of female photographers at midcentury, magazines like *Popular Photography* and *U.S. Camera* spoke primarily to men.

The photography magazines quickly took up an interest in television. In 1949, one camera club contest (sponsored with a prize from *U.S. Camera*) invited shutterbugs to compete for the best photo (or home movie) that depicted the photographer's new TV set.[22] More generally, as I discuss in chapter 2, photography magazines promoted the new hobby art of shooting snapshots off the TV screen, and they also taught readers how to create other photographic "TV crafts." In such ways, the expert advice on photography linked the television set and the snapshot camera, promoting their use as companion technologies in postwar homes.

Amateur interest in photography was encouraged by the midcentury period's more general elevation of photography to an art form. In 1944, the Museum of Modern Art (MoMA) mounted the first US exhibition of snapshot photography, *The American Snapshot*. Curated by MoMA's first director of photography, Willard Morgan, the show included numerous family snapshots (the exhibition catalog opens with a photo of baby "Butch"). In 1955, MoMA's *Family of Man* became a major source of public fascination. Created by Edward Steichen (MoMA's director of photography from 1947 to 1961), along with a board of midcentury luminaries (including anthropologist Margaret Mead), the uniquely staged exhibit displayed 503 photographs of people from around the world, and it traveled to thirty-seven countries across six continents.[23] For those who did not attend the show (or else wanted to relive it), *The Family of Man* was the subject of a 1955 CBS TV documentary and was also memorialized in a best-selling book that could be found on coffee tables across the nation.[24] The exhibit's use of the word *family* in the title, and the numerous photos of children and kin, no doubt resonated with the family photography that ordinary people shot in their homes. Despite its humanist intentions, critics debated (and continue to debate) the exhibition's political and ideological complexities, particularly regarding colonialism, racism, and "first world" displays of "others."[25]

Nevertheless, across the nineteenth and twentieth century, photographers of color had a major influence on the medium, and at midcentury, photography was increasingly central to the politics of race, nationalism, and civil rights. Deborah Willis's 1994 pathbreaking anthology *Picturing Us* highlights the importance of photography for Black publics across the nineteenth and twentieth centuries.[26] As Willis writes (in a separate essay), "A number of black people felt that there were no representative images of their experiences published in periodicals or on postcards. Thus some felt it necessary to address this visual omission by setting up photography studios, writing editorials, and posing for the camera."[27] In her oft-cited essay "In Our Glory," bell hooks claims, "Cameras gave back to black folks, irrespective of our class, a means by which we could participate fully in the production of images. . . . Access and mass appeal have historically made photography a powerful location for the construction of an oppositional black aesthetic. In a world before racial integration, there was a constant struggle on the part of black folks to create a counter-hegemonic world of images that would stand as visual resistance, challenging racist images."[28] Speaking specifically of home-mode pictures, she adds, "Photographs taken in everyday life, snapshots in particular, rebelled against all of those photographic practices that re-inscribed colonial ways of looking and capturing images of the black 'other.'"[29]

Given the diverse range of families who made TV snapshots, and especially the numerous African American TV snapshots that appear on the collector's market, it seems important at the outset to consider the different historical experiences against which snapshots resonate. As Stuart Hall argues in his essay on vernacular studio photographs of diasporic publics, even if such photographs are highly generic, they call for a "politics of reading" on the part of the critic and an effort to understand the historical context of the people posing in them, to see the photos from their point of view.[30] Although I don't think it's possible to fully understand the experience of the people in the snapshots I've collected, nevertheless, both photography and television had different meanings and uses for differently situated publics. Hall's concept of "articulation" is especially useful here as it allows for an understanding of how media forms can resonate differently in their connections and attachments to different histories, memories, and lived practices.[31] Even while I acknowledge my limited perspective, in this book I speculate on family photos in the context of historical scholarship as well as primary documents (such as the Black press) that shed light on race, photography, and television (mostly with reference to African American publics).

At midcentury, Black art photographers and photojournalists explored everyday portraiture in ways that encouraged African American publics to see their own lives through the pictures. *The Sweet Flypaper of Life* (1955), with photographs by Roy DeCarava and text by Langston Hughes, is a canonical example.[32] A photo poem about daily life in Harlem, the book features, for example, a child playing at an open fire hydrant, couples dancing in kitchens, pedestrians walking down streets, a mother washing dishes, teenagers around a jukebox. Hughes's poetic narration presents Harlem through the eyes of grandmother Sister Mary Bradley, who serves as a framing device for the photos, speaking conversationally in female talk about her family and neighbors. Published in the same year as *The Family Man*, *The Sweet Flypaper of Life* pictured life in a community of color created in the context of segregation, migration, and Jim Crow, marking experiences that were not universal (as with the theme of Steichen's exhibit) but rather formed through historical circumstance. The book's focus was on ordinary daily experience as opposed to the often-sensationalized portraits and stereotypes of Black life in mainstream photojournalism.

Over the course of the 1960s, as Black photographers, curators, and critics protested the closed world of museum photography and came to have increased presence in that world, the ordinary snapshot camera continued to resonate against the larger meanings of photography as a tool for oppositional voices and practices.[33] Along these lines, hooks emphasizes the quotidian nature of the family portrait and especially its role in homemaking: "Most southern black folks grew up in a context where snapshots and the more stylized photographs taken by professional photographers were the easiest images to produce. Significantly, displaying those images in everyday life was as central as making them. The walls of images in southern black homes were sites of resistance. They constituted private, black-owned and -operated, gallery space where images could be displayed, shown to friends and strangers. These walls were a space where, in the midst of segregation, the hardship of apartheid, dehumanization could be countered."[34] In practices of home decoration, the family photo made counter-hegemonic ways of looking part of the domestic interior.

Although it would be a vast act of overinterpretation to say that African American snapshots are always acts of self-conscious resistance to racism, snapshot cameras nevertheless provided ways to reappropriate racist practices in mainstream visual culture and, as hooks suggests, to feel at home with one's image. Given television's own legacy of racism (a subject to which I will return), the snapshot camera offered a home-mode antidote to network television's omissions, stereotypes, and hegemonic acts of inclusion. With a snapshot camera, it was possible to intervene and talk back to TV. By posing in their TV settings, African Americans, as well as other underrepresented people of color, could make themselves the subjects of pleasing representations with a medium that often failed to please them.

Throughout this book, I see TV snapshots as a site for the creative production of images, social identities, pleasures, and lived historical experiences. That said, found photos can be stubborn things to understand. Certainly, as John Berger argues, "Photographs bear witness to a human choice." The photograph "is already a message about the event it records. . . . At its simplest, the message, decoded, means: 'I have decided that seeing this is worth recording.'"[35] Yet, human choices—as actor-network theory reminds us—are bound up with objects and technical affordances that play a role in social practice.[36] For example, a snapshot camera's shutter speed limited the range of action in a snapshot and helped to determine how humans posed for the camera; even moderately fast movement could result in blur, so people had to avoid quick facial expressions, stand relatively still, or *imitate* doing things (like reading a book or feeding a baby). Kodak's color film was based on the bias of its Shirley card tests (which used a white model as the standard), binding photographic techniques, as Shawn Michelle Smith has shown, to the history of eugenics, in which whites used photographs to reinforce racist beliefs in white beauty hierarchies.[37] In this sense, while photos register a field of human choices, they nevertheless are imbricated in the agency of things (what devices can and can't do) and with human-object relations. Moreover, as found images, TV snapshots are a complicated archive, always resisting empirical claims and always open to interpretation.

LOST, FOUND, AND RE-COLLECTED: THE EVERYDAY ARCHIVE

This book is a product of serendipity—the various turns of good fortune I've had in my search for lost things. Nevertheless, found photos pose challenges. Most of the snapshots in this book come from anonymous trade routes and are ripped from their original contexts. Online dealers or vintage shop owners accumulate them at estate sales and break up collections.[38] While dates are often stamped on the photos, in many cases they are not (and, therefore, I have made educated guesses).[39] Offering little to go on, snapshots remain enigmatic.

These snapshots are collectibles, but not always, or even primarily, because they feature TV sets. Instead, they are part of a more general collectors' culture around found photos. My search for TV snapshots on Google produced examples uploaded to share sites like Flickr and Pinterest and to various photography and collector's blogs.[40] In the material spaces of flea markets, thrift shops, and vintage stores, TV snapshots are typically strewn among many other sorts of snapshots, so that searching for them is needle-in-haystack research. I decided, therefore, to check eBay in the hopes that its searchable site would allow me to find my objects of desire in a more focused way. On a hunch I typed in "TV snapshots." Jackpot! That search term resulted in a steady flow of photos sold by online vintage stores and photo dealers.

While the search terms I use designate my interest, other people who buy TV snapshots are not necessarily concerned with TV. They may just as well be interested in snapshots featuring midcentury fashions, furniture, or cats—all of which are also search terms that often result in snapshots that feature TV sets. In this respect, the archive I have amassed is searchable online, but the search terms I use do not refer to a preexisting archive; instead, the search has the curious effect of creating the archive, or at least facilitating my collection as such.

In its role as a repository and trading post for found photographs, eBay has become an everyday experience for an online collectors' culture.[41] While eBay characterizes itself foremost as a virtual store, it also assumes the other meaning of the word *store*, operating as an archive formed through an impulse to save objects—or more specifically, photographs of objects—that appear on the site. In addition, eBay is a social media site on which sellers weave tales about objects to make them more desirable, and eBay's community board lets buyers swap stories of their own. My use of eBay as a research tool, therefore, is framed by this everyday online experience where shopping, storytelling, and storing the past are interrelated activities.

Even though I was surprised to find so many snapshots, my collection of roughly five thousand should not be regarded as a representative sample in the empiricist sense. Instead, I use terms like *a lot* and *numerous* to indicate general trends or iconographic subgenres (such as dress-up photos or trick shots). This may be annoying to readers who want statistical generalizations, but it would be pointless and misleading to quantify things that can't be counted but that still, I argue, "count" as important materials through which to understand the past. As I write this book, new TV snapshots appear online every day. Like many digital archives, this one is not finite. It is generative. While I do think the relatively large collection I have amassed helps confirm the significance of the practice, it is impossible to know how many TV snapshots people produced compared, say, with snapshots of their poodles or pianos. This is, however, not my concern. Instead of calculating general trends, I explore snapshots as iterations of a popular practice through which people visualized themselves and their new TV homes. Moreover, I examine photos that seem to divert from photographic trends and family snapshot norms. Such snapshots offer counter-memories to the reigning historical narratives about TV as a sentimental family medium. By looking at snapshots in relation to each other and alongside adjacent media (like pinups or art photography), I hope to give them significance beyond the stray example, and to show how family snapshots speak to absent (or silenced) voices in television history. By reading them in their varied historical contexts, I hope to understand them from the point of view of their posers (even if that is often more conjecture than fact).

In *Image Matters*, Tina Campt considers the unwieldy nature of family photographs and the difficulties entailed in interpreting their relevance to their posers and for history more generally. Based on historical collections of snapshots of Black German families and studio portraits of West Indian migrants in England, Campt reconstructs their affective resonance and the historical experiences they suggest. Rather than view the photos just as strays or singular *orphans* (a term often used in film studies to consider found objects like home movies), Campt argues we should examine them as *sets* that resonate with each other and speak to the material, affective, and haptic experiences of people who posed in and made them. Like Hall, Campt sees historical contextualization and the politics of reading as central concerns, and she demonstrates how the photos in her study speak to "fugitivity," alterity, counter-narratives, and the everyday struggles and pleasures of publics whose voices were rarely documented or saved in archives.[42] In this regard, collections of family photos can mark the significance of everyday life in ways different from, and sometimes in terms more compelling than, canonical works of photographic art. As Campt suggests, family photos are complex texts that demand close textual analysis, a method that I employ here.

Given their intimate and personal nature, snapshots pose ethical concerns. Archivists and historians often negotiate the complexities of making personal images public. This is easy to forget at a moment when digital photos have made snapshot photography into a public act in which people display their private lives willingly, gleefully—and share photos online with others they may have never met. The found photos I explore in this book are pictures of other people's homes and were created in the context of intimacy. In other words, they weren't meant for me (or you as readers) to see. Therefore, at the start, it seems important to acknowledge the sense of eavesdropping or even surveillance I often feel when looking at photos of families that aren't mine. This is especially the case in relation to families of color, for whom photography was historically connected to the politics of intimacy and resistance against hegemonic visual practices. And it seems equally important to acknowledge that photography has also historically been used as a disciplinary means of surveillance disproportionately against people of color.[43] Looking in other people's houses, then, is not an entirely innocent practice.

For many readers, TV snapshots may well evoke "kitschy" sensibilities. Readers may find themselves laughing at or nostalgic for the clunky TV consoles, flamingo pink curtains, pompadours, go-go boots, miniskirts, and yellow shag rugs. While I don't want to police the joys of nostalgia (which I believe can at times serve redemptive and even critical functions for thinking about the relations among the past, present, and future), it's important to remember that people at the time did not likely experience their lives as kitsch. I return to these issues of history, memory, counter-memory, kitsch, and nostalgia in chapter 5 as I look at the memory cultures and art practices surrounding TV snapshots today.

At the most practical level, my selection of snapshots is governed by copyright laws that make it possible for me to reprint snapshots (as long as I own them) that were produced up until 1977, when copyright laws changed. Nevertheless, TV snapshots date well into the 1990s (even if the practice was less typical).[44] In addition, while I focus on US photos, this is largely because of my location, my historical frame of reference, and the fact that online stores (like US eBay) sell mostly US snapshots. But because I have found snapshots from places around the world, I have decided occasionally to discuss or display these in various sections of this book. While I cannot address the specificities of national broadcasting systems in the scope of this project, readers should be aware when looking at international examples that broadcast systems manifest at different times and were differently organized across the globe. Even in the United States, in the late 1940s and early 1950s, television was mainly available in big cities and surrounding suburbs, and across the decades, the number of stations in different regions of the country was uneven.

More generally, when writing this book, I've grappled with choices and arrangements. Should I publish the blurry images, crooked angles, cut-off heads? Or should I display the more legible snapshots that approximate some of the basic standards set forth in instructional manuals? In some way this choice is decided for me in advance, as most dealers sell only the "good" (or most legible) photos because they are worth more on the collectors' market. But in many cases, my selections really come down to my own attractions and tastes. Which little girl in which party dress is the perfect example? The French provincial color TV or the sleek modern portable? The cat lying in front of the TV or the canary cage placed on top of one? These may seem inconsequential choices, but selection and arrangement of documents is a major issue for all historians. As a space of what Jacques Derrida calls "consignation," the archive makes choices, classifies, confers meaning, inscribes the documents of the past with the concerns of the present.[45] As much as it preserves, the archive also destroys and silences pasts not chosen for inclusion and display—an issue I discuss in more detail in chapter 5.

What is the difference between an *archive* and a *collection*? For Derrida, who traces the etymology of the word, the archive is both a place (a house, consistent with the archive's etymological ties to architecture, shelter, or the Greek *arkheion*) and a source of official power or *commandment* (the *arkhe*—an authority or "place from which order is given"). Here, I use the term *archive* in both ways. The snapshots are literally pictures of houses, but they remain homeless, torn from their original home-mode forms of collection (the album, the box, the dresser drawer) but not yet housed in an official museum or archive. This book, then, is not the same as a personal collection, but it is also not based on the sorts of things typically found in archives. *TV Snapshots* is best categorized as a re-collection, literally a collection of other people's collections; figuratively, a history that straddles the lines between an official archive and a family album.

In the course of my research, colleagues recommended I use software programs to compile searchable lists and logs. I did try. But my attempt to mimic official archiving escaped me. I found the software alienating. The searchable logs were too systematic, unable to grasp the affective range of the snapshots, at least as I understood them. How do you, after all, make the *punctum* searchable? I did, however, find a way to organize the pictures. I saved and arranged my TV snapshots in ordinary family photo albums. This home-mode form of preservation was appealing to me, perhaps because the albums evoke the intimacy and women's pleasures through which family photos were historically saved. Without essentializing my preservation practices as feminine, it does strike me that my choice must have been related to what Daniel Miller calls "the comfort of things."[46] I like touching and holding the material pictures, putting them in and taking them out of albums, more than I like them when they appear digitized as JPEGs and metadata on my computer. The family album is familiar to me, the way I saved photos for most of my life. It inspires me to think about TV snapshots in relation to the people who made them, selected them, wrote funny little remarks on them, and preserved them in their own albums.

In the past two decades, photography studies has taken a material turn. Historians and theorists like Elizabeth Edwards and Janice Hart, Margaret Olin, and Christopher Pinney see photographs not just as images, but also as three-dimensional things that people touch, trade, and put in other things (like albums). Snapshots accrue meaning and affective resonances in the process of their circulation and manipulation, literally as they are handled and change hands.[47] Handling torn, faded, used snapshots literally means physical touching, but it also involves the more affective sense of being touched by a photo. And because TV snapshots are other people's photos, I am touched secondhand.

In its appeal to ordinariness and the materiality of things, *TV Snapshots* especially finds inspiration in Ann Cvetkovich's *An Archive of Feelings*.[48] As

Cvetkovich envisions it, the archive of feelings suggests an archive composed of collections made of things and sensations not typically saved in official archives. Her immediate concern is with lesbian cultural artifacts and the memories, traumas, and pleasures they evoke. Her archive includes ephemera like diaries, films, videos, and pamphlets that contain counter-memories and clues into the affective relations among people whose lives went undocumented by official archives. Although Cvetkovich finds ephemera in material places (like LGBTQ community centers), her concept of the archive is more expansive. She sees artifacts of lesbian visual culture (films, videos, photographs) as ephemeral archives that record memories, histories, and affects that are not saved or stored in physical sites. As she argues elsewhere, photographs also store affect.[49]

The word *affect* has a complicated genealogy and a range of uses.[50] Photography scholars variously use the term to think about how photographs (as images, objects, and social practices) can resonate culturally and not just in relation to individual emotions. Given the TV snapshot's relation to the sensations and textures of everyday life, in this book I especially draw on Kathleen Stewart's *Ordinary Affects*. She writes, "The ordinary is a shifting assemblage of practices and practical knowledges. . . . Ordinary affects are the varied, surging capacities to affect and to be affected that give everyday life the quality of a continual motion of relations, scenes, contingencies, and emergences."[51] Stewart (like many others interested in affect theory) sees affect as being "akin to Raymond Williams's structures of feeling."[52] But following the more Deleuzian-inspired sense of the term, she also suggests that ordinary affects are less a structure than "an animate circuit" of intense and banal encounters, and a "contact zone where the overdeterminations of circulations, events, conditions, technologies, and flows of power literally take place."[53] Stewart composes her book as an "assemblage of disparate scenes" of everyday life, stitching together affective experiences she claims are "patchy" and without closure.[54]

In this book, I patch together an assemblage of other people's daily scenes. Although they are often taken on occasions (Christmas, birthdays, etc.), snapshots engage a dialectic between the rhythms and rituals of dailiness and those times marked as special (or what Kodak called "Kodak moments"). In the pages that follow, I try to capture moments of everyday life in TV homes just as a photographer might snap a picture.

Admittedly, this mode of image capture grasps at things that can't really be neatly bundled or "framed." Henri Lefebvre called his theory of everyday life the study of "what is left over," literally that which remains after the academic analysis of specialized and structured activities (like the law or the economy).[55] The everyday is ephemeral, contingent, habitual, not easily subjected to historical time. The desire to know it (my desire here) can reify everyday experience as a *thing* and lose its ephemeral nature. There is always the danger of essentializing the things of everyday life and holding them up as "authentic" even though most of the objects are manufactured and sold on mass markets. Michel de Certeau's focus on the creative reappropriation of mass-produced goods and the spaces of daily life has been central to the conceptualization of the everyday as a field of actions, iterations, and potential resistance to (or at least divergence from) the more sedimented spaces of institutionalized power. Drawing on de Certeau, Edwards and Hart see the materiality of photographs in terms of "the operations of everyday life," arguing that "even the most pragmatically engendered materialities, such as photograph frames and albums, come to have meaning through habitual reiterations of engagement with them."[56]

Theories of the everyday have also been key to my home field of television studies for quite some time. Interest in the everyday spans methods of ethnographic and historical research on television households and textual analysis of programs. British cultural studies had a profound influence on the study of television as a lived practice, not just in terms of TV programs but also what Raymond Williams (in 1975) famously theorized as the "flow" of textual materials in the context of the home reception environment.[57] Sociological and ethnographic studies by scholars such as David Morley, Roger Silverstone, and David Gauntlett and Annette Hill helped to define a field of inquiry into the dynamic of TV watching at home, and studies in varied international contexts have been central to this work.[58]

Feminist television scholars (who are a major influence for my book) have laid the groundwork for much of this project, and they continue to invent new directions. Pathbreaking scholarship on broadcast-era soap operas and other daytime programs by authors like Tania Modleski, Charlotte Brunsdon, Dorothy Hobson, Christine Geraghty, Marsha Cassidy, and Elana Levine demonstrate the everyday pleasures these programs afforded their mostly female audiences as well as the industry's attempts to capture women's attention by integrating programs into what Modleski calls the "rhythms of reception" in the home.[59] Historians and critics like Ernest Pascucci, Amy Villarejo, Quinlan Miller, Lynne Joyrich, Ron Becker, and Gary Needham have considered how broadcast television addressed—or failed to address—the everyday life of LGBTQ publics, whose daily experiences did not always square with the networks' obsessive focus on heterosexual family audiences (especially in the period I investigate here).[60] Analyzing more recent postnetwork TV, scholars such as Misha Kavka, Frances Bonner, Laurie Ouellette, Racquel Gates, Brenda Weber, Ann duCille, Mimi White, Amy Holdsworth, and Karen Lury examine such genres as lifestyle and makeover shows, court TV, dating shows, game shows, reality home shows, and children's programming in relation to neoliberal self-care, race, sexuality, and modes of intimacy, affect, and pleasure.[61] In much of this scholarship, the quotidian aspects of TV—its structures of feeling and structuring influence on lived routines, as well as its use for the playful unstructuring of daily grinds—opens compelling, if thorny, questions about the medium's place in everyday life.

Regardless of the objects of study, access to the everyday is limited, and especially so for historians. Cultural historians often explore diaries, letters, or scrapbooks to understand the experiences of ordinary people, whose lives are not archived in the ways that the lives of kings, stars, or presidents are. Similarly, television historians examine audience fan mail or letters to the editors of fan magazines, which offer glimpses into viewers' thoughts about TV. But these sources are tricky in their randomness and lack of contextualization.[62] Snapshots are also tricky things. In this sense, I view snapshots as clues to questions rather than answers, as ways to see things typically thought so inconsequential as to go unseen.

Across the chapters of this book, I explore snapshots as creative acts and textual forms that bear traces of everyday life with TV. I begin in chapter 1 by broadly considering television's "thingness" as a material object in the home and how people—as picture takers—incorporated it into family portraits and displays of interior décor. This chapter also initiates my interest in the spatial orientations toward the TV set, its use as a setting for family activities and camera poses.

Chapter 2 looks more specifically at television's role in staging human poses and its use as a theatrical backdrop against which people performed everything from wedding ceremonies to dance recitals. I consider the snapshots in relation to midcentury theories of everyday life as *dramaturgy* put forth by midcentury sociologists (most prominently Erving Goffman). In addition to performances in front of the set, I explore performances with cameras as a mode of hobby art. I look at TV trick shots (in which, for example, people used optical tricks to picture themselves performing on TV), and I examine the hobby art of screenshots, in which people captured images of programs and media events off TV. Throughout, I explore the dialectic between liveness (on TV) and stillness (in photos), and I analyze the uncanny mergers between human posers in the home and the ethereal performers that emanate from the TV screen.

The next two chapters look at the performance of gender and sexuality in front of the TV set. In chapter 3 I discuss what I call dress-up snapshots and the everyday glamour that women enacted as they posed in front of TV screens. Drawing on fashion theory as well as film and television history, I analyze the dress-up poses in relation to women's everyday life, arguing that women often used the new medium to direct the gaze at themselves (as opposed to programs on TV) and to fantasize about glamour inside and outside the home. I also explore photos that "queer" the family album by presenting people in nonconforming, nonheteronormative gender performances in front of the TV. Chapter 4 picks up on this interest by considering more explicitly sexualized pinup photos featuring women in various stages of undress posing in front of TV sets. While many of these appeared in men's magazines like *Playboy*, others were "homemade" pinups shot with ordinary snapshot cameras. These pinups raise questions about the sexual and erotic life of the TV home, a subject barely broached in TV history, which has mostly focused on TV's status as a family medium.

I end this book by reflecting on issues of TV history, the archive, and the memory cultures that form around TV today. Chapter 5 focuses on photoshare sites where people post and discuss midcentury TV snapshots and where contemporary photographers exhibit their own "retro" TV snapshots, so that the history of the form has now become a photographic art practice in itself. I consider these practices in addition to more general theoretical concerns about the digital photo archive and its relation to TV memory and history. In the brief conclusion, I draw out analytic frameworks of the book and think about the archive I've amassed in the memory practices of my own everyday life. In this sense, my history of TV snapshots is also history of the present. Throughout this book, I've found it impossible to separate history from memory fully, and rather than try to do so, I'm interested in the interactions between the two that snapshots bring into focus.

As anyone reading this book will observe, the television set is no longer the same object that it was in the twentieth century. Its midcentury object form now appears as an antique, a vestige of a Jurassic world without mobile screens or streaming media. But my sense is that the scholarship on the history of TV and everyday life is not really done. Discovering these snapshots confirmed my desire not only to know more but also to know *differently*, from another perspective. Given the fact that TV snapshots generally focus on what is happening in front of or next to the TV set, this book *reorients* television studies away from the programs on-screen and the act of watching TV. Instead, I explore the home as a theater of everyday life, where people used snapshot cameras to make TV pictures of their own (figure I.4).

FIGURE I.4 1961.

1

TV PORTRAITS

PICTURING FAMILIES AND
HOUSEHOLD THINGS

On October 17, 2015, the *New York Times* ran a front-page story titled "The Lonely Death of George Bell."[1] A recluse and hoarder, upon his death, Bell was a forgotten man. A photo of his living room displays takeout cartons, clothes, a briefcase, garbage bags, picture frames, appliances, packing papers, and more—much more—strewn on the floor of Bell's apartment, the place where he grew up and lived nearly his entire life (figure 1.1). A TV set is buried in the pile, barely visible yet perhaps still in use, with a few videotapes stacked on top and tossed inside a plantless decorative planter. The space is drenched in a bleak, almost clinical, light that streams in from two large windows, their venetian blinds pulled up and hanging catawampus. A large bear head mounted between the windows dominates the wall, terrifying the room with a frozen growl. The caption reads: "Sniffing a field of odor, George Bell's neighbor called 911. Once firefighters had jammed the door, the police squeezed into a beaten apartment groaning with possessions."[2] The

pile, the smells, the groans all signal a life gone wrong through a patholog-
ical relation to things. The article goes on to tell the story of Bell's life and
death, illustrated with more photos that survey the scene as if through the
eyes of the police. But one photograph—a family snapshot pulled from the
rubble—harks back to happier times some sixty years before.

The snapshot pictures Bell as a teenage boy posing with his father in the
same room. Sitting in front of a TV set, the young Bell looks toward the camera (figure 1.2). The same two windows with the same venetian blinds form
a backdrop, but the blinds are drawn down in their intended fashion, and
floral drapes shelter the room in a feminine feel. A decorative plate hangs
above the TV (in the same spot where the bear head now growls). Holiday
greeting cards adorn the set, and instead of the videotapes, a large leafy plant
sits inside the decorative planter, adding signs of life to the scene. A tinseled
Christmas tree, skirted by gifts, stands next to the TV, marking the ritual time
of a festive family occasion. The scene looks like countless other TV snapshots from the 1950s. But its presence in the *New York Times* serves a particular rhetorical function. Juxtaposed with the criminalizing rhetoric of the
death scene surveillance-style photos, this family snapshot is a reminder of
the "right" relation to objects that the hoarder Bell had somehow failed to
maintain. Whether Bell is actually happy in the snapshot is hard to say. (No
one is smiling.) But the TV snapshot is the only photo in the story that shows
Bell's home in a human and lively light—the rest are images of decay. To use
Mary Douglas's terms, the TV snapshot signals "purity," but the photo of the
hoard spells "danger"—a cultural binary she uses to describe taboos around
dirt (and why people code specific objects and people as "dirty" and "out of
place") in Western culture.[3]

I begin with Bell's story to capture how TV snapshots often function as
signs of normative relations to the object world. That is, they signify object relations that are socially sanctioned, that are "pure" and in their proper
place. For that reason, Bell's TV snapshot is easily recognized as what Barthes
calls a "studium," the element of a photograph that depicts a whole way of life
that is easily recognized by anyone from the same culture looking at the shot.
The *New York Times* story uses the TV snapshot to evoke this whole way of
life. Over the course of the 1950s, television became a standard and often idealized domestic object—something that often signified family togetherness
and the bounty of postwar consumer pleasures. Television also increasingly
shared the spotlight with, or entirely displaced, objects with which families
traditionally posed (pianos, fireplaces, and Christmas trees)—the things that
belonged to "Kodak moments." As it functions in the *New York Times*, the TV

FIGURE 1.1
(*above*) From
N. R. Kleinfield,
"The Lonely
Death of George
Bell," *New
York Times*,
October 17, 2015.
Photographed
by Josh Hanner.
Reprinted with
permission from
the New York
Times/Redux.

FIGURE 1.2
(*left*) Snapshot
of George Bell
and father, 1956.

snapshot humanizes Bell by giving him what appears to be a typical middle-class childhood past. But while the article provides endless detail about the rancid objects in the hoard and delves into the personal trials that led Bell to this life of squalor, it says nothing about any of the objects in his childhood snapshot. The implication is that there is nothing to say precisely because the image has been so internalized and so routinized as to be common sense by now—hardly relevant for analysis.

In this chapter I examine how snapshots came to portray television as a family object. I explore how people arranged and photographed the TV set in relation to other household activities and things, and I consider how people presented their families as they assimilated the new media object into domestic spaces and routines. My goal is less to psychologize the reasons that people took TV snapshots (although some of that may be inevitable) than it is to understand the cultural logics of the TV snapshot as a typical representational practice for the midcentury family—so typical that it is even retrieved intact from the hoard of Bell's putrid remains.

CONSPICUOUS CONSUMPTION?

Personal portraiture has a long history with objects. Since the nineteenth century, photography has had a special relationship to the presentation of self via things. Drawing on practices of bourgeois portrait painting, studio portraits portrayed human subjects alongside furniture, vases, plants, carpets, and other studio props (or personal objects brought to the studio) that imbued photographs with both visual interest and symbolic meaning. Backdrops for studio portraits were often designed with Victorian parlors in mind, thereby evoking bourgeois decor and decorum. "Any article of furniture which may have been used in the drawing room would always be in good taste" in studio portraits.[4]

Snapshot photography follows these protocols of studio portraiture. Kodak handbooks and how-to magazines often recommended the use of furniture, telephones, toys, and other domestic objects as props. In *Snapshot Versions of Life* (1987), Richard Chalfen considers the relationships among snapshots, consumerism, and display: "There is a tendency to attend photographically to certain new items of material culture. Snapshots will be made of adults standing next to, or sitting in, the new car, motorcycle or van, a new motorboat, sailboat or yacht. . . . While celebrating new material acquisitions, these snapshots are calling attention to the fact that life is progressing along a successful path." Although Chalfen claims that snapshots "generally neglect daily life around the house," and that they rarely show people "listening to a radio or stereo, watching television, [or] playing cards or board games," the photographs in my collection suggest otherwise.[5]

When I show my snapshots to colleagues or friends, the first thing they usually say is that the people who posed for these snapshots did so to "show off" their new TV sets. In other words, they subscribe to the theory of "conspicuous consumption," a term first coined by Thorstein Veblen in his book *The Theory of the Leisure Class* (1899). For Veblen, conspicuous consumption was tied to a new way of life in industrial culture in which time away from work could be configured as class privilege via the display of one's leisure and the accumulation of material things.[6] In postwar America, the theory of conspicuous consumption found a second life among critics and sociologists (from Harry Henderson to David Riesman to William H. Whyte) who mobilized, revised, or refuted the concept in the context of the booming consumer culture and postwar suburban expansion.[7] Throughout the 1950s and 1960s, conspicuous consumption was often colloquially conflated with the more conformist notion of "keeping up with the Joneses."

The snapshot camera had a double meaning in this context; it was itself a consumer object promoted as a form of conspicuous leisure, a means of documenting family vacations or quiet afternoons at home. But snapshots were also a medium through which to display other acquisitions—presents under Christmas trees, new dresses, birthday gifts, all sorts of household things. In the 1951–52 edition of *How to Make Good Pictures*, Kodak told readers to use cameras to display domestic plenty, stating, "New living room furniture and decorations call for new [snapshot] pictures."[8] Although Kodak did not mention television, for many people the TV set was the ultimate living room object of desire.

After World War II, advertisers promoted television as a sign of one's ability to acquire not just things, but also family togetherness facilitated by consumerism. Ads (like the one I displayed in the introduction) showed families circled around the new TV console in sentimental poses of leisure-time pleasure. In 1954, NBC president Sylvester "Pat" Weaver called television "the shining center of the home," suggesting its symbolic function as a sun around which the family might orbit as well as an instrument of progress and enlightenment (Weaver was especially keen to use TV for education and cultural uplift).[9] Beyond its status as a thing to display, as Weaver's enlightenment metaphor suggests, TV signified a distinctly modern way of seeing the world. This was so not only in the United States but also in numerous national contexts (including, for example, Sweden, the Soviet Union, West Germany, Argentina, England, India, Cuba, Canada, Australia, Italy, and Japan), as TV entered households at different times across the globe in the 1950s through the 1980s.[10]

In TV snapshots, the twin values of consumerism and modernity were registered in images that feature people posing as the proud possessors of TV sets. Sometimes people frame the set as the sole subject of the shot, and occasionally they write inscriptions on the back like "Our TV" or "new RCA," indicating the significance of the first TV.[11] While these sorts of photos typically date from the late 1940s to the late 1950s (the first wave of adoption), similar portraits of TV sets continue into the 1960s, as planned obsolescence aged the first TV and innovations in technology and product design (such as portable and color TV) began to flood the market.

In some photos, people demonstrate the technical operations of the new TV set, turning tuning knobs, or pretending to do so (figure 1.3). In many cases, one person points to the screen, turns the knob, or selects a channel on the dial while others look on or assist with the procedure (figure 1.4). These photos continue into the 1960s, as the purchase of a second TV likely offered an occasion for a new demonstration. A 1963 snapshot depicts a woman (probably a mother) looking on as a girl (probably her daughter) tunes the TV, even pulling the skirt of her dress as if curtsying to an audience as she performs the task (figure 1.5).

FIGURE 1.3 (*opposite*)
Circa 1949–55.

FIGURE 1.4 (*left*) Circa 1950.

FIGURE 1.5 (*below*) 1963.

While such snapshots do "show off" the new TV set, they are much more than portraits of conspicuous consumption. They are also social vignettes in which people demonstrate and perform their technical ("tuning-in") knowledge of how the TV works (something that interested the first wave of TV consumers, who often marveled at test patterns). Moreover, and most important to my interests here, people in these snapshots enact their relationships with each other (mother-daughter, romantic partners, friends, and, of course, poser and camera operator) through their mutual engagement with the new TV.

More generally, snapshots suggest the sociality that TV inspires. Being "first on the block" to own a TV often meant visits from neighbors who came by to watch, a dynamic reported in sociological studies of the period and in the popular press.[12] Amy Vanderbilt's *Complete Book of Etiquette* (1952) gave women rules for how to host TV parties.[13] In snapshots, the sociality of the TV set is registered in the gestures of posers and in the inscriptions on the back. One snapshot (dated January 1, 1950) shows a couple standing behind a large TV console (figure 1.6). The couple are engaged in what appears to be a happy and romantic exchange of looks, and the woman points directly at the man (not the TV). The inscription on the back reads: "New Year's evening at Dorothy & Warren's—This is their new T.V. set" (figure 1.7). Even if the TV set is central in the frame, the pose and the inscription suggest the convivial nature of television's innovation. Here as elsewhere, TV snapshots were consistent with the repertoire of camera "hospitality" recommended by companies like Polaroid ("the party camera") and Kodak (which often promoted picture taking as a means of entertaining guests). Posing for pictures was a form of amusement at social occasions, and as such, snapshot cameras documented, memorialized, and helped to produce the fun at TV parties and neighborly visits that often accompanied the acquisition of a new TV.

As might be expected, some snapshots show people (almost always children) watching TV together in scenes that suggest social interaction and family bonds (figure 1.8). But much more typically, people pose in action shots doing other things in front of the TV. For example, they read (or pretend to read) newspapers or books while posing in front of the TV set (figure 1.9). (The prevalence of such photos may be a function of photography magazines and Kodak manuals often advising readers to use books or magazines as props in "doing something" poses that would make people seem less frozen and more natural.)[14] In such scenarios, the TV set is not the main object on display; rather, it is a setting in which some other action or object takes center stage.

FIGURES 1.6 & 1.7 Visitors pose with hosts' new TV; inscription on back, 1950.

Given that TV snapshots are embedded in a field of social practices (like TV parties) and are not always centrally focused on the TV set, conspicuous consumption turns out to be a rather unsatisfying explanation. It is not wrong, but it is weak. It cannot account for the complex uses of TVs and cameras as companion technologies and the range of social practices registered in the photos.

Moreover, conspicuous consumption neglects the volatile and disputed nature of television in postwar culture. Far from just a simple status symbol or sign of family bliss, the television set was an ambivalent thing, a site of utopian hopes (as in Weaver's enlightenment discourse) but also dystopian fears (of, for example, surveillance and mind control). Rather than either of these extremes, debates around TV more typically revolved around daily struggles in the home and related political struggles in the nation across gender, class, ethnic, and racial lines.

For African American families, television was a particularly contradictory object. On the one hand, ads for TV sets in *Ebony* presented television sets as objects of racial pride. Whereas ads for high-ticket items in *Ebony* usually featured white models posing with, for example, cars or washing machines, for much of the 1950s, ads for TV sets featured Black families viewing TV and

FIGURE 1.8
(*opposite*)
Circa
1949–55.

FIGURE 1.9
(*left*) 1957.

African American performers on-screen.[15] Meanwhile, the African American press tracked TV success stories of entertainers like Hazel Scott and Bob Howard who (briefly) hosted shows on local stations, as well as network TV "firsts" (like Nat King Cole's short-lived program in 1956).[16] More broadly, African American newspapers often expressed cautious optimism for television's status as a medium. As jazz singer and bandleader Cab Calloway told the *New York Amsterdam News* in 1950, TV "isn't Utopia now, but [if people speak up, listen, and act] . . . it may be Utopia yet!"[17]

On the other hand, as numerous historians have demonstrated, television was a site of racial protest.[18] African American organizations like the NAACP and critics in the Black press protested demeaning stereotypes (as in *Beulah* [ABC, 1951–53] and *Amos 'n' Andy* [CBS, 1951–53]). And despite TV's utopian promise, the press routinely challenged broadcasters' failures to hire Black executives or to make Black stars leads of programs.[19] (Alvin Chick Webb's 1954 five-part study, "Jim Crow in Radio and TV," which ran in the *New York Amsterdam News*, is an aptly titled example.)[20] By the 1960s, Black critics, activists, and viewers grew increasingly disappointed by the limited sorts of roles African Americans could play on and behind the camera. Nevertheless, many continued to see television as a field of possibilities, both for cultural expression and for the concerns of civil rights movements.[21] Throughout the civil rights period, African American, Latinx, and Native American organizations battled the racism of the network system, and some people of color used TV strategically, producing or appearing in TV programs they made for their communities at local or educational stations.[22] In this sense, television's status as an object in the home—and as an object in snapshots—has to be read in the context of the varied and disputed political meanings attached to it in the nation as a whole.

Even within mainstream white culture, TV precipitated intense disputes, especially around gender and youth. As I argue in *Make Room for TV*, women's magazines debated TV's effects on children, the romantic life of couples, and women's domestic labor. And rather than a status symbol, for some people TV was an object of shame. While TV was a "rich man's toy" in the 1930s and 1940s, by the early 1950s—as television became available at lower prices and via credit financing on the mass market—some people shunned it. "Highbrow" (and even "middlebrow") critics often denigrated TV as a sign of debased tastes and educational status. In a classic case of Bourdieu's "distinction," some people distanced themselves from the objects of the "masses."[23]

In all these ways, as both a medium and an object, television was replete with multiple and charged meanings, never just a simple object of conspicuous display. By extension, TV snapshots resonate in contradictory ways, often with ambivalence. Rather than being sites for conspicuous consumption, the snapshots are better understood in relation to changing practices of everyday life in the new TV home, practices like homemaking, childcare, socializing, and interior design that were all in some way unsettled by the new medium. Snapshots picture these everyday practices in the space of a frame. Snapshots are what de Certeau calls "spatial stories," by which he means things like maps and tours that literally, but also figuratively, move people and chart their everyday itineraries.[24] TV snapshots move us affectively while also providing maps and tours of domestic spaces and the social itineraries of residents. Photographs don't just record the spaces and objects of everyday life; they also transform them (for example, people move furniture or clean rooms for poses). Still, snapshots are not always "picture ready." While they often seem to crystalize moments of family bliss in the tidy, picture-perfect postwar home, the snapshots in my archive lead us in another direction, to a more complicated messy repertoire of picture taking that framed TV in myriad iterations of everyday use.

TV DECOR AND LIVED-IN-NESS

In a 1951 special issue devoted to TV, the trade journal *Interiors* (aimed at high-end designers) called television a "Cyclops" that "hogged" visual attention in the home by demanding it be placed as the focal point. The editors continued, "Television attacks the American eye, and the American eye, to our military way of thinking, is something for the designer to worry about."[25] While hyperbolic, the military metaphors suggested an all-out design war on television, and (to continue the military metaphor) numerous designers offered ways to camouflage the set. Inspired by the minimalist and streamlined styles of twentieth-century modernisms, industrial designers and architects like John Vassos, Marcel Breuer, George Nelson, and Charles and Ray Eames integrated radio and television into furniture arrangements or designed custom cabinets and built-in shelving that made media recede from view. Rather than conspicuous display, the designs spoke to modernism's penchant for minimalism and to (the mostly male) modernists' association of decorative styles with women's frivolous tastes. These modernist media designs echoed the masculine rejection of femininity that design historian Penny Spark argues was central to modernist design hierarchies. (Nelson, for example, specifically associated overstuffed living rooms and fancy Chippendale radio cabinets with women's preferences and middlebrow design flaws.)[26]

Although ads for TV sets often displayed television as the focal point of living room settings and promoted decorative cabinet styles, popular home magazines took cues from the high-end designers, telling readers how to hide TV sets in walls of books and behind paintings (masking the mass medium behind "higher" intellectual and artistic pursuits). In their 1945 bestselling book *Tomorrow's House* (aimed at the growing ranks of young middle-class or middle-class aspirant homebuyers), Nelson and *Architectural Forum* editor Henry Wright instructed people to hide radios (as well as phonographs and home movie projectors) in Nelson's new architectural feature he called the "storagewall."[27] Designed specifically for housewives overwhelmed by possessions in their newly built small postwar homes, the storagewall stored everything from mops to tennis rackets to board games. In the storagewall, media machines mingled alongside the more general mess of everyday life. Picking up on the concept, well into the 1970s, popular decorating manuals taught readers how to build makeshift shelving versions and recommended camouflaging TV sets in this way (figure 1.10).[28] Histories and ethnographies of television in varied national contexts (for example, Sweden, Chile, and England) observe similar decorative attempts to camouflage the set via shelving and wall units or else by hiding the TV set in the private areas of the home (like bedrooms or closets) so that visitors would not see it.[29] Media machines are central to what I have elsewhere called the "modern history of clutter," in which objects associated with mass media were deemed unsightly and swept away through modern "clean" design.[30]

The rooms in TV snapshots seem at least somewhat inspired by socially aspirant design ideals, but they also offer a glimpse into the way people arranged their homes for TV, displaying a wider range of tastes and design practices than those pictured in magazines, handbooks, and design journals. Rather than replicate the design ideals, most snapshots indicate the kind of "making do" that de Certeau discusses in *The Practice of Everyday Life*.[31] Although people may have relied on the experts' advice, they nevertheless improvised on it, creating their own articulations of TV decor.

FIGURE 1.10 The modern media wall as featured in *The Practical Encyclopedia of Good Decorating and Home Improvement*, 1970.

While set manufacturers fashioned TV cabinets to blend with trendy furniture styles, snapshots demonstrate eclectic arrangements of period styles (a Chinese modern set mixed with a colonial furniture ensemble or a French provincial console accenting modern decor).[32] Some snapshots feature makeshift media walls and TV shelving that apparently attempt, with varying degrees of success, to approximate the modern design ideal (figure 1.11). Other snapshots display idiosyncratic tastes like a safari-themed room with a TV placed next to a ceramic elephant and an actual monkey on top of the elephant (figure 1.12). Some photos diverge from aspirational TV decor altogether, featuring bare-bones makeshift arrangements, with TV sets placed awkwardly on a table not designed for that use, sometimes spruced up with a decorative doily, giving a feminine touch to the manmade machine. Nevertheless, the fact that people photographed such rooms suggests their pride in their TV decor. That said, some snapshots indicate that the TV was by no means the most important object in the room, as is the case in a photo featuring a man posing next to a huge statue of Jesus while a tiny portable TV hides on the floor behind him (figure 1.13). Although the living room is by far the major location, TV sets also appear in dining rooms, dens, basements, bedrooms, and kitchens (figure 1.14). Taken together, the snapshots remind us of the heterogeneity of lived practices.

In addition to providing insights into tastes and decorative schemes, snapshots indicate TV's role in producing an *empty space*—that is, the place in front of and around the TV. On the one hand, this empty space was created for practical reasons: people needed to create unobstructed sight lines from which to look at the screen. On the other hand, people used this empty space as a field of social action, where they did things other than watch television.

In *The Production of Space*, Henri Lefebvre argues that even while space may be perceived as an "empty container," in effect "space is never empty; it always embodies a meaning." Space "plays a socializing role" because it is formed through the "architectronics" of larger social "networks" that govern it.[33] Speaking of the modern home, Lefebvre argues that it is networked to public infrastructures such as gas, electricity, and water, as well as radio, telephone, and television networks that link the house to the outside world and make it less an immutable, static, private space waiting to be filled by occupants than a "complex of mobilities" connected to outside forces.[34] Similarly, the fields of architecture, home building, interior design, and product design (including the design of TV sets), as well as the communication infrastructure of the postwar home, helped to produce the midcentury interior as a media space before it was ever occupied. Still, the point here is

FIGURE 1.11
(*above*) Colonial-style TV set clashes with modern built-in shelving and "mod" ornament, 1968.

FIGURE 1.12
(*right*) Circa 1960–65.

FIGURE 1.13 (*left*)
Circa 1960–65.

FIGURE 1.14 (*below*)
Circa 1955–60.

not that space is determined a priori by political-economic forces or public infrastructures. Rather, in Lefebvre's account (and in my estimation) space is produced through a complex set of determinations and procedures, and ordinary people still play a role in the way space is occupied and imagined.

Lefebvre's conceptualization of social space as embodied meaning (even in places that appear empty) is especially useful for thinking about television as an object embedded in a field of social action, and not just a "shining center" of the home. The empty space around the TV set is not a void, but rather an arena for the performance of what de Certeau calls "spatial practices."[35] Spatial practices include the practice of snapshot photography. As a field of vision, the empty space around the TV lends itself to being framed by the viewfinder so that snapshots disclose activities around TV that normally are overlooked.

In candid shots, the empty space around the TV is a play place for board games, card tables, and all sorts of festive activities. Children push toy trucks, write on blackboards, set up train tracks, twirl Hula-Hoops, pick up pickup sticks (figures 1.15–1.18). The empty space around the TV is a place of caregiving, where mothers feed children or supervise birthday parties. These images contradict received wisdom about television's destruction of social interaction and its rendering of humans (especially children) into passive viewers, which circulated in both popular and academic criticism of television at midcentury (and which often gets repeated even today). Instead, the snapshots corroborate ethnographic studies that argue against the idea of passive viewing. But while much of that scholarship focuses on fan activities or interactive video gaming, the snapshots show that even in the midcentury home, the television space was a place of play and social interaction that exceeded TV watching alone.[36] Even when the TV set is turned on, people are engaged in other activities, perhaps attending just sporadically to the screen or using TV as an ambient sound source. Often, someone in the room watches TV while others do different things. Sometimes, someone looks at the camera rather than the TV set so that taking a picture is more exciting than anything on TV. As opposed to a field of direct vision focused on TV, the empty space around the TV is a place of divided attention. In many snapshots, the TV set is far in the background, a vanishing point at best.

While television scholars often talk about TV's simulation of life—its *liveness*—TV snapshots demonstrate something different. Snapshots display the *liveliness* of people engaged in social activities other than watching programs. TV snapshots reorient television from the dominant uses (of watching) and spatial practices (of sitting in place) promoted by the TV industry.

FIGURE 1.15 (*top left*) Hula-Hooping, 1959.

FIGURE 1.16 (*top right*) Playing Twister, 1972.

FIGURE 1.17 (*bottom left*) Triffic Traffic toy, circa 1962–70.

FIGURE 1.18 (*bottom right*) Writing on chalkboard, circa 1955–60.

That said, one of the main things people do in TV snapshots is pose in front of TV sets. But, unlike the picture-ready poses in decorating manuals and women's magazines, the act of posing for snapshot cameras often reveals the *lived-in-ness* of television, the signs of everyday use in the space around it.

TV MESS

As communication media, snapshot cameras reveal how people want others to see their rooms and television's newfound place there. In snapshots that are intentionally posed, people often frame their TV homes in the best light. They tidy rooms when posing for cameras, and they also dress children. Given that Kodak routinely suggested that women were in charge of photographing, saving, and displaying family pictures, the presentation of the home in snapshots was—as Nicola Goc argues—specifically configured as a mode of women's work.[37]

Yet, even in carefully composed snapshots, television's presence often provides a direct contrast to designers' rigorous—even militant—attempts to eliminate signs of clutter and daily use. Instead, snapshots often belie the mess of television in daily life, especially the electrical cords that dangled on walls or ran across floors. Exposed in the snapshots, the cords reveal TV's fundamental incompatibility with the architectural and electrical infrastructure of the postwar family home. Wiring and outlets in traditional housing stock—as well as in the small homes of the new mass-produced suburbs— were simply not arranged in ways that allowed for the clean design recommended in both high-end and middle-class design venues. While architectural photographers for home magazines never showed outlets or electrical cords (in glamour shots of the home, the TV set seemed to operate magically without them), the snapshots reveal the unsightly jungle of electrical paraphernalia that accompanied the presence of media machines.

The clash between design ideals and electrical infrastructure is paradoxically most evident in posed shots that aspire to picture-ready ideals. One family poses three children in front of the set, which is placed next to a telephone stand so that the devices are linked in a makeshift communication center. But the gaggle of wires disrupts the scene, drooping along the wall (figure 1.19). Another snapshot presents a little girl all dressed up, posing with her doll carriage in front of her TV (figure 1.20). The picture is designed to portray the girl at her best, and she must have been proud of her pose because she signed the snapshot and addressed it to her aunt. But her dress-up pose is cluttered. A TV antenna sits on top of the set, and cords run between an electric organ and a phonograph with a doily on top.

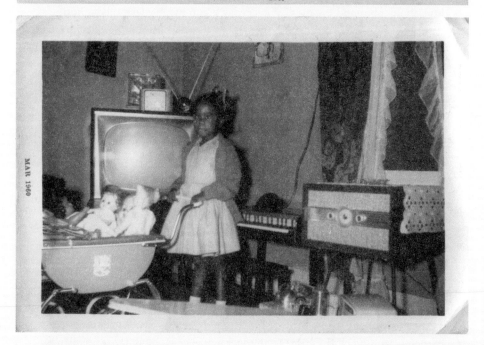

FIGURE 1.19 (*top*) 1958.

FIGURE 1.20 (*bottom*) 1960.

In snapshots like these, the tangled mess of cords, plugs, and other electrical gizmos are what Ann Cvetkovich (discussing the work of artist Zoe Leonard) calls the "low punctum" of the photograph. While Barthes's "punctum" (the incidental detail that "pricks" and evokes emotion) speaks to the deep wounds of mourning and trauma (especially in Barthes's discussion of his mother's photograph), Cvetkovich's "low punctum" refers to "emotional effects that are ordinary"—in my examples, the emotions that accompany the failure to live up to the picture-ready ideal.[38] Although decidedly not the chaotic hoard that signals "danger" in George Bell's photo, the low punctum of mess in TV snapshots suggests something not quite "pure." In TV snapshots, the low punctum manifests in the little batches of everyday clutter in media homes, the thorn in the side of women's household labor.

In addition to electrical cords and gizmos, the mess of television includes traces of women's labor as mothers, cleaners, cooks, and play pals. For example, while figure 1.20 is designed as a portrait of a child at play, women's work is evidenced by the ironing board and other utilitarian objects piled up on the lower border of the frame (apparently caught accidentally by the camera). The cords, ironing board, and piled-up objects evoke the mother's household labor and the mess of everyday life in the modern media home.

In other snapshots, the mess of media is registered in stray objects that accumulate on the TV set or in the empty space around it. The space around the TV set is what home manuals and time-motion studies called a "traffic area" for family activities. As the term implies, the traffic area is subject to congestion. In the snapshots, the TV set and empty space around it are dumping grounds for toy trucks, dolls, half-eaten bags of potato chips, laundry baskets—all sorts of leftover stuff. One snapshot shows an iron on top of a TV with the cord dangling across the screen, as if the TV set has become a makeshift worktable for household labor (figure 1.21). Meanwhile, in the same photo, children enjoy an assortment of toys (trucks, blocks, plastic bowling pins, a chalkboard) scattered around the TV, so that the space is a chaotic mix of domestic work and play. Still other snapshots reveal hair curlers, dishrags, empty plates, or baby bottles tossed willy-nilly on or around the TV set. While the mess in these snapshots usually is part of the general mise-en-scène of the photograph, in several cases people seem intentionally to document their TV mess (perhaps finding it amusing). In some photos, women are caught (likely by their husbands) in candid shots, vacuuming the carpet or ironing clothes next to the TV (figure 1.22). In all these snapshots, the "low punctum" of ordinary affects and the mess of everyday life disrupts

FIGURE 1.21 1972.

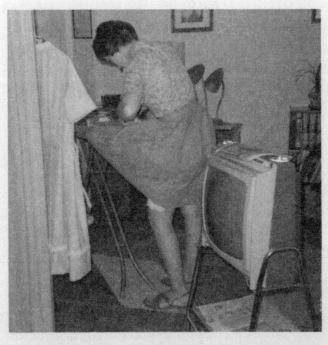

FIGURE 1.22
1965. Printed with
permission from
Mary and Leigh
Block Museum of
Art, Northwestern
University, Gift of
Peter J. Cohen, 2019.17.
Photo scan: Repository
and Digital Curation,
Northwestern
University Libraries.

the ideal depiction of TV homes as featured in ads, decorating manuals, and women's magazines.

The vacuum cleaner and ironing board snapshots (and others like them), with their focus on domestic labor, reorient the leisure-time spaces of watching TV and the (assumed) position people adopt as spectators. These photos make us look at people *not looking* at TV. Put another way, such photos suggest what Sara Ahmed calls a "queer orientation" to objects, through which people experience the object world in ways that go against the dominant norms of experience and perception.

In her book *Queer Phenomenology*, Ahmed begins by considering Edmund Husserl's phenomenological account (in which he thinks about his own relation to his desk). Ahmed argues that his theory is based on his subject position as a male philosopher who experienced the desk as a writing tool (and from a spatial position oriented toward his role as a writer). But, Ahmed argues, his phenomenological account had a blind spot; he could not see the desk from the position of people in his home (such as women laborers in the kitchen) who did not experience the desk in the same way. (For them, we might imagine, the desk was a thing to clean.) It is, however, the "concealed labor" in the background of the home (or what he perceives as the background) that supports his privileged male position as a philosopher, "that gives him the capacity to 'think' about the writing table." "In a way," Ahmed argues, "a queer phenomenology is involved in 'turning the tables' on phenomenology."[39] Ahmed especially thinks about object orientations in relation to queer sexual orientations (a point to which I return in chapter 3). But I find her concept useful in a more general way.

In one sense, as a genre, all TV snapshots could be considered for their "queer orientation" to TV, as they suggest a way of using television against the grain of the spatial orientation of television spectatorship. But the photos that feature women's labor are especially interesting in this regard. In the ironing board snapshot, for example, the woman's relation to television is literally backward. Although the TV set may provide audio accompaniment (perhaps she is listening in), her labor reorients her relation to the TV screen and TV spectatorship. We can only imagine what TV meant for domestic servants who did not actually own the TV and who may have been listening in from other areas of the house where the homeowners gathered around it. (To maids, perhaps, other people's TVs were just unwanted noise.) As I suggested at the outset, TV snapshots demonstrate spatial and object relations that depart from practices of sitting in place and watching TV, the practices broadcasters and advertisers expected. Instead, as I show throughout this book, the snapshots place bodies in all sorts of alternative spatial arrangements and positions. Moreover, they reorient the perspective from which we (as historians) look at TV.

From the perspective of women's domestic labor, the snapshots also capture how twentieth-century household technologies created what historian Ruth Schwartz Cowan calls "more work for mother."[40] While the appliance industry promoted stoves, fridges, washing machines, and the like as time-saving devices that would free women up for leisure-time pursuits, in reality, women's labor was redistributed. Childcare experts demanded that mothers spend more time on children, including the work of amusing kids. Ironically, even media machines that were intended for household leisure created more work for mother. The introduction of television was replete with debates about its effects on household chores. Women's magazines even suggested that tele-addicted housewives who neglected their chores were subject to the scrutiny of nosy neighbors who might peer into a window and see their mess.[41] This gendered logic of labor and leisure continued with the widespread introduction of the VCR in the 1980s as mothers assumed the role of housekeeper, cleaning up and organizing videotapes that accumulated on the floor around the television set.[42]

Even before the VCR, the assemblage of media technologies around the TV was itself a mode of media mess, a blight to the pristine home decoration seen in ads for TV or decorating books. TV snapshots often display a bricolage of old and new technologies stacked on top of each other, often in willy-nilly arrangements that look more like hordes than decorative ensembles. Phonographs, clocks, radios, stereo speakers, and telephones are piled on the TV set or organized beside it in improvisational arrangements of tables, stools, or stands (as in figure 1.19). Sometimes these arrangements appear to be makeshift attempts to simulate the sleek clean media walls promoted in decorating manuals or the combination TV-stereo-radio "entertainment centers" sold by TV manufacturers. Yet, in effect, these media assemblages often multiply the mess. Phonograph records spill over on a table not meant to hold them. Wires and extension cords tangle over each other as they vie for juice in a single outlet. At times, older media machines (worn-out radios or record players) just sit on the floor beside the TV pitifully, as if they have lost their eminence in the home.[43]

Snapshots even feature TV sets piled on top of each other. These assemblages evoke a complex media archaeology, as people literally layer new TVs on top of the old. One set of three photos shows a woman who stacks her TVs over time (figure 1.23). Dated 1961, the first shows the woman sitting next

FIGURE 1.23
Woman posing
with her TVs in
1961, 1968, and 1972.

to her console TV. A TV manual in her lap suggests that the console is new. The second snapshot, dated 1968, shows the same woman sitting next to the same TV console, only now there is a smaller portable TV on top. Taken in 1972, the final snapshot shows the same woman sitting next to the same TV console, but now the portable model has been switched out for a newer portable TV that sits on top of the original console. Cords run from the TV to a stereo and a clock on the credenza next to the set, revealing the mess of the media ensemble. Still, the fact that this woman posed three times in almost the same way with her TVs suggests that she was proud of her arrangements.

It seems likely that there were varied reasons for this practice, which appears, from the number of snapshots that display two TVs, to be fairly widespread. But, to take my own grandmother as an example, the logic (for her) of the double TVs had to do with sentimental ties to her broken color television set, which she regarded as a beautiful piece of furniture as well as a keepsake from my grandfather (who purchased it shortly before his death). When the color set broke down, rather than having it fixed, she purchased a new portable model and placed it on top of the TV my grandfather had bought her (alongside a commemorative porcelain bell for her golden wedding anniversary). She also posed for pictures while sitting near the double TVs (figure 1.24). I have vivid memories of her double TVs, and when I look at these photos, what I see is not the TV set so much as the figure of my missing grandfather. In other words, the TV snapshots stir affectionate memories for a family member I cherish. Judging from other photos like this, I would guess that at least for some people, similar issues of memory and attachment were at the heart of what now appears as a curious design practice of stockpiling machines that are entirely redundant, and an equally curious photographic practice of taking pictures of the double TVs.

TELE-DECORATIONS AND THE TV STILL LIFE

As my grandmother's snapshot suggests, the television set was often used as a vehicle through which to display other household things that were meaningful to their owners. In many photos, the object on display is not the TV itself but the things on top of, next to, or in front of it. Figure-ground relations in the snapshots, as well as posers, draw attention away from the TV set and toward other objects. A snapshot featuring a German couple shows them standing in front of their TV with a vacuum cleaner (figure 1.25). The photo has a handwritten note on the back that indicates it was sent to a friend or family member. The (translated German) text reads:

FIGURE 1.24 My grandmother with her two TVs, posing with my sister and nephew, 1983.

Dear Friedel,

You wanted to know about my vacuum cleaner. It is a Hoover vacuum cleaner. Paul built the bookcase with glass sliding doors. The beat up rug under the TV is 11 years old.

With Love, Ella & Paul, 1967.

While the TV is prominent in the pose, Ella and Paul mention it only as incidental. Instead, the inscription draws attention to the utilitarian object associated with women's work, and secondarily to the man's do-it-yourself handiwork. The real source of pride is the cleaning device and bookcase, not the TV.

In other snapshots, TV sets are adorned with things that express family sentiment, cultural heritage, personal achievements, and acquired taste. Trophies, dolls, family photos, souvenirs, vases, and religious tokens are often the central focus of attention in the snapshots. Functional accessories like TV lamps (a popular consumer object at the time used to enhance vision) appear on top of the TV; yet even these were designed to look like decorative keep-

FIGURE 1.25 Showing off the Hoover, 1967.

sakes (model ships, ceramic animals, and mermaids were among the many options). Many of these photos feature just the TV sets and tele-decorations on them or on the walls behind them (figure 1.26). In its use as a display medium, the TV set usurps the function of other furniture and architectural features (most notably mantelpieces and pianos) that had traditionally served as surfaces for household treasures. (And, sometimes, TV shares this function with the traditional fixtures of display.) In some photos (for example, in figure 1.27), dangling wires or utilitarian objects tossed on the TV set (like newspapers) belie the mess of television in the otherwise pristine ornamental displays. Nevertheless, in all these photos, bric-a-brac tells a family story.

Like shop windows that change their displays for the seasons, TV sets were "dressed" for holidays. Halloween pumpkins, little Christmas trees, na-

FIGURE 1.26 (*above left*) Tele-decoration snapshots hailed from many parts of the world. Germany, 1958.

FIGURE 1.27 (*above right*) Circa 1958–62.

tivity scenes, and Easter baskets adorn the TV (figures 1.28 and 1.29). Christmas cards, birthday greetings, and valentines are displayed on top of the set, or tacked to walls around it. Television merges with traditional ritual adornments to become the center of festive celebration and religious life. One Christmas snapshot depicts an emptied-out TV set whose chassis has been replaced with a nativity scene and rosary beads. A statue of the Virgin Mother prays on top (figure 1.30).

Historians and anthropologists have previously observed how people used television sets as a vehicle for symbolic expression. In an early and prescient essay on the topic, Ondina Fachel Leal examines Brazilian homes where TV sets are decorated with plastic flowers, and she explores TV sets and tele-decorations as signifiers of social class and modernity. In her influential book *Ambient Television*, and in related essays, Anna McCarthy argues we should pay attention to the "thingness" of television in public sites like stores, bars, or waiting rooms. "The television set is a kind of semiotic magnet in social space, a place to put stickers, posters, plastic flowers, real flowers, and written signs that communicate something about the space to others."[44]

TV snapshots confirm the ornamental use of the TV set as a symbolic vehicle. But the fact that people did not just decorate TVs, but also *photographed*

FIGURE 1.28 (*above left*) 1952.

FIGURE 1.29 (*above right*) Circa 1954–59. Printed with permission from Mary and Leigh Block Museum of Art, Northwestern University, Gift of Peter J. Cohen, 2019.17. Photo scan: Repository and Digital Curation, Northwestern University Libraries.

FIGURE 1.30 (*left*) 1957.

their tele-decorations, tells us something we did not know. The snapshots suggest people's urge to document, memorialize, and share their decorated TV sets—*as images*—with others. These snapshots demonstrate how the domestic gaze could easily shift points of attention from the programs that were on TV to the material "thingness" of the objects on top of and around the set.

Many snapshots of decorated TV sets are part of the *still life* mode, a category of snapshot photography promoted in photography manuals and advice literature for amateur photographers. The still life snapshot inherited its compositional strategies from still life painting, featuring pictures of everyday things like floral arrangements in vases or fruit bowls on tables. For camera enthusiasts of the early twentieth century, the still life was a form of

FIGURE 1.31 (*right*)
Circa 1961–65.

FIGURE 1.32
(*opposite*) Circa
1970–75. Purchased
from photo dealer in
Russia.

artistic expression. As *Kodakery* advised amateurs in 1922, "There is no more telling way to express one's individuality and artistic feeling with the camera than by still life studies." The arrangement should display a "texture" of material things, a "tone," and can add a "storytelling message that draws the eye and rivets the interest."[45] By the 1950s, as indoor lighting became simpler, the still life snapshot was a quotidian art for anyone interested in displaying the objects in their homes. In the 1951–52 edition of *How to Make Good Pictures*, Kodak told readers to "group interesting objects in a harmonious relationship, [thereby] achieving beauty in the pattern of shapes, shadows, and textures."[46]

As in the traditional still life scene, the TV snapshots capture the textures and tones of everyday life. Notably, many of these snapshots are devoid of human posers, and the main subject of the photo is not the TV. Instead, the TV still life presents the TV set as just a table for other things. Some photos cut off the TV or present just the top of it (figures 1.31 and 1.32).

Art historian Norman Bryson argues that still life paintings are a means of "looking at the overlooked," a way to see the details of daily life so seemingly inconsequential as to be disregarded. The first modern still lifes date from the 1600s and depict the household's affluence with such "things as fruit, baskets, goblets, bowls, as independent pictures (not just details or margins

in religious scenes)." Bryson speaks not just about the objects in the scenes, but also about the "culture of the table" that still life paintings present (images that, he argues, date back to antiquity's xenia, scenes of the household that depicted tables with food, and in later versions, serving instruments).[47] The modern still life draws from this "culture of the table," but it also deploys elements of theatricality, staging, and framing of objects in ways that suggest a self-aware aestheticizing of everyday life.

To be sure, TV snapshots are a long way from Bryson's early examples. But his analysis helps to place the snapshots within a genealogy that speaks to their wider cultural meanings and mediations of the quotidian objects in the home. The still life snapshots both documented and aestheticized television's "tabling" role in the representation of the midcentury household. Inviting people to look at the overlooked, the snapshots turn the TV set into a medium for artful displays and personal iterations of home. While it's impossible to know the gender of the camera operator, these photos sometimes feature women as the director of a scene, "dressing" TV sets as if dressing a set for a stage play, movie, or TV show (figure 1.33). In their various iterations, the camera setups suggest at least some familiarity with the codes of still life photography and, often, a deliberate striving for artfulness in everyday life.

FIGURE 1.33 1955.

Given the aesthete sensibilities of these photos and the still life's more general currency in the how-to discourses of Kodak manuals and photography magazines, these snapshots might even be considered as home-mode
forerunners to artists' renderings of TV sets that began to appear at the end
of the 1950s and early 1960s (for example, in the work of Richard Hamilton,
Tom Wesselmann, and Nam June Paik). Most directly, the snapshots resonate with Lee Friedlander's black-and-white photographs of TV settings and
tele-decorations in his series *The Little Screens*, produced in the early to late
1960s. Friedlander's photos are an uncanny foil to TV snapshots, not only
because of his chosen medium, but also because of how Friedlander stages
domestic scenes and decorates TV sets, often using darkly lit spaces with the
camera exposed for the brighter screen. For example, *Aloha, Washington,*
1967, features a bedroom setting with a television set (figure 1.34). The top of
the TV is adorned with a mix of intimate things (framed studio portraits of
children, a small alarm clock that sits on top of a lace doily) and a metal TV
antenna (which is also rendered decorative as it sits on top of another lace
doily with little cherub figurines and plastic flowers around it). Because the
photograph cuts off the bottom of the TV set, the top of it and its decorations
form a main attraction. Nevertheless, the quotidian feminine decor of this
bedroom TV sharply contrasts with the TV news image of President Lyndon
B. Johnson, whose face is pictured in an extreme closeup on the screen. John-

son's talking head is a menacing presence in this TV interior not only because it suggests the troubles of the outside world (Johnson's association with the TV coverage of President Kennedy's assassination and Vietnam) but also because the screen image of President Johnson is prominently featured (it takes up almost the entire bottom half of the photograph). The top and bottom halves of the photo induce a state of cognitive dissonance by contrasting the quotidian time of TV decoration (and TV still lifes) with the monumental/heroic time of TV news.

Friedlander's photographs are unsettling images. In 1963, Walker Evans called Friedlander's photos "deft, witty, spanking little poems of hate."[48] Conversely, the TV snapshots are welcoming and sociable; they invite the onlooker (i.e., family and friends) to see an intimate portrait of homey things. The TV still life belongs to the world of home decoration and domestic crafts, which were at the time perceived as women's domains. Rather than the modern art gallery, with its often ironic (if not hateful) attitude toward TV, the TV still life is made for the joys of the family album.

FIGURE 1.34 Lee Friedlander, *Aloha, Washington*, 1967. © Lee Friedlander, courtesy Fraenkel Gallery, San Francisco, and Luhring Augustine, New York.

SENTIMENTAL TRANSMISSIONS

Like the childhood snapshot of Bell and his father, many TV snapshots are arranged as sentimental family poses, striving for the picture-ready look of domestic bliss. These sorts of photos are today so iconic that they function as cultural shorthand for what it meant to be an ideal family in the 1950s. While I have spent much of this chapter exploring photographic practices that merged families with television sets and other household things, the family portrait remains the most ordinary, yet in my view also uncanny, sort of TV photo. It is at once so familiar and yet so strange. If, as Bourdieu claims, family photos integrate the family by rehearsing its eminence in front of the camera, in these snapshots, family photos also integrate TV into the group, making it a kind of para-human thing.

In group snapshots, family members line up next to the set or huddle in front of it or beside it, making TV appear not merely as a machine, but rather as an integral member of the family pose (figures 1.35 and 1.36). Conversely, especially in pictures of children, humans become thing-like. Snapshots often feature parents holding up newborns as prize possessions (figures 1.37 and 1.38). This is not surprising given that baby photos constitute a main share of family photos. (In 1960, for example, baby pictures accounted for an estimated 55 percent of 2.2. billion photographs taken in the United States.)[49] As should already be obvious, children often pose in front of or next to the TV. They are sometimes dressed in color-coordinated clothes that harmonize with flowers or other things on top of the TV so that humans blend with TV decor (figure 1.39). Some snapshots even show children sitting on top of the TV set, as if they are themselves tele-decorations (figure 1.40). In these scenarios, the status of children as sites of conspicuous reproduction in the nuclear family home is the central focus of display. In such cases, the new TV and the children enter into reciprocal relations; they each represent objects of desire for achieving the postwar American dream.

These photos resonate with the objectifying, even deadening, power of photography, as discussed, for example, by Walter Benjamin (in relation to his childhood portrait taken in a photography studio) and by Barthes in *Camera Lucida*. Discussing Benjamin's recollection of his childhood fears of posing for studio cameras, Esther Leslie claims that Benjamin viewed the bourgeois world of commercial photography as one where "humans become mere props."[50] Barthes's statement is even more direct. He writes that the pose (or as he puts it, "the photograph I intend") "represents that very subtle moment when, to tell the truth I am neither subject or object but a sub-

FIGURE 1.35 1957.

FIGURE 1.36
Circa 1957–60.

ject who feels he is becoming an object: I then experience a micro-version of death."[51]

In TV snapshots, the uncanny reversals between animate and inanimate things are presented in tropes of domestic sentimentality and even humor. In addition to children, people take pictures of pets, often to humorous effect. A dog lunges for the screen; or is he reaching for the birdcage perched on top of the set? A cat sits on the TV as if bric-a-brac (figures 1.41 and 1.42). The child and pet portraits resonate with broader discourses about the new medium. During the 1950s, commentators often called TV a "baby," "pet," "babysitter,"

FIGURE 1.37
Circa 1953–59.

FIGURE 1.38
Circa 1965–70.

"new family member," "nurse," and "guest," anthropomorphizing the new TV and thereby domesticating it.

Yet, there is more to this than anthropomorphism. In snapshots, the TV set plays an active role in mediating (or perhaps even broadcasting?) people's relationships with one another. The production of family sentiment in the photos is not just a reflection of people's authentic emotions; rather, sentiment is produced through complex relays between human posers and TV sets (their object design, reflective screens, tuning knobs, and tele-decorations), as well

FIGURE 1.39
Circa 1970–73.

FIGURE 1.40 1970.

as the technical affordances, operations, and protocols of use for snapshot cameras.

Snapshots often show family members at either side of the set, leaning on or gently touching it. Children hold hands (as in figure 1.40), hug, or kiss while posing with the set (figure 1.43). Couples lean in on the set as if embracing each other through it, or they gaze fondly at one another (figure 1.44). In such cases, television is not just a *mass medium* for the transmission of programs. Instead, the television set becomes an *intimate medium*

FIGURE 1.41 (*above*)
Circa 1952–60.

FIGURE 1.42 (*right*)
Circa 1967–72.

for the transmission of human emotion between the people pictured in the pose. The set draws them closer and figuratively broadcasts their sentimental bond.

Certainly, family photos can also evoke alienation, resentment, estrangement.[52] In TV snapshots, the camera often catches people in the act of "bad" performances of family (as, for example, when people don't smile, or when they stand apart from the group). In some TV snapshots people stand frozen with the set between them, as if the new object has cut off human expression and touch. In such photos, the TV set appears as a source of disconnection and alienation. The details in such snapshots can provoke the punctum (as they sometimes do for me) of family discord. But whether mediating family bonds or estrangement, TV sets help to produce the affective relations among the people in the photographic frame.

Recent scholarship on photography has emphasized the tactile and haptic nature of the medium. As I noted in the introduction, photographs are liter-

FIGURE 1.43 (*below left*) 1959.

FIGURE 1.44 (*below right*) Circa 1955–60.

ally handled, and the signs of their wear (as with a loved one's photo) are part of their material history as things. In *Touching Photographs*, Margaret Olin argues that the tactility of photographs gives rise to metaphors about the ways in which we are *touched* by them, and photos form relational communities among people who are touched by them in similar ways. In addition, Olin argues, photographs imply tactile operations and gestures (someone behind the camera or iPhone snapping the picture).[53]

Olin's concept of "touching photographs" is useful for thinking about how snapshots can evoke feelings among people looking at them, even in cases such as mine, where the photos depict strangers from the past. This is often true when it comes to people touching each other (as when a couple embraces in a snapshot). As Campt suggests, "The tenderness, joy, and connection that structures" photos of friends or loved ones can "touch us quite literally because of and through the physical touches they depict and the affective relations they solicit: [people] touch head to head, head to shoulder, arm to shoulder, shoulder to chest. Affect registers in these images through touches of demonstrative affection that enact an intimate haptics of embrace."[54] In TV snapshots the "haptics of embrace" is not limited to human bodies. It is often the TV set itself that is touched by the people in the frame, and that in turn

FIGURE 1.45 1954.

FIGURE 1.46 1956.

elicits the sentimental nature of the family bond. TV snapshots call attention to the communicative agency of photographed objects, their ability to transmit affect and sensual relations among people and things, and in turn, their ability to touch us.

Some of these touching photos are composed as group shots in which family members gather around the set. In one example (what appears to be a mother-daughter photo), a woman kneels with her arm around a girl while the girl has her arm around the TV set (figure 1.45). In such photos, the human gestures evoke closeness, almost a caress with and through the TV set. Some children appear to hug the TV as if it were a parent, teddy bear, or pet (figure 1.46).

The "tabling" function of the TV set and the tele-decorations on it also play a role in transmitting sentiment in family poses. One family portrait features children gathered around a TV set with a birthday cake on top (figure 1.47). The children on the left hold hands and caress (their hands meet on top of the TV); the girl on the right presses her fingers on top of the set; and the oldest boy stands behind the TV and the cake, holding up and pointing to a can (which appears to be the subject and action he wishes to communicate). While used as a utilitarian table for a birthday celebration, in the photo the TV set becomes a "TV cake"—a ritual object that joins the foursome together and helps to mediate the touching relations in this intimate family scene.

Sentiment is transmitted in especially curious ways when family photographs are themselves the decorative objects on top of the TV. For example, in figure 1.37 (the snapshot of parents holding up newborns), the couple's love for each other and their children is conveyed not only by their embrace or gaze at each other, but also by the wedding photo on top of the TV, which doubles the scene of their affection. In other shots, parents pose next to or in front television sets that have framed portraits of their children placed on top, completing the family scene. In some photos (as in figure 1.39), the framed studio portrait on top of the TV appears to depict a younger version

FIGURE 1.47 1958.

FIGURE 1.48 Circa 1950–55.

of the poser in the snapshot. In the TV set's role as table for other photos, it becomes a kind of time machine that depicts posers at different moments of their lives. In still other cases, studio portraits of soldiers rest on top of the TV, perhaps signaling memories of loved ones who died in combat or are stationed overseas (figure 1.48). More generally, the photos on top of the TV set are virtual stand-ins for absent family members or prior selves (who appear in snapshots as memories and remind us of the passing of time).

As Gillian Rose argues, snapshots are never just about family integration; they are also about absence and distance.[55] Especially when framed as a decorative object, or arranged in a family album, family snapshots evoke memories of faraway people or lost loved ones. Snapshots bring missing people closer through the tactile experience of handling the photo and the visual experience of looking at it. For Rose, the spatial and temporal play between here and there, now and then, constitutes an especially important dynamic for the presentation of families in snapshots and suggests a more complex form of family integration than Bourdieu imagined. TV snapshots that feature family photos on top of the set are an especially profound example of family integration by proxy. These photos are all about the *representation of absence*; the missing loved ones in photos on top of (or on the wall above) the set are made present as they mingle with people posing in front of the TV. Given television's role as a medium that conquers distance—bringing faraway places and people near—the entire scenario speaks to how TV and snapshot cameras work together as companion technologies in a unique "assemblage of the social" that constitutes everyday experience in the midcentury media home.[56]

FIGURE 1.49 Circa 1948–55.

Certainly, the performance of sentiment could occur with any cherished object. For example, a couple stand near their newly purchased car, touching it but not each other. Nevertheless, the photo may still evoke the love between the people (and not just their pride of purchase). In this sense, a television set is not uniquely capable of evoking emotion between posers, nor is it the only object capable of eliciting affective responses in people looking at the pictures. But unlike most other objects, the television set serves as a table for other sentimental things; in this regard, its evocation of affect, memory, and family bonds is overdetermined. Moreover, unlike other objects, television is a medium that transmits "live" moving images and performances into the home, which makes it both an inanimate and animate object at the same time. More than a photographer's prop, the TV set appears itself to pose for the camera along with the humans in the frame. Lined up next to people, the TV screen at times appears as a kind of extra face, waiting to express itself for the camera. Its screen "eye" stares back at the camera, and when the TV is switched on, the performers on-screen become part of the family portrait. And they sometimes seem to look at or pose with posers (figure 1.49). Even when the TV is off (which seems to be the case in many photos), the glass screen often catches the glare of a camera flash, the reflection of the camera operator, or other people in the room.

In this sense, while TV snapshots are "touching," they are never just that. Their sentimentality is complicated by the doubling, reflection, and refraction of images. These photos often call attention to camera technology and mediation. Although most are not intentionally self-reflexive, TV snapshots evoke and often index the fact that people are operating cameras and performing for them. I want to turn now to this performative dimension of TV snapshots and the configuration of domestic space as a theatrical space, or what people at the time often referred to as a home theater.

2

TV PERFORMERS

A THEATER OF EVERYDAY LIFE

In 1957, the Kodak company discovered the new photo opportunities that television offered as the ultimate family medium. At a time when programs were often financed by single or alternating sponsors who integrated commercials into shows, Kodak established a long-term relationship with early television's longest-running family sitcom, *The Adventures of Ozzie and Harriet* (ABC and CBS, 1952–66). Based on a real-life family playing themselves on TV, the program dealt with the daily mishaps of Ozzie, Harriet, and their sons, David and Ricky, a white middle-class family living in a fictional Midwest suburb. Promoting the merger of actual and fictional worlds, the couple used their own colonial-style house in the Hollywood Hills for exterior shots, while the sitcom's interior settings, which were located on a sound stage at Hollywood Center Studios, were designed as a replica of their real-life home. Week after week, the Nelson home doubled as a Kodak showroom. In the opening credit sequence, Kodak introduced "America's favorite

FIGURE 2.1
Ozzie, Harriet, Ricky, and David Nelson in advertisement for Kodak cameras, 1958.

TV family" with an image of the Nelsons exiting their house, and then (via an optical trick) they were "snapped" into the familiar white frame of a Kodak snapshot. At various points in the sitcom, the Nelsons (in their real-life personas) showed audiences the family pictures they took with their cameras, hawking everything from the Kodak Brownie and Kodachrome film to slide projectors and home movie cameras. Cross-promotions with print advertising and store displays ensured that audiences would have ample opportunities to see the Nelsons posing with Kodaks and to imagine their own families within Kodak's frame (figure 2.1). Even if most people did not have their own TV sitcom, anyone's family could pose for a snapshot camera.[1]

I begin this chapter with *Ozzie and Harriet* not only because it was one of Kodak's primary advertising vehicles, but also because the program and commercials highlight the subject at hand: poses and performance. The midcentury period was nothing if not self-reflexive about the performative nature of everyday life. On television the boundary between real life and the performance of real life was porous. Like Ozzie and Harriet, other celebrity couples (George Burns and Gracie Allen, Jane and Goodman Ace, Stuart Erwin and June Collyer, and television's most memorable sitcom spouses, Lucille Ball and Desi Arnaz) played versions of themselves on early TV. When Ball gave birth to Desi Arnaz Jr. (by C-section), her sponsor Philip Morris synchronized the date with the arrival of the fictional Little Ricky on the show, and millions tuned into CBS to see this quasi-real/quasi-staged media event. Picture magazines published endless baby pictures of the real-life Desi Jr. One publicity photo even shows Desi (senior) snapping a photo of Ball and their son in their real-life home. The blessed event was thereby staged both for TV cameras and for snapshot cameras, blurring distinctions between Hollywood and home-mode poses.

Star persona often merged with (and at times overrode) realist character construction in these sitcoms, which made performance segments central to their plots and premises. *Ozzie and Harriet, I Love Lucy*, and *Burns and Allen* all featured the talents of their stars by using the domestic setting as a stage for performance. In *Lucy*, Desi Arnaz (as nightclub bandleader Ricky Ricardo) and Lucille Ball (as "wannabe" showgirl Lucy Ricardo) often performed in the fictional Tropicana nightclub, which was a standing set on the *I Love Lucy* sound stage. But performance sequences just as often took place in the domestic settings. All sorts of everyday things—couches, chairs, lamps, desks, pillows, vases—became props or costumes for music, dance, and comedy routines.

The showbiz family sitcoms spoke to American culture's larger fascination with the performative nature of everyday life, which could be found not only in popular media but also in midcentury social theory, which took a decidedly dramaturgical turn. In 1955, sociologist Nelson Foote wrote an article titled "Family Living as Play" in which he argued, "The family home may be most aptly described as a theater." The members of the family, he suggested, were performers in a play enacted for each other: "The husband may be an audience to the wife, or the wife to the husband, or the older child to both." Acknowledging the introduction of television into this family theater, Foote nevertheless argued, "By no means is this concept [of the home as a theater] to be reduced to watching television. . . . The ration of time spent by family members as an audience for the performance of each other as against time spent in watching commercial portrayals may signify how well the home rates as a theater in their own eyes."[2]

Foote's essay fluctuates between two meanings of play: one, a theatrical performance; the other, the ritual modes of play that sociologist/psychologist

Gregory Bateson (1955) deemed central to social interaction. For Bateson, play was a form of metacommunication based on a linguistic paradox that was performative in nature. In play, people understand their acts are make believe, and therefore "the statement 'This is play' looks something like this: 'These actions in which we now engage do not denote what those actions *for which they stand* would denote'" in ordinary contexts.[3] During play, actions (such as fighting) that denote conflict and produce fear when performed in nonplay situations (such as combat) no longer suggest such literal cues or cause such responses. Although Foote did not cite Bateson (their articles were published in the same year), the slippage in meaning between play as social activity and play as theater was central to the postwar fascination with social interaction in everyday life. (Bateson himself goes on in this essay to talk about movies and spectatorship.) In Foote's theatrical framework, there is a ludic and ritual dimension to family performance in which people understand that the roles they assume are not the roles they normally play.

One year later, in 1956, Erving Goffman published the first (Scottish) version of what would become his seminal 1959 book, *The Presentation of Self in Everyday Life*.[4] Like Foote, Goffman drew on literary critic Kenneth Burke's theories of symbolic action for his inspiration, but he laid out a much more sweeping sociological treatise on the nature of social relations. Goffman observed the "front region" and "back region" (or "backstage") behaviors that defined the field of social relations. So-called authentic expressions of self were an effect (rather than the essence) of self-presentation, and they involved what he called "impression management." Whether at home, at work, at school, in hotels, or in any other social context, people and groups of people (or "teams") performed roles in "settings," and if considered "sincere," the setting corresponded to how the performance was delivered. For example, if visiting a middle-class family home, one would expect the manner to be polite and respectful. But fundamentally, even if people believed themselves to be sincere, social life was based on performing roles. It was "dramaturgy." Not coincidentally, Goffman began his book with an epigraph about masks.

Goffman's dramaturgical approach to social relations would come to have a major influence on the direction of modern sociology, and even today it helps to explain social relations and "impression management" in digital culture.[5] But in Goffman's book, his thoughts on media are restricted to several mentions of broadcast productions and news reports. He never mentions the one major domestic medium through which people staged themselves and managed impressions of the household: the snapshot camera. This connection—

between theater, performance, masks, and cameras—would come later, in Barthes's *Camera Lucida*.

POSING PLACE

The midcentury obsession with showbiz family sitcoms, and the sociological focus on dramaturgy in everyday life, form a historical context for thinking about TV snapshots.

As I suggest in chapter 1, studio photographers and Kodak manuals often conceptualized family portraits in theatrical terms, surrounding picture takers with quotidian "props"—furniture, rugs, vases, and so forth—or adorning them in Sunday-best attire that functioned as costumes in pictures. Moreover, television's presence in snapshots follows the longer history of performative poses with media objects like telephones, magazines, or radios, which were also used as props.[6]

In *Camera Lucida*, Barthes writes that when being photographed, "everything changes: I constitute myself in the process of 'posing,' I instantaneously make another body for myself, I transform myself in advance into an image. This transformation is an active one."[7] While all poses may be performative, the addition of a television set to the pose creates new pictorial possibilities. The photos I explore in this chapter speak to the increasing mediatization of home life in postwar culture—the plethora of screens and live transmissions— and in this context, they engage new opportunities to make "another body" for oneself. People perform in front of the set, and they use TV as a prop and backdrop for the presentation of self and family. People also delight in performing optical tricks with their TV sets in ways that go beyond documenting the family and toward a self-reflexive mode of acting for the camera and "family living as play." In the TV home, snapshots visualize the concept of home as theater, and in so doing, they become quotidian enactments of the dramaturgical theory of everyday life.

In rather literal ways, performance snapshots invert the normative object and spatial relations between viewers and TV sets. People who pose in these photos assume what Ahmed calls a "queer orientation" to objects. Rather than watching actors perform on TV, people watch each other perform in front of it, beside it, and even—in trick shots—inside the TV. In these photos, the empty space around the television set essentially becomes a *posing place* in which people play roles and engage in acts of everyday pretend.

Kodak manuals and how-to books had traditionally recommended families pose in front of fireplaces or windows, both of which provided theatrical backdrops that framed human subjects. Although the manuals continued to recommend these spots in the postwar period, in snapshots the television set often usurps the role of previous domestic posing places. In part, this is likely the result of the shrinking size of the postwar suburban home. Given limitations of space, television sets were often placed next to windows or fireplaces, the traditional focal points in a room. In some snapshots, the TV set is even placed inside the hearth, which apparently has gone out of use. Moreover, many of the new suburban homes were built without fireplaces, so that TV sets became the sole focus of attention. Yet, in a more figural sense, both the fireplace and window became metaphors for television. In the parlance of the era, television was both a "window on the world" that brought views of far-off places to the home as well as an "electronic hearth," the center for family togetherness.[8] TV snapshots literalize these metaphors.

The fireplace is an especially interesting case given its historical associations with family sentiment. As a posing place, television shares or takes on the ritual functions previously performed at the hearth. Christmas, Easter, Halloween, Mothers' Day, New Year's Eve are all occasions for poses in front of or next to the TV. (The Easter and Christmas snapshots in chapter 1 are examples.) Ritual moments of life cycle are celebrated in the TV setting. Children and teens blow out birthday candles or appear in ceremonial costumes like graduation regalia and confirmation dresses (figures 2.2–2.4).

FIGURE 2.2
Circa 1972–75.

FIGURE 2.3
Circa 1952–59.

FIGURE 2.4
Circa 1952–59.

In *Stuff*, Daniel Miller argues that rather than focus on the symbolic meanings of objects, material culture studies should instead attend to how objects form backdrops for the performance of social relations. Drawing on Goffman and art historian E. H. Gombrich, Miller argues for a "frame" analysis that explores how objects recede from view to become social settings that create an "exterior environment that habituates and prompts us" to act in certain ways. Referring to his ethnographic case study of pots in an Indian village and their iconic use at a wedding, he notes that his informants told him that his desire to understand the meaning of the pots made him miss their larger social import. "As the villagers were telling me again and again the pots are not the point, they are the frame. Material objects are a setting. They make us aware of what is appropriate and inappropriate. . . . But they work most effectively when we actually don't even look at them, we just accept them." "The surprising conclusion," he argues, "is that objects are important, not because they are evident or physically constrain or enable, but quite the opposite. It is often precisely because we do not see them. The less we are aware of them, the more powerfully they can determine our expectations, by setting the scene and ensuring proper behavior."[9]

Picture taking is critical to the ways in which objects and architectural features become frames and backdrops for family performance in the home. As television takes the place of previous posing spots, it melts into the background. Rather than watch actors perform on TV, people act out roles in the TV setting and use television sets as a prop for performance. The performance of family rituals is often rendered in camera images that display the repertoire of actions, expressions, and gestures involving the TV set. For example, one snapshot shows a "just married" couple who place their wedding cake on top of their TV and pose for a picture staged for the camera (figure 2.5). A "touching photo," (much like the photo of the birthday cake TV in chapter 1), the snapshot communicates love between the posers through the intermediary device of the TV set. But the pose is also a ritualized and gendered enactment. Standing behind the set (so that the cake on top of it is fully in view), the couple perform the ritual cake-cutting ceremony, with the groom feeding a slice to the bride. Television plays a crucial part in "setting the scene" of the photo and "ensuring proper behavior."[10]

Snapshots show people performing—or *pretending* to perform—all sorts of daily activities in front of the TV set. Children pretend to ride bicycles, throw footballs, wheel doll carriages. In the context of the 1950s Davy Crockett craze (in part spurred by Disney's TV shows and Disneyland's Frontierland), kids dress in cowboy and cowgirl costumes and pretend to shoot toy

AUG 1962

FIGURE 2.5 1962.

guns. Even when not dressed in western gear, boys and men shoot toy—and real—guns (figure 2.6). One man (likely a policeman) captures the performance of killing so well that it's hard to tell if the gun play is a pretense (figure 2.7). More generally, however, playing at doing something creates a kind of *magic circle* around the TV in which people understand they are mutually engaged in acts of make believe and role play (much as video games, computer games, and alternate reality role-playing games operate today).[11]

TV SHOWS?

Snapshots often literally picture people performing as entertainers in their homes. In these photos, the TV screen is a backdrop for family recitals and amateur shows. Photos portray people playing instruments or dancing (or pretending to do so) while posing in front of or next to the TV set. These per-

JAN 65

FIGURE 2.6 1965.

OCT · 62

FIGURE 2.7 1962.

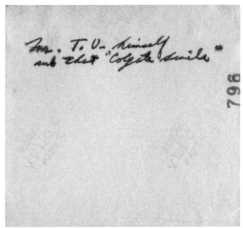

FIGURES 2.8 & 2.9 "Mr. T.V." with inscription on back, circa 1950–55.

formance photos literalize Barthes's claim that rather than cinema or painting, the photograph is most like theater.

In numerous shots, furniture appears to have been moved to set the area around the TV as one would set a stage. One photo features a man who sits on a chair that's been moved in front of the living room TV. Smiling for the camera, he strums his guitar. The inscription on the back of the snapshot reads, "Mr. T.V. himself and that 'Colgate smile'" (figures 2.8 and 2.9).

The popularity of amateur talent shows on network and local television must have encouraged people to consider television as a space for quotidian performance. But rather than play piano or croon pop tunes for TV's mass audience, in snapshots people perform in front of TV for an intimate group of family and friends. Some snapshots present family members and guests watching the performance. A man plays (or pretends to play?) his accordion next to his TV set (figure 2.10). The photo includes an audience for the performance by way of a large mirror on the wall just behind him. The mirror reflects a second man (just his head) who appears to be sitting and watching the accordion performance. His gaze is reflected in a reverse field of vision. In this and similar photos, the mirror functions as what Michel Foucault calls a "heterotopic" space, an "other space" that reorients and reorders the dominant spatial arrangements in everyday life.[12] The important point in relation to the snapshots is the way in which the mirror reorders the home and turns it into the "other space" of the theater. As pictured in the snapshot, the mirror reflects, but also reconfigures, social relations of domesticity in terms of spectator reactions to a performance. When mirrors hang on the wall behind the TV, they sometimes reflect people gazing at other people performing in front of the screen, and they also at times reflect the camera operator shooting the "show." In some snapshots, the TV screen itself takes on the mirror's function, offering faint glimpses of spectators sitting on sofas watching people perform in front of the TV for the snapshot camera.[13] Whether in the mirror or through the screen, reflections of spectators highlight how a TV home can easily morph into a home theater.

Given the midcentury's focus on cultivating the talents of children, it's not surprising that snapshots often feature kid acts. Boys (always boys) play accordions, guitars, drums, or horns (figures 2.11 and 2.12). Girls (always girls) sit at toy pianos that have been moved into the empty place around the TV (figure 2.13). The writing on the back of one such photo calls attention to the child's make-believe performance. In a child's scrawl, the text reads, "Dear Daddy and Mommy, A simple remembrance of my recital. Love, Daphne." Other girls wear tutus, striking ballerina or tap dancing poses (figure 2.14).

FIGURE 2.10
Circa 1957–62.

FIGURE 2.11
(*above*) 1956.

FIGURE 2.12
(*right*) 1964.

FIGURE 2.13
Circa 1952–57.

FIGURE 2.14 1955.

As is obvious, these snapshots are also a performance of gender, even if some posers seem to achieve the midcentury picture-ready gender ideal more than others.

Performance photos are part of a more general focus on theatricality and cinematic appeals in home-mode photography after World War II. In her discussion of 1950s home movies, Patricia Zimmermann shows how photography manuals taught readers to create storytelling plots akin to those found in Hollywood movies. Even though snapshots could not literally move, how-to advice on still photography similarly proposed ways to simulate Hollywood narratives by staging scenes in a cinematic fashion.[14] As a 1950 article in *Popular Photography* told readers, "Sequencing tells the story." Bearing in mind the slow speed of the low-end camera, the article recommends a "leisurely sequence of a child opening a present."[15] In 1959 the same magazine told readers to shoot photos in "chronological order" and "make a storyboard" to plan out action for family pictures.[16] More generally, the photo magazines conceptualized family members as stars of their own photos, and they applied the language of theatrical exhibition. The 1959 "storyboard" article told readers to "decide what audience you're interested in. Is it children? Adults? Make the slant pleasing to the audience."[17]

The postwar camera guides, with their focus on storyboarding, acting, and audiences, can be better understood when considered in the context of interdisciplinary scholarship that considers relationships between performance and photography (and other forms of documentation).[18] In her pathbreaking book *The Archive and the Repertoire*, Diana Taylor considers the relation between performance and documentation (including photos) by drawing on theories of "performativity," especially what Derrida called the citational and iterative acts entailed in the performance of language and "the event of speech."[19] For Taylor, Derrida's provocation opens up ways to think about embodied performances as not just ethereal and spontaneous to a moment but rather as iterations of a repertoire of bodily gestures and expressions that exist in cultural memory. For instance, a poser might "cite" gestures common to stage acting, drawing on a repertoire of cultural memory while also archiving (or documenting) this in a photo. Taylor also considers the activity of taking photographs as itself a performative act that, I would suggest, also entails citation of a preexisting repertoire. For example, a person taking a photo may "cite" similar poses in film or television but create specific iterations of them. Finally, Taylor investigates the meanings and affective resonances this has for posers, camera operators, and people looking at the photo. The interdisciplinary scholarship on performance and photography often focuses on photography of live events or video recordings of performance art, but the concepts of iteration and citation, and the concerns with the performativity involved in picture taking, are useful for thinking about family snapshots as well.

When considered from this perspective, TV snapshots are not just pictures of a performance; they are, more specifically, *performative.* These snapshots cite and reiterate a repertoire of culturally coded modes of performance (found in theater, in ceremonial rituals, in fashion magazines, in films, and on TV itself). But they are not mere mimicry of some more professional mode. Instead, the snapshots are quotidian iterations of performance experienced via the everyday repertoires of home-mode picture taking.

Snapshots taken in sequence in the storyboarding mode provide clues into the repertoire of actions entailed in staging these performative poses. One little boy, dressed in his Sunday best, poses for three pictures, apparently taken in succession on the same occasion (figure 2.15). The three photos are rendered in the storyboard mode, and they appear to cite a virtuoso performance that might take place at a public recital. Although it's impossible to know which one of these photos came first, the sequence suggests that the camera operator must have deliberated on each pose. One features the boy with a violin in one hand and his bow in the other. A television set is behind him. A second snapshot moves in closer to frame the scene in detail. Now standing nearer to the TV set, the boy poses with his bow on the strings, as if performing for the camera. A third photo shows the boy on his mother's lap as she sits in a chair. The main action in this shot is one of affection, as the boy kisses his mother's cheek. The triptych offers a glimpse into how these performance snapshots functioned as do-it-yourself domestic recreation, a means of family bonding, and a way to showcase a child's talents. Each photo is a citation and iteration of a performative repertoire, and the presence of the mother as diegetic audience embodies the affective response to the scene solicited from the people who will eventually look at the picture. Presumably, the family would share these performance photos with others and in so doing "publicize" their little "stars."

Performance photos often evoke the sonic traces of everyday life. The image of the little boy with his violin suggests the musical sounds of his bow across the strings as he first prepares and then executes (or mock executes) the performance. Despite the doubling of mass-media sound devices (there is a radio on top of the TV set), the three snapshots direct attention to and anticipate the acoustic sounds of the boy's violin rather than the technologically transmitted sounds of broadcast entertainment.

FIGURE 2.15 A sequence
of snapshots in storyboard
mode, 1972.

The acoustic dimension of TV was often registered in snapshots that depict dancers. In such photos, the empty space around the TV effectively becomes a dance floor. It is often unclear if the implied music comes from the TV or some other domestic sound source, but the TV set serves as a setting for the performance. In one photo, a woman appears in front of a TV apparently doing the twist (a dance craze popularized in Chubby Checker's 1960 hit single "The Twist"). Perhaps caught in the act, she nevertheless looks at the camera, aware that her dance is also a pose (figure 2.16). The wall decorations above the set (plaques of ballet dancers and stencils of dancing girls), as well as dancer figurines on top of the set, reinforce the centrality of dance in the home and mark the TV setting as a stage set for the woman's dance routine.

Photos of dancers often register the presence of a home audience watching the scene. In figure 2.16, a camera flash goes off in the mirror, indicating the presence of the camera operator as an audience for the woman's rendition of the twist. In another snapshot, a man (likely a father) dances in front of a TV with a little girl (likely his daughter). Other children circle around them as if watching and participating from the wings of a dance floor (figure 2.17). Although she is mostly cut off by the viewfinder, a woman sitting in a chair forms an additional audience member (her legs reach into the right side of the frame). The main subjects of the snapshot appear to be aware that they are performing not only for people in the room, but also for the camera. The girl looks at the camera, and both she and her dance partner appear stilled in a pose.

Although people of various ethnicities, races, and nations danced in front of their TV sets, the snapshots of African American dancers resonate with the unique status of Black musical performance in the period. Television's association with the burgeoning record market for African American jazz, pop, and soul artists was a major selling point in advertisements for home entertainment aimed at Black consumers. *Ebony* ran ads for hi-fi/TV combination models, some tailored specifically for the African American market, with Black performers on the screen.[20]

Some snapshots succinctly capture this articulation of television with hi-fi culture and Black musical performance. One photo presents a boy in a white shirt and bowtie who appears to tune in the TV set while a dapper toddler in a striped sports jacket rifles through jazz LPs (figure 2.18). Nat King Cole's *Unforgettable* (1954) is pictured prominently on the floor. Although it is hard to tell if the photo is a candid shot or a deliberate pose (the boys look at each other as opposed to the camera), the formal attire indicates a special occa-

FIGURE 2.16 1963.

sion and gives them a camera-ready look. The camera operator frames the scene in such a way as to picture the boys as masters of ceremonies for home entertainment, with one child tuning in the TV while the other performs as a disc jockey sorting through LPs. A little girl seated on an ottoman forms a diegetic audience, her gaze ambiguously directed at the TV screen and the boys. Even the baby she holds seems to look at the boys and the screen, so that everything is framed around spectators and performers.

While photos such as this one present fleeting moments of everyday life, they become more meaningful when considered in terms of television's racist casting system. In the late 1940s through much of the 1960s, the television industry provided few lead roles for performers of color. While Black talent often appeared in network variety shows like *The Ed Sullivan Show* (CBS, 1948–71) or on dance programs like *American Bandstand* (ABC version, 1957–87), the casting system made clear distinctions: whites could command the stage as hosts, while African Americans, as well as Latinx or Asian performers, appeared almost exclusively as guest stars (subject to invites and callbacks from white producers). When they did appear on network stages, performers of color were often presented as racialized, exoticized, or Orien-

FIGURE 2.17 1961.

talized others.[21] While the performers did at times assert their agency (for example through linguistic code switching), the guest star system worked to contain them within hegemonic narratives of inclusion and assimilation.[22] Ann duCille observes that even while some white hosts hoped their stages would be spaces of integration, regardless of individual politics, the guest star system was also a savvy business practice that allowed networks to hire, at relatively low cost, some of the most talented stars, many of whom were Black.[23] Studio audiences were also subject to racist practices. As Matthew Delmont points out in the case of *American Bandstand*, even while the program presented Black musical groups, when it transitioned from local TV to the ABC network in 1957, it regularly blocked Black teenagers from its studio audience and dance floor until 1964.[24] More generally, the networks often capitulated to network affiliate stations in the South that objected to seeing white and Black bodies dancing together on TV.

The African American press alerted readers to discriminatory Jim Crow hiring practices while also singling out several local shows with Black hosts and praising network firsts like Nat King Cole. But given the rarity of these shows, more typically, the press cleverly responded to the networks' racist

FIGURE 2.18 Circa 1958–62.

star system by foregrounding the pleasures TV offered Black viewers. The *Chicago Defender*, the *New York Amsterdam News*, and *Jet* published TV schedules that were edited to feature Black guest star performers, telling viewers, for example, which Black musicians were on TV variety shows at what time, a strategy that suggests the excitement of seeing Black performers on the new medium and a relative disinterest in white headliners. Television producer and actor Tim Reid recalls: "Somebody would yell, or we would know through the grapevine that some black person was going to be on television that night and we watched it. The rest of it we didn't watch, I mean there was nothing that related to us or we could relate to so we didn't watch it." Similarly, cultural critic Patricia Turner says: "I can remember my mother, my aunts, and my neighbors. If they heard that a black person was going to be on television or if they saw one come on the screen, they would dash to the phone and start calling each other so that the neighbors and the aunts wouldn't miss it."[25]

When seen in the context of television's racist star system, the performance snapshots take on new dimensions. Like the strategic viewing of Black talent promoted in the African American press, the snapshots were a means by which people reimagined the Jim Crow practices of network TV's guest star system. Even if television cameras displayed Black performers as guest stars on a white man's stage, with a snapshot camera, African Americans could host their own performances in their own homes. Although perhaps not intentional or conscious acts of resistance to TV racism, the snapshot camera gave African Americans agency and control over images that the white-dominated television industry historically denied.

While not always charged with these political meanings, all the performance snapshots invert the normative relations between TV performers and TV watchers. In snapshots, people used TV figuratively to "broadcast" themselves and to steal the show away from the programs on-screen. Or in the words of my previous example, they demonstrate how people picture themselves as "Mr. T.V." Whether strumming guitars, tinkling little pianos, dancing in tutus, doing the twist, or pretending to do so, people used TV as a backdrop for self-presentation. Nevertheless, it's important that the TV set and not some other thing is present in the picture. Unlike a wall, fireplace, or window, the TV set is itself a performance medium so that its presence in the snapshots overdetermines the reading of the pose as stagecraft, keying the spectator to understand it as such.

While I have so far been thinking about TV as a prop or frame, its status as a medium is often registered in these performative poses. The snapshots don't just picture residents performing at home; they also often capture images off the TV screen so that people seem to pose with TV performers. By depicting the home as a scene of dramaturgy and quotidian performance, the snapshots blur distinctions between the homebodies in domestic spaces and the bodies that dwell in the ethereal spaces of television. In the rest of this chapter, I explore how people used cameras creatively and playfully to reflect on their new home theaters and the relationship between the *lived* space in front of the TV set and the *live* space of TV transmission.

HOME THEATERS: FROM TABLEAU VIVANT TO TV LIVENESS
Performance snapshots follow on practices of domestic amusement that date back to the Victorian home and the parlor theatricals that women arranged for family members and guests. Advice books on domestic amusements and etiquette manuals on the art of hostessing recommended that residents follow scripts for plays that could be staged by ordinary people in their homes. In particular, the performance snapshots resemble the Victorian art of the *tableau vivant*, literally a living picture of a human subject frozen in a still pose that rendered a dramatic scene (such as a battle) or was allegorical, spiritual, or expressive of feelings (such as hope or motherly love).[26] While the tableau vivant was not confined to domestic space (it was also a public art),

the parlor versions—with their rendering of domestic space into stage space and, of course, their dramatic "stillness"—bear striking relations to photographic poses.

In *Camera Lucida*, Barthes makes a direct comparison between the tableau vivant and the photograph, claiming, "Photography is a kind of primitive theater, a kind of Tableau Vivant, a figuration of the motionless and made-up face beneath which we see the dead."[27] Barthes is concerned with the formal stillness of the tableau vivant as an analog for photography and its relation to death. But the domestic versions that concern me here have an important resemblance to snapshot photography in terms of the quotidian and gendered aspects of both practices. Both were coded as feminine arts made by and for women, and both required women to learn technical crafts of staging, lighting, and posing. Domestic advice manuals told women where to buy scripts and the items (costumes, props, lamps) needed to mount these amusements. In other words, like the first Kodak cameras and the Kodak Girls, tableaux vivants were an early form of women's consumer culture.

By the early decades of the twentieth century, home amusement machines (phonographs, radios, home movie projectors, and cameras) increasingly took over the role played by the parlor theatricals, importing industrialized modes of theatrical experience into domestic life. As a medium that transported distant images and sounds "live" into the home, television had a unique role to play in the theatrical conception of domestic space. As early as the late nineteenth century, futurologists predicted the advent of a televisual-like device, enthusing about the images transmitted over the ether. In 1912, the mass periodical the *Independent* announced the imminent arrival of the "Future Home Theater" through a combination of film and disc (or "talking pictures") sent through the telephone wires to "every home, so that one can go to the theater without leaving the sitting room."[28] In the postwar period, the home theater became both a common practice and an industrial metaphor for the TV experience. Advertisements for television sets routinely referred to TV as a "home theater," and programs adopted titles like *Goodyear Television Playhouse*, *Texaco Star Theater*, and *Admiral Broadway Revue*. The performative and theatrical TV snapshots resonate with this televisual context. They also resonate with the emphasis on *liveness* and live performance in the production of and discourses on early TV.

In the 1950s, broadcasters and TV critics especially valued television's liveness—not just TV's technical capacity for live transmission, but also the aesthetic construction of intimacy, immediacy, and simultaneity that makes viewers feel as if they are transported to live events or performances unfolding in real time. The television industry promoted liveness as an ontology, ideology, and artistic ideal that made TV different from the "pastness" of cinema.[29] Even while television was increasingly shot on film by the mid-1950s, liveness remained a routine aspect of TV. Television set manufacturers often advertised liveness as a phenomenological feature of the TV experience by, for example, showing television performers popping out of the TV set or residents in the home giving televised dogs biscuits right through the screen (figure 2.19).[30] In its ideal form, TV would give audiences a feeling of "being there" on the scene or what media theorists now refer to as *telepresence*.

In snapshots, the telepresent places and performers on the TV screen often seem to merge with the material space of the home and the residents in it. Here, TV's liveness is coupled with the *liveliness* and *lived-in-ness* of domestic life depicted in snapshots. The significance of this merger takes two related photographic paths: The first is rooted in the conflation of private and public life and the performance of national rituals as media events on

FIGURE 2.19
Advertisement
for GE television,
1951.

live TV. The second is a function of the virtual, and often uncanny, nature of liveness. Both entail distinct photographic hobby art practices that engage conundrums of telepresence.

PHOTOGRAPHING TELEPRESENCE: SCREENSHOTS

In *Radio, Television, and Modern Life*, Paddy Scannell considers broadcasting's "doubling of space," the interplay between a live event on-screen and the reception space of the viewer. From a phenomenological standpoint, Scannell focuses on how television helped to change people's experience of public events, essentially allowing the viewer to be in "two places at once." As an ex-

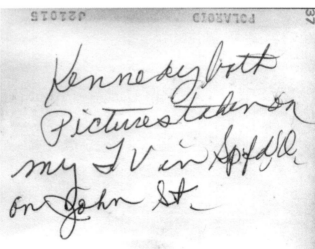

FIGURES 2.20 & 2.21
Screenshot of
President Kennedy
and inscription on
back, circa 1962.

ample, he cites the 1953 coronation of Queen Elizabeth II and the sacralization of an official public ritual through domestic viewing. Viewers, for example, may drink beer, yell at the queen (or president), and wear pajamas while watching a national media event in their homes. Meanwhile, public officials had to anticipate and stage TV cameras for the performance of national ceremonies like the coronation.[31]

Snapshots provide new clues for understanding how people experienced this doubling of space, especially how they documented public performances visually, in effect making these media events into their own creative forms of photographic witnessing. In TV snapshots, the doubling of space is less about the nation's attempt to stage official events for TV cameras than it is about the viewer's role in restaging televised events that were transmitted into the home. This is especially pronounced in the screenshots of televised events people snapped off TV.

Variously referred to as *video portraits*, *off-the-screen photography*, *video photography*, and *armchair photography*, screenshots were a popular hobby art. Magazines like *Popular Photography* and *Popular Science* ran how-to columns, advising their mostly male readers on the new photographic art that could be accomplished with a snapshot camera and some amateur know-how. The hobby was a way to perform with a camera, and the magazines and camera clubs held contests and amateur shows in which shutterbugs could compete. Winning photos were displayed in the magazines and sometimes in local venues. In this sense, the screenshots were a form of para-TV performance, in which people could use TV to showcase their own image repertoire and achieve a modicum of fame on the amateur photography circuit. Many screenshots feature run-of-the-mill variety show performers or scenes from dramas, while others capture live sports or media events. Although with different goals from the TV still life, the screenshots were also a mode of "stilling" TV, in this case by capturing moving images in time. Screenshots were a way to preserve ephemeral TV broadcasts before the advent of the VCR.[32] Nevertheless, the screenshots are not just shots of screens; many also include depictions of the TV set, the domestic setting around it, and the tele-decorations on top of it.

One such screenshot (ca. 1962) features President John F. Kennedy. (The photographer actually snaps two almost identical photos, most likely to choose the best result.) Each photograph depicts a televised headshot of the president. Rather than just snap the image of Kennedy, the camera operator instead framed the snapshot so that the whole TV (a modern walnut console with two built-in stereo speakers) is visible. Decorative wallpaper peeks out behind it, and the carpet beneath it is also in the frame. A potted plant and curios (which are arranged in pairs) sit on top of the TV. In other words, the image is both a screenshot and a TV still life, and it incorporates background elements of the domestic space. Taken as a whole, the image is not just a picture of a national media event (a new president talking on TV). Instead, it captures the doubling of space that Scannell theorizes. It is about both the ceremonial space of the nation and the intimate space of the home. This is further suggested by the inscription on one of the two photos. "Kennedy" is penned in cursive writing on the front white border of this Kodak print (figure 2.20). On the back of the photo, in the same penmanship, the inscriber writes "Kennedy[,] both photos taken on my TV in Springfield on John St." (figure 2.21). The inscriber specifically locates the picture in the home; what is meaningful to this person is not just that the photo captures Kennedy but that it captures Kennedy on *their* TV, in *their* city, and on *their* street. Although no resident poses in this picture, the snapshot nevertheless is about the dweller. The photo is a record of their personal itinerary. The person who shoots this snapshot is ultimately documenting their own relation to a national TV event as it unfolds live in real time in their home. This is, in the end, a presentation of self as witness to the presentation of a public figure performing on TV.

At the present moment of digital reproduction, it may be hard to fathom the skill required to shoot still images off an analog screen without the aid of VCRS or DVRS, with their pause buttons and freeze frames. Even while people who made screenshots often used high-end snapshot cameras, arresting a moving image on TV was difficult at best. TV sets were subject to contingencies of bad reception, and even if reception was good, the scan lines and screen glare made it hard to get good results. Screenshots required knowledge of the tricks of the trade, which magazines like *Popular Photography* provided by instructing readers on lighting, aperture, shutter speed, and film stock as well as the use of special equipment like tripods. Shooting off TV also demanded knowledge of TV tuning (how to adjust contrast and brightness knobs); how to compensate for screen shapes (like the curved screens on portables); and how to avoid quick blur when TV cameras panned, dollied, or zoomed in for a close-up. Offering these and other insider tips, a 1960 feature story in *Popular Photography* told readers how to "record history as it is made by shooting your TV screen." The article presented a close-up of President Kennedy taken off the screen (much like my example). It also recommended that if frames from programs were shot in sequence, photographers should make sure to take pictures of program titles (or *telops*) off the screen and "include them in albums" designed with specific themes in mind (like Kennedy's assassination or sports events).[33]

The repertoire of skills required for the screenshots is most apparent in photos that were taken in sequence. Such snapshots freeze the flow of media events on-screen. For example, four snapshots follow the news coverage of President Kennedy's death in November 1963 (figure 2.22). (Along with the 1969 moon landing, this seems to be the most photographed US TV event in the decade.) One photo in the sequence captures a frame from the title art for CBS *News Special Report*. The other three snapshots feature screen images taken at different times during the week of Kennedy's death. One displays CBS news anchor Walter Cronkite (who first broke the news of the assassination); another captures CBS news anchor Harry Reasoner talking on the telephone to newscasters in Dallas about the condition of Lee Harvey Oswald (this is a snapshot version of what became an iconic newsroom photo of Reasoner learning that Oswald had been gunned down); the fourth screenshot shows the casket being carried in the funeral procession. Unlike the news still, however, the TV snapshot locates the media event in the time and place of the home. As with the previous example, each photo displays the camera operator's domestic setting. The television set is decorated with a potted plant and a ceramic squirrel. The photographs also feature a table with a lamp and a vase of flowers; a partially visible painting on the wall; part of a brick fireplace; and wires dangling on the floor. Taken in intervals across the four-day coverage of Kennedy's death, these four snapshots chart the relation between the time and space of the nation and the quotidian time and space of watching TV (the time of the viewer at home).

In these and other examples, screenshots speak both to TV's *liveness* and its *lived-in-ness*. Although no actual residents are included in the pictures, the experience of home is everywhere in these photos. By documenting a national event within the frame of their own domestic setting, people performed their personal orientation toward it. Television shutterbugs saw public rituals as an occasion for locating—and performing—their unique relation to the media event as they witnessed it in their homes. Rather than just shots of remote places and events, these screenshots are quite literally about people's own whereabouts, their experience of being telepresent.

With several new twists, the practice continued across the decades. One woman snapped 120 screenshots of the popular soap opera *Another World* (all from the early 1990s) and placed them into a miniature-sized photo album devoted to the program. Each snapshot is labeled with actors' names and the roles they played. The woman who made this album (Mrs. Robert

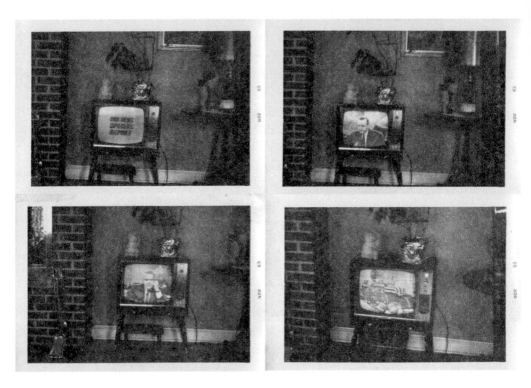

FIGURE 2.22 Screenshots of TV coverage of the Kennedy assassination, 1963.

Waldman from Bloomsburg, Pennsylvania) also typed up the lyrics to the theme song, which are pasted on the inside cover. An act of TV fan fiction, this iteration of the TV screenshot is also about the personal itinerary of the picture taker. The album cover features two labels: one, the title of the program; the other, the picture taker's full name and complete street address. Once again, these screenshots are not just pictures of a TV program; they are more specifically about the woman's experience—*her* home and *her* TV. All the photos include the brown wood frame of Mrs. Waldman's TV set (and some also include the VCR on top of the TV). These soap opera screenshots turn TV's seriality into the serialized production of a TV diary that tracks the woman's daily television viewing and snapshot rituals. As with the other screenshots, these video portraits of soap opera stars turn out to be a performance of self.

To put this in a broader conceptual frame, the screenshots can be understood within the context of the interdisciplinary work on performance and photography I mentioned earlier. The Kennedy photos resonate with Taylor's concerns in *The Archive and the Repertoire,* and especially her last chapter, which deals with photos that New Yorkers snapped while witnessing and mourning the events of 9/11. Taylor claims that taking pictures was a way for people who did not participate in the event as heroes or victims to nevertheless become part of it—or as she puts it, to make themselves "there" in it.[34] The performative act of taking a picture also helped people cope with a national trauma via the creation of personal iterations of the mass-produced images seen in newspapers and on TV screens. The Kennedy photos can be seen in a similar light. Nevertheless, rather than photos taken on the scene, the TV snapshots are at one remove: they are photos of images on a screen. Rather than confirming one's presence at an event and on the streets, they mark one's telepresence at home.

In their aesthetic function as *representations* of telepresence, the screenshots also resonate with what Margaret Iversen calls "performative photography," by which she means photography that "tracks and records a contemporary event."[35] Iversen focuses on photographs and videos by artists who experiment with documenting live performances or unfolding events, often with random and unknown futures, sometimes with simple scripts or instructions, and often in relation to quotidian environments and personal itineraries. For example, she analyzes Vito Acconci's *Following Piece* (1969), in which he follows a randomly selected stranger walking down a street, and in one version records this on a camera. Like Taylor, Iversen sees performative photography as that which "signals an awareness of the way the present gesture is always an iteration or repetition of preceding acts."[36] Finally, with its focus on unfolding events, performative photography treats "the camera . . . like an instrument of discovery, such as a telescope."[37]

Although there are significant differences between the artworks that Iversen discusses and the screenshots, the concept of "performative photography" resonates with home-mode photography.[38] As a quotidian form of performative photography, screenshots allowed people to "discover" fleeting moments transmitted on-screen and to capture, reiterate, and reorder televised images. With screenshots, people record their personal itineraries as TV spectators in domestic spaces and commemorate their telepresence at the public events that TV brought (virtually) home.

THE UNCANNY SCREEN: TRICK SHOTS AND TV GHOSTS

The second path of telepresence as it relates to snapshots is imbricated in the virtual nature of the images on-screen. To return to my remarks at the end of chapter 1, snapshots call attention to TV's uncanny transmissions. Television is not alive, but its ability to turn on makes it *lifelike*. The industry's investment in TV *liveness* at midcentury made it only more so. In snapshots, where TV screens are switched on, people in the home appear to be performing with the actors on-screen. A photo from Germany shows a young woman posing in her living room next to her TV, which transmits a remarkably clear image of a man who forms a strange sort of couple with her (figure 2.23).[39] A Halloween snapshot presents an eerie scene, as the children seem to pose along with a TV weathercaster who is broadcast live on the TV screen. Because of the holiday ritual, the glowing pumpkin on the television set turns TV liveness into a creepy celebration of the dead (figure 2.24).

TV snapshots do a curious thing. Both the posers in the home and the telepresent people on-screen take on the same *indexical presence* in the photo. They are both traces of what Barthes calls the "that-has-been" of photography. Physical presence in the home and telepresence on-screen both "have been" and they "have been" precisely at the same interval in time—the moment they are mutually captured by the snapshot camera. For Barthes, the "that-has-been" of photography points to death. His comments on the tableau vivant capture the sense of photographic motionlessness, stillness, and arrested temporality that he compares to the corpse. The "that-has-been" of photography (for example, the likeness of his deceased mother in the photograph he longs to retrieve) makes him think of the inevitability of his own death. Despite the photographer's desire to capture life (Barthes notes the attempt to capture lifelike action poses), photographs objectify, "embalm," and transform the poser into a "specter."[40] "Photographers," Barthes writes, "are the agents of Death." "This is the way our time assumes Death: with the denying alibi of the distractedly 'alive,' of which the Photographer is in a sense the professional."[41] Barthes was not alone in relating photography to death. Walter Benjamin, André Bazin, and Susan Sontag offered similar analogies.[42] Paradoxically, when TV liveness is captured on still cameras, liveness becomes an indication of the "that-has-been," the impending agent of death.

The "living dead" nature of TV snapshots is in many ways a function of the difficulty of capturing moving images with snapshot cameras. Numerous photos present people posing next to screens with washed out or fuzzy pictures of performers who look almost like TV ghosts.[43] Out-of-focus shots have the effect of blurring the posers, provoking visual equivalences between them and the ghostly images on-screen. Embodiment and disembodiment mingle in these photos as the domestic space merges with the space of TV transmission. A snapshot of three women (most likely a mother and her two daughters) is a perfect example. Sprawled out on the floor with the TV set be-

FIGURE 2.23 (*left*) Germany, circa 1960–65.

FIGURE 2.24 (*below*) 1961.

FIGURE 2.25 1969.

tween them, their faces are almost on the same level with the talking head on-screen, a blurry—and ghost-like—image of President Richard Nixon (figure 2.25). The picture makes for an eerie group shot. As in Freud's seminal essay on the uncanny, such photos turn the most familiar and homey of pictures (the family scene) into something *unheimlich*, or unfamiliar, even scary and strange.

The uncanny nature of telepresence is the subject of myriad trick shots. On their own, trick shots were a popular practice among camera enthusiasts. Kodak manuals and photography magazines taught people how to arrange optical illusions, sometimes in advice to skilled amateurs but also via simple homemade means that required no dark room or special devices. Television seems to have spurred new possibilities for trick shots, at least judging from the variety I have found. In TV snapshots, tricks draw attention to telepresence and virtual embodiment, and they often present this in self-reflexive, or at least self-consciously playful, ways.

In the simplest versions, people paste pictures of themselves onto the screen so that they appear to be performers on a TV broadcast (figure 2.26). This mode of trickery was encouraged by the television industry's exploitation tactics. At the dawn of commercial television, in 1947–48, RCA enticed early consumers with a promotional Christmas card designed to look like a TV set, into which people could insert their own family photo. In subsequent years, photography magazines offered how-to tips for TV cards. In its December 1950 issue, *Popular Photography* told readers, "Television is growing popular as a greeting-card theme." The magazine displayed a Christmas card with a snapshot of a woman pasted onto an illustration of a TV set. A cartoon drawing underneath the TV shows her husband, children, and dog sitting on a sofa and "watching" her on TV.[44] People made their own iterations, turning family snapshots into playful holiday greetings (figure 2.27). The "Look, I'm on TV!" photo was popular in several national contexts, including in the Soviet Union, India, and Egypt. In these places, they were created in the 1970s or 1980s, and rather than families, they are individual portraits (often 8 × 10) and are sometimes used for postcards or, as in one Soviet example, calendar art (figure 2.28).

Even before the rise of commercial television, the thrill of seeing oneself on TV was the basis for popular attractions at world's fairs and international exhibitions, which offered the public chances to look at their own image broadcast via closed circuit TV. This was one of the major draws at the RCA pavilion at the 1939–40 New York World's Fair, and the thrill wasn't gone for quite some time. The RCA color TV exhibition at the 1964–65 New York World's Fair similarly promoted the new color system by allowing people to see themselves broadcast on RCA's "living color" TV cameras. Whether this suggests the fundamental narcissism at the heart of people's relation to the screen is, of course, a complex question and one that, I must admit, is less interesting to me than the ways in which people delighted in the game of telepresence and (as Scannell suggests) television's capacity to double space, to allow people to be in two places at once. World's fair exhibitors found a way to market, popularize, and stage telepresence and combine this with self-performance.

Even more so than novelty cards or fairground attractions, trick shots evoked the uncanniness of telepresence by turning the resident's body into an image that appeared to be transmitted on a TV screen. Some of the more self-reflexive snapshots even seem to comment on the trick, as, for example, when a young woman poses for a picture and tapes a photograph of herself to the screen (figure 2.29). Can she be in two places at once? The optical illusion seems to answer yes and no, and maybe all at once. The trick is ultimately related to the uncertainty of TV technology and of snapshot cameras as mutual forms of optical illusion. Even if they are steeped in the promise of

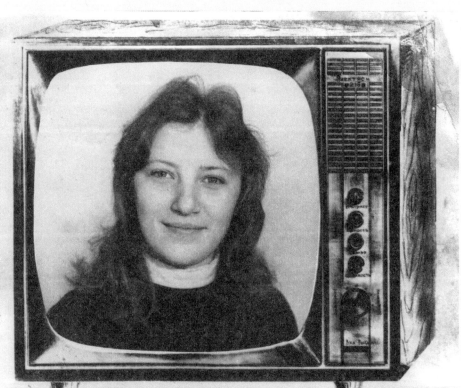

1917 60 ЛЕТ ВЕЛИКОЙ ОКТЯБРЬСКОЙ СОЦИАЛИСТИЧЕСКОЙ РЕВОЛЮЦИИ **1977**

ЯНВАРЬ	ФЕВРАЛЬ	МАРТ	АПРЕЛЬ	МАЙ	ИЮНЬ
3 10 17 24 31	7 14 21 28	7 14 21 28	4 11 18 25	2 9 16 23 30	6 13 20 27
4 11 18 25	1 8 15 22	1 8 15 22 29	5 12 19 26	3 10 17 24 31	7 14 21 28
5 12 19 26	2 9 16 23	2 9 16 23 30	6 13 20 27	4 11 18 25	1 8 15 22 29
6 13 20 27	3 10 17 24	3 10 17 24 31	7 14 21 28	5 12 19 26	2 9 16 23 30
7 14 21 28	4 11 18 25	4 11 18 25	1 8 15 22 29	6 13 20 27	3 10 17 24
1 8 15 22 29	5 12 19 26	5 12 19 26	2 9 16 23 30	7 14 21 28	4 11 18 25
2 9 16 23 30	6 13 20 27	6 13 20 27	3 10 17 24	1 8 15 22 29	5 12 19 26

ИЮЛЬ	АВГУСТ	СЕНТЯБРЬ	ОКТЯБРЬ	НОЯБРЬ	ДЕКАБРЬ
4 11 18 25	1 8 15 22 29	5 12 19 26	3 10 17 24 31	7 14 21 28	5 12 19 26
5 12 19 26	2 9 16 23 30	6 13 20 27	4 11 18 25	1 8 15 22 29	6 13 20 27
6 13 20 27	3 10 17 24 31	7 14 21 28	5 12 19 26	2 9 16 23 30	7 14 21 28
7 14 21 28	4 11 18 25	1 8 15 22 29	6 13 20 27	3 10 17 24	1 8 15 22 29
1 8 15 22 29	5 12 19 26	2 9 16 23 30	7 14 21 28	4 11 18 25	2 9 16 23 30
2 9 16 23 30	6 13 20 27	3 10 17 24	1 8 15 22 29	5 12 19 26	3 10 17 24 31
3 10 17 24 31	7 14 21 28	4 11 18 25	2 9 16 23 30	6 13 20 27	4 11 18 25

1 января — Новогодний праздник, 8 марта — Международный женский день. 1 — 2 мая — День международной солидарности трудящихся. 9 мая — День Победы. 7 ноября — 60-я годовщина Великой Октябрьской социалистической революции. 5 декабря — День Конституции СССР.

FIGURE 2.26 (*opposite top*) Circa 1950–55.

FIGURE 2.27 (*opposite bottom*) Circa 1952.

FIGURE 2.28 (*above*) Calendar art, Soviet Union, 1977.

FIGURE 2.29
1957.

indexicality, eye witnessing, and documentary truth, cameras ultimately are always about technical and optical tricks, and these home-mode trick shots take pleasure in that paradox.

Other people create a trompe l'oeil by posing (or appearing to pose) inside their sets. One woman empties out the chassis, climbs into her television cabinet, and mimics a TV commercial, holding up a bottle as if demonstrating a product (figure 2.30). The eBay dealer who sold me this snapshot described it as an imitation of the classic "Vitameatavegamin" performance on *I Love Lucy* ("Lucy Does a TV Commercial," 1952) in which Lucy Ricardo removes the guts of her TV set, ventures inside it, and appears on-screen as the Philip Morris bellboy (the mascot for *I Love Lucy*'s sponsor). (In keeping with the blurring of fiction and reality, later in the plot Lucy performs in a fictional commercial for Ricky's fictional TV show in which she holds up a bottle of Vitameatavegamin, a fictional tonic.) Whether the woman in the snapshot is actually mimicking Lucy, the comparison does suggest the close relation between the sitcom's theater of everyday life (and its melding of star personae with fictional characters) and the snapshot's own playful trick, which revolves around the relationship between actual and telepresent bodies.

FIGURE 2.30
Circa 1952–55.

Similar tricks go in slightly different directions. In what appears to be another spoof on TV commercials, one camera operator places their cat alongside a can of dog food inside a hollowed-out Motorola TV set (figure 2.31). The incompatibility of cats and dogs is central to the prank that this pet owner plays on the poor cat, who has a wonderful look of bemusement (or is it anger?) on her face. But the photograph is itself a ruse played for a laugh. Other trick shots are composed as family portraits. A mother holds her infant up behind a TV console with an emptied-out chassis (figure 2.32). The console is decorated with curios and a lamp. A picture of a soldier (likely the father) hangs on the wall just above it. The snapshot is a typical domestic scene, save for the optical illusion rendered through the emptied-out TV. The baby is visible behind the screen as his mother holds him up inside the set (we see her right shoulder in the TV). But the mother's head and left shoulder are visible just outside the console, giving lie to her hoax. Another family scene features a little girl sitting on a chair that is placed behind an emptied-out RCA TV console (figure 2.33). She appears in a headshot as if performing on-screen. Another girl (her older sister?) stands in the living room, gesturing as if about to tune in (or turn off?) the TV, and she smiles for the camera. The younger girl's legs dangle off her chair underneath the TV cabinet,

FIGURE 2.31
(*above*) 1953.

FIGURE 2.32
(*right*) 1956.

FIGURE 2.33 Circa 1952–58.

revealing the otherwise clever trick. In all the trick shots, the TV set takes on the novelty status of a photo booth at an amusement park, but as family snapshots, the fun is entirely rigged up at home by human hands.

More generally, the ludic nature of trick shots is evoked through their comic doublings and reversals of humans and TVs. One snapshot (taken some time in the late 1940s in Britain) shows a little boy and a woman (likely his mother) posing for a camera outdoors. The boy is wearing a TV set (the dealer who sold me this photo explained that the faux TV set was a costume he wore for a "fancy dress" party). The TV set costume covers his entire body save for his face, a sliver of his shoulder, and his feet, which peak out. His face is framed by the costume's TV screen (figure 2.34). Given the time of the photograph, TV is clearly still a novelty (the BBC began daily TV broadcasting in 1936 but was slowed by the war). In this sense, the costume must have been conceived as an innovative gag. But as a picture, this snapshot is all about the double take and the uncanny doubling of human and machine. It seems safe to assume that even if people at the time would have understood that the boy was in a costume, people looking at the photo would still have had this sort of double-take reaction. Picturing a walking TV set, the photo plays tricks on the eye.

FIGURE 2.34 Britain, circa 1947–52.

The TV trick shots hark back to the history of late nineteenth-century magic acts that presented animated furniture and other household objects in awesome but often also humorous scenarios, which Patricia Pringle calls "entertaining interiors." Exploring Jean-Eugène Robert-Houdin's *Soirées Fantastiques*, which he presented at the Palais Royal in Paris between 1845 and 1848, Pringle considers the optical tricks he used to fool his publics. His hermetically closed-off "box set" stage ("designed to create the most complete illusion of reality") was furnished as a drawing room into which he invited "guests," who marveled at the automata and objects that appeared to move on their own (but were actually rigged with secretly controlled trap doors, pistons, counterweights, ceiling wires, and other technical apparatuses). "The fact that the stage had no flies and no apparent connection to any other space beyond it must have reinforced the impression of looking in to an enchanted room whose obedient furnishings sustained effortless magical production and where Robert-Houdin was seen . . . performing a gradual choreography partnered by tables, walls, floor, and ceiling, his dexterous maneuvers concealing their secret spaces and mechanisms."[45] Pringle considers this and similar conjuring acts (some more sadistic renditions of, for example, furniture torturing humans) as prototypes for early trick films. She focuses on Segundo de Chomón's *Hôtel Électrique* (1908), in which animated furniture, suitcases, and grooming tools (with high-tech sentient powers) attack and scare hotel guests.[46] Although she does not suggest it, Robert-Houdin's box set stage, the drawing room setting, his configuration of his audience as guests, the animated (lively) things, and the resulting illusion of reality all also speak to a proto-televisual vision.

Pringle's analysis is especially interesting in relation to television and TV trick shots because she argues that this history of entertaining interiors should be seen in terms of the history of furniture itself, from the eighteenth-century French rococo style (with "curving lines and delicate legs" suggesting "the appearance of animation") to late eighteenth-century furniture that came with moveable parts (such as swiveling mirrors, secret doors on springs, or convertible piano-beds that opened up for sleep) through to modern patent furniture (like foldable chairs and murphy beds).[47] Pringle notes one popular late nineteenth-century pantomime act that used a trick convertible piano to seemingly dissect a human body. At midcentury, TV sets quickly became a figure in animated optical tricks. The science fiction/comedy film *The Twonky* (Arch Oboler, dir., 1953) features a sentient TV that struts around on girlish French provincial legs and wreaks havoc on its male owner.

The trope extends from popular culture to art photography. In Friedlander's *Little Screens* series, he often plays with the animate nature of TV as furniture and moving image. In *Nashville*, 1963, for example, he fills the bright screen with a woman's face that pops out (as if alive) against an almost black background (figure 2.35). The woman's eyes stare outward, reversing the normal relations of TV spectatorship by seeming to watch the room. The TV set assumes a lifelike quality, appearing to pose for the picture and look back at the camera (and out at the viewer). The TV set is on a table with spindly, even "girlish," legs, which makes the TV face even more creepy; the legs suggest TV's status as something that can move around, something in between animate and inanimate forms. The antenna that rises from the set gives the entire arrangement an alien feel, while the white shirt hanging from the door gestures toward something human but only through disembodied cloth, the prankster's ghostly white sheet. While produced through aesthetic practices and optical tricks, Friedlander's photograph captures something of the more ordinary affects in TV trick shots. But rather than Friedlander's menacing interiors, TV trick shots turn TV sets into "entertaining interiors" for everyday poses at home.

Although people may have recognized that trick photography was fake, the presence of a TV set in trick shots makes it difficult to decide with certainty about the veracity of the image.[48] However humorous, the trick shots spoke to something disturbing about TV's presence in the domestic interior as well as its own questionable status as a photographic medium. Despite its claims to "window on the world" realism, as a new technology, TV was itself a mystery, often considered a magician's trick. Advertisements frequently called TV a "magic mirror" or a "magic window," and some featured magicians, snake charmers, swamis, or magic carpets—turning TV into an orientalist mystery.[49] As in Freud's description of the uncanny, these discourses on television harked back to animistic belief systems, even while TV was the ultimate expression of modern science and reason.[50] The magical thinking around TV—the idea that it could truly come alive—is connected to the longer tradition of magic that coupled humor with the uncanny dread of something hidden, even frighteningly so (as in the case of the nineteenth-century trick piano that cut a man in parts). The trick of the trick shot is not necessarily innocent fun, even if (to use Bateson's formulation) people understand the metalinguistic rules of tricks to be a mode of pretense and play.

Although the people who made TV snapshots did not explicitly theorize their camerawork in this way, the trick photos implicitly question the episte-

FIGURE 2.35
Lee Friedlander, *Nashville*,
1963. © Lee Friedlander,
courtesy Fraenkel Gallery,
San Francisco, and Luhring
Augustine, New York.

mology and ontology of television. In other words, how do we know what is inside the TV set, and where do TV images come from? These questions were not just philosophical ponderances; they were also on the minds of postwar publics, who knew little about the inner workings of the machine. In the postwar era, technical discourses in magazines like *Popular Science* and *Popular Mechanics* instructed male tinkerers how to "crack open the set" not only to fix it, but also to explore it as field of knowledge.[51] Rather than watching TV, just looking inside it could be a form of visual pleasure in itself. Addressing the man of the house, in 1955 one TV owner's manual advised, "Be satisfied one evening just to unscrew the back and to snoop inside. . . . Use a table lamp or a flashlight because there's a lot to see."[52] Here, as elsewhere, the desire to see inside the set (to ask how it worked and where TV pictures came from) was central to popular discourses that surrounded television's introduction.

In trick shots, answers to these ontological and epistemological questions come in the form of oblique gags. The complex technology inside the "black box" and its ethereal transmissions are humorously reconfigured in a human form (the poser) who occupies the mysterious place inside the TV. Virtual embodiment through the airwaves is rearticulated as actual embodiment in the set. In a related way, trick photos confuse boundaries between screen space and material space. Their humor is in part created through the mayhem of this confusion.

Along these lines, numerous snapshots feature toddlers walking into the screen's ghostly abyss, an image that readers may recall was central to Tobe Hooper and Steven Spielberg's *Poltergeist* (1982), in which a little girl is sucked into her TV set by angry household ghosts. Long before that famous ghost story, poltergeist snapshots presented the figure of a child—or a pet—who appears to have an innocent curiosity about what is real versus televised space. Children stare into the TV abyss, pressing hands or faces on the set and screen, and they stand mesmerized before it (figure 2.36). Cats stand on two paws and scratch the glass as if hunting for prey inside the box (figure 2.37). While most of these photos are not intentionally staged as tricks shots, the serendipity of circumstance clearly allowed camera operators (likely parents or pet owners) to catch their loved ones unawares, and they also understood that the scene they were lucky enough to witness would—as a photograph—look like a clever optical trick.

Even if not intentionally staged, these poltergeist snapshots hark back to nineteenth-century spirit photography, which, as Tom Gunning argues, tended to "collapse and dissolve conventional space and undo familiar orientations," much in the way I am suggesting that the TV snapshots merged telepresence with material spaces and reoriented normative (spectator) relations to TV.[53] In line with the snapshot's use as home entertainment, domestic homemaking manuals of the late nineteenth and early twentieth centuries recommended spirit photography as a popular amusement at parties. At midcentury, women's magazines and advice manuals like *Party Games for All* (1946) continued to promote "ghost" photographs as a fun form of camera trickery.[54] Spirit photography used aesthetic techniques such as double exposure, photomontage, and superimposition, but novice amateurs could deploy less technically complex methods to achieve results. Reducing the practice to its bare-bones core, Kodak's *How to Make Good Pictures* told readers to dress a poser as a ghost and sit them at a "séance" table in a darkly lit room.[55]

In his book *Haunted Media*, Jeffrey Sconce discusses the uncanny and often frightening aspects of electronic "presence" in stories about telegraphy,

FIGURE 2.36
Circa 1950–60.

FIGURE 2.37
Circa 1952–57.

radio, television, and new media. Sconce's notion of hauntings and the dread of the "electronic elsewhere" or "void" in popular stories about TV is especially useful for thinking about the snapshots, which similarly posit an electronic elsewhere and the ghostly possibility that electronic presence is somehow haunting the home. Sconce relates this not to fears about women (as in Freud's link between the uncanny and the threat of castration), but rather to women's own fears (at least as expressed in 1950s popular fiction) of being trapped by television and other electronic media (a metaphor, he argues, for being trapped in the suburban home and restrictive gender roles).[56] While Sconce considers horror and science fiction tales (including *Poltergeist*, cult classics like *The Twonky*, and 1960s episodes of *The Twilight Zone* and *The Outer Limits*), the snapshots mitigate against the frightening aspects of the uncanny. Trick shots and poltergeist shots resolve in comic realism rather than in science fiction or horror.[57] (We know the photograph is a trick played by the camera operator and are never actually afraid that the children or pets will be swallowed up by a TV ghost.) Snapshots veer away from the realm of the ghoulish and toward the territory of the cute. Nevertheless, these photos speak to the fantastic possibility that lived space and TV space are one and the same. They point toward the realm of an "electronic elsewhere" inside the box.

While trick shots are not frightening, they still operate by turning what is home-like or familiar into something *unheimlich* or strange. Although it's hard to know who shot and staged these photos, the fact that women and children seem to have been the central posers in trick shots is interesting in itself. Perhaps these photos of women trapped in TV were staged as popular jokes that used women and girls as "butts" of the humor. Or maybe the photos were a response to the "trapped housewife" and "trapped by television" stories that Sconce analyzes. At any rate, in midcentury trick shots, women and girls seem to delight in turning the horrors of TV entrapment into their own home-mode comic performances and optical tricks.

In the end, TV snapshots fundamentally question what it means to be at home with television. The ritual poses, performances, screenshots, trick shots, and poltergeist photos turn attention away from the actors on-screen and toward a reverse field of self-presentation. Created in a historical context in which sociologists increasingly conceptualized social relations and family life in terms of dramaturgy, theater, and play, TV snapshots became a vehicle through which ordinary people could imagine themselves as stars of their own making. But the snapshots are more than a reflection of midcentury social theory. As home-mode images and stories, they also call into question the status of TV transmissions and, with that, the relationship between the material spaces of the home and the ethereal spaces and mediated events on-screen. Trick shots and poltergeist shots turn these epistemological and ontological questions into a ludic form of creative image making. As women climb into consoles and children walk into screens, the boundaries between real life and lives lived on TV dissolve. Snapshot cameras and TV sets were tools in a theater of everyday life. Judging from the photos, it seems people enjoyed this mode of "family living as play," perhaps as much as, if not more than, they liked watching stars perform on TV.

In fact, by 1969, TV set manufacturers began to recognize the ordinary pleasures of seeing yourself perform on TV. A remarkable contraption, Sylvania's Scanner Color Slide Theatre let you "put your family album on TV" (figure 2.38). Like the performance and trick shots before it, but now packaged in a readymade machine, the device allowed people to make themselves the headliners in a TV show. Or, as the ad put it, "Instead of watching the stars hamming it up on TV," Sylvania's "amazing machine" lets you "go Hollywood." It even came with a built-in tape recorder so that families could add "a sound track of swashbuckling background music to liven up [slideshows]" of mundane domestic scenes. One-part color TV, one-part slide projector, one-part tape recorder, Sylvania's Scanner Color Slide Theatre was clearly a precursor to home video. But, in its own time, it spoke to the television industry's increasing attention to the relationship between TV sets and snapshot cameras as companion technologies in the home. Combining the two and adding the third element of audio tape, Sylvania's home entertainment machine is testimony not only to the company's clever orchestration of media technologies, but also to the performative nature of everyday life in the midcentury TV home.

FIGURE 2.38 Advertisement for Sylvania
Scanner Color Slide Theatre TV, 1969.

3

TV DRESS-UP

FASHION POSES AND
EVERYDAY GLAMOUR

In 1951, *Life* magazine ran a two-page photo spread titled "Clothes for TV Watching." Warning women of the potential fashion disasters TV might cause, *Life* observed:

> A lot of woman who used to dress formally to entertain at home have found themselves and their guests sitting on the floor after dinner to look at television. This position is not graceful in a short tight cocktail dress or practical in an elaborate evening gown. A successful solution for floor sprawling TV fans is "in home clothes," which are colorful, comfortable fashions in which a hostess can casually relax on the rug. . . . Adding elegance to comfort, they are worn with dressy shoes, plenty of jewelry and usually have necklines low enough to compete with almost anything on the TV screen.

The accompanying photos feature five women in their made-for-TV ensembles as they lounge on color-coordinated "TV hassocks" (figure 3.1).[1]

Two models strike graceful poses on the floor. Referring to one as a "strapless slacks floor viewer," *Life* enthuses over her red "one piece" pantsuit, set off by a jeweled black sweater and strappy black sandals. A long cigarette holder poised in the palm of her hand embellishes her seductive—if still well-mannered—pose. To her right, a second "floor viewer" balances a demitasse cup and saucer while modeling a strapless flannel formal, accented by jeweled black slippers. Other photos present outfits for sedentary viewers. Sitting cross-legged on her hassock, a third model looks surprised (perhaps by something on-screen?) as she poses in her plunging V-necked velveteen sweater and "soot" black pants "brightened" by gold sandals and an orange hostess apron. On her far right, the trendiest of the group perches on a hassock in her striped harem trousers and velveteen top (also with a plung-

FIGURE 3.1 Fashion spread in *Life* magazine, January 29, 1951.

ing V-neck). Her horn-rimmed glasses, combined with an abstract drawing resting at her feet, finishes her quasi-beatnik look. In the center of the layout, a final model assumes a motherly (if still modish) style. Accessorized by a young boy (presumably her son), she looks elegant in her "blanket plaid" skirt, which matches the three plaid hassocks next to her in the shot.

Although the outfits had relatively lofty price tags for the time, *Life* tapped into popular practices of everyday TV glamour that could be found not only in fashion photography and picture magazines, but also in snapshot photography. TV snapshots often show women dressed up for the camera, using the television set as a background from which to exhibit their clothing and allure. To be sure, long before the television set, ordinary women dressed up and posed glamorously for snapshot cameras. But the arrival of television in the postwar home offered housewives and young girls new possibilities for self-display and related dynamics of visual pleasure in domestic space. In fact, more than just an anomaly of the *Life* photo spread, TV fashions were a strategy for the sale of women's clothing. In 1951, *Cosmopolitan* fashion editor Virginia Williams echoed *Life*'s concerns with the "TV hostess [who] nearly always ends up sitting on the floor," and she suggested an array of "at home" fashions (hostess gowns, wide skirts, slacks, and "dressy housecoats") that would "carry you through any occasion with flair, flattery, and distinction." Speaking to fashion industry insiders, the trade journal *Women's Wear Daily* reported in 1949, "Greater interest in television sets for home use throws fresh emphasis on clothes to wear for tele-viewing," and "home television means more impromptu entertainment" of guests. The new "At-home clothes for television" included "hostess pajamas for . . . formal entertaining" and "at home costume[s]" like "television coats" (or housecoats) that housewives could throw on "over a negligee" when unexpected company arrived.[2] The use of the word *costume* is especially noteworthy because the article describes the practice of dressing for TV as a sort of female masquerade in which women become quick-change artists who literally cover up their private, more intimate homebody selves with TV wardrobes that can be thrown on in a hurry for an audience—not only for TV—but also for the housewife's own bodily display.

As the marketing of TV fashion suggests, visual pleasure in the TV home was not always aimed solely, or even primarily, at the images on the TV screen. In fact, the *Life* fashion spread did not even depict a TV set. Instead, the domestic gaze focuses on the body of the female TV viewer who must look good for her guests.[3] Moreover, as a sign of her TV hospitality, the housewife must offer her female visitors opportunities to show off their own visual appeal by providing them with optimal viewing conditions and accessories (like TV hassocks) that will enhance their beauty, even while lying on the floor. The entire scenario is aimed at redirecting attention away from television and toward the female bodies in the room so that, as *Life* puts it, women can "compete with almost anything on the TV screen." Low-cut V-necks, strapless dresses, sparkly jewels, and "touch me" fabrics (like velveteen) are women's weapons in a beauty contest—if not all-out war—with TV.

The snapshots take this visual competition one step further by orienting the woman's body so that she is no longer even feigning interest in the act of watching TV. As with the performance poses of accordion players and little ballerinas, the women in the dress-up snapshots steal the spotlight from the TV screen, using TV as a backdrop—a posing place and a theatrical setting— as they direct attention onto their own sartorial splendor. Even if the TV set is turned on in these shots, the focus is not on the screen image but on the woman's fashion choices and her ability to strike an enticing pose.

Inscriptions on the back of photos typically remark on the outfits, not on the television set. Posing in a pinkish-white party dress, set off by glass slippers, a young woman stands in front of her TV set (figure 3.2). Cursive writing on the back of the photo expresses her pride in the dress: "Flawless Formal." Another snapshot features a teenage girl wearing white socks, a crisp white dress, and a matching sweater as she stands before her TV console (figure 3.3). (For reasons I cannot guess, she is cradling a stuffed animal in her arms.) The back of the photo reads, "Sophomore dress up day." It's also clear from the inscription that this girl was proud enough of her snapshot to share it with others (perhaps her classmates?) because the back of the photo instructs the borrower to "please return" it.

With a similar focus on fashion, a woman remarks on her dresses in two separate TV snapshots taken four years apart (figures 3.4 and 3.5). In the first photo, she poses before her television set in a black empire-waist sheath with a bodice of contrasting black and white stripes. Her white gloves and two-tone high-heel sandals indicate a special occasion outside the home. In cursive script on the back of the photo, she writes: "May 1952. Me. On Williamson Ave. Black and white dress." In the second photo, she returns to her TV set and poses in another black empire sheath, this one with a white bodice set off by a black bolero jacket. The outfit is accessorized with the same sandals and white gloves as she wore in the prior photo. Penned in the same handwriting, the back of the photo reads: "May. 1956. Me standing [in] our front room on Wilson Ave. Black and white dress." The time lapse between

FIGURE 3.2
"Flawless formal"
written on back, 1960.

FIGURE 3.3
"Sophomore dress
up day" written on
back, 1959.

the photos suggests that the TV space had become a habitual setting for this woman's home-mode fashion shoots, a routine practice of her everyday life. Similarly, in another set of snapshots dated March 1961, a woman uses her TV setting for a full-color fashion shoot, with one photo depicting elegant daywear and the other glamorous evening attire (figures 3.6 and 3.7). Snapshots such as these indicate the poser's familiarity with (or at least informal knowledge of) figure poses, and some suggest a playful adoption of fashion and glamour photography for home-mode purposes.

The practice continues across the decades, indicating the ritual nature of the TV setting as a space for the presentation of fashionable selves. In 1968, a young woman poses in a white mini dress with over-the-knee gold boots (figure 3.8). A few years later, another girl stands in front of her portable TV striking a glamorous fashion model pose in her 1970s-era wide-leg jumpsuit (figure 3.9). Some women and girls even went to the extra expense of developing dress-up snapshots in 8-by-10 pinup size, suggesting that these TV dress-up poses were among their most prized self-portraits. Women and girls strike glamour poses in everything from prom gowns and cocktail dresses to minks and trendy casual wear to more revealing clothes like bikinis (and, as I discuss in the next chapter, sometimes women posed nude).

FIGURES 3.4 & 3.5 Woman models two different black-and-white dresses, 1952 and 1956.

FIGURES 3.6 & 3.7
Woman models day
wear and evening
wear, both 1961.

The dress-up snapshots I explore in this chapter present fashion and glamour as an ordinary domestic practice, yet at the same time, the women posing in these pictures make spectacles of themselves. Turning the tables on TV's normative uses and orientations, when posing for these pictures, women demand that the camera operator, as well as other people in the room, watch them as opposed to watching TV. In this sense, the dress-up snapshots especially resonate with scenarios of visual competition between housewives and television to which the *Life* fashion spread spoke.

Life was not alone in this regard. As I detail in *Make Room for TV*, midcentury women's magazines often portrayed television as a "hypnotic eye" that would seduce men and destroy women's romantic lives. The TV-fixated husband, ignoring his wife and ogling glamour girls on-screen, was a common figure in postwar popular culture. Everything from TV sitcoms and movies to comic books and ads for TV sets repeated the scenario. The visual "competition" between women and TV extended past the literal depiction of glamour girls on-screen to a broad range of TV attractions—especially wrestling matches and baseball games—that occupied men's undivided attention. Whether literally or figuratively, TV was the "other woman"—a powerful force to be reckoned with in the home (figure 3.10).[4]

Meanwhile, the presence of the "glamour girl" on the TV screen was a constant source of anxiety for regulators, industry executives, and TV critics. Controversies raged over plunging necklines—the exact issue that the *Life* fashion spread singled out as women's number one source of visual/sexual competition with TV. Discussing female viewers' complaints about sex on TV, NBC's top censor (director of continuity acceptance) Stockton Helffrich observed in 1957, "When [women] see some plunging décolletage on a TV gal, they think she's competing with them."[5] Television personality Faye Emerson, known for her décolleté dresses, was a flashpoint for critics (who often ogled her cleavage). But given that Emerson was a frequent "fem-cee" on daytime shows (she began her TV career with a fifteen-minute fashion show), she gradually toned down her explosive femininity, adopting a more down-to-earth sort of feminine charm that television producers thought would better appeal to housewives.[6] Similarly, in 1954, the NBC network took special care when casting its fem-cee for its afternoon program *Home* (1954–57). Rather than hire what one NBC executive dismissed as a "glamour struck" type, the network opted for the more ordinary and matronly Arlene Francis.[7]

That said, midcentury television programs certainly had their share of glamorous and sexualized women, from the scantily clad variety show danc-

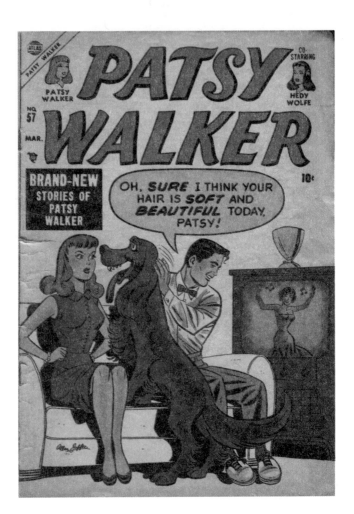

FIGURE 3.10
Patsy Walker, no. 57,
comic book cover,
March 1954.

ers, like the Billboard Girls on *The Jackie Gleason Show* (CBS, 1952–57 version) and the Golddiggers on *The Dean Martin Show* (NBC, 1965–74), to the "bad girl" seductresses on noir-inspired cop shows like *Johnny Staccato* (NBC, 1959–60) and *77 Sunset Strip* (ABC, 1958–64). But television tended to diffuse the threatening aspects of Marilyn Monroe bombshell femininity or even the more girlish sort of Audrey Hepburn glamour that was popular on midcentury movie screens. A notorious example is Mary Tyler Moore's sitcom character Laura Petrie on *The Dick Van Dyke Show* (CBS, 1961–66). According to Moore, when she and the show's producer Carl Reiner decided to dress Laura in sexy capri slacks, CBS said, "You know we're afraid that housewives are going to be a little annoyed because she looks so good in pants."[8] Conversely, TV producers pandered to what they perceived to be women's desire to ogle "beefcakes" and "dreamboats" on dramatic shows like

Dr. Kildare (NBC, 1961–66) and *Route 66* (CBS, 1960–64). In a 1964 interview, Madelyn Martin (a head writer for *I Love Lucy* and Ball's subsequent sitcoms) explained, "You can't package a dramatic show around a woman because women want to look at a man, and they don't want their husband to look at other woman."[9]

While television scholars like Christine Becker, Denise Mann, Alex Doty, and Mary Desjardins have analyzed glamour and fashion on early TV programs, my focus is on the other side of the screen, where women staged their own bodies as sites of visual display.[10] Starting in this chapter with snapshots of women posing in scenes of everyday glamour and moving in chapter 4 to more explicitly sexual pinup poses, I compile a forgotten archive of images that offers clues into gender performance and the "sex life" of TV.

EVERYDAY GLAMOUR

As a photographic genre, the modern glamour shot finds its lineage in star publicity pinups, fashion and fan magazines, and more explicit borderline materials (such as the pinups in men's "girlie" magazines). Like fashion itself, the aesthetics and social meanings of glamour photography changed over the course of the twentieth century, and snapshot photography was itself embedded in these shifts.

In her history of Kodak, Nancy West argues that snapshot photography and fashion shared a parallel history rooted in "modernity's cult of individuality" and fashion's centrality to the creation of the "new woman." Kodak's early marketing campaigns (circa 1900–30) portrayed the Kodak Girl as an icon of modern haute couture and affluent leisure lifestyles.[11] Her costumes (especially her most iconic blue and white striped dress) became a popular fashion trend, with stores selling knockoffs to eager consumers.[12] Consistent with practices that would soon become central to Hollywood's star system and glamour pinups, in the early 1900s, Kodak Girl model Maude Marguerite McConnell rose to fame as an international celebrity in her own right, appearing in fashion columns and on the covers of *Ladies' Home Journal* and *Woman's Home Companion*.[13] Although West claims that Kodak's investment in haute couture waned in the 1930s in favor of marketing campaigns that focused on domesticity, ads for Kodak and other camera companies still displayed well-dressed (if more casually outfitted) women in well-appointed homes. Rather than high fashion, midcentury snapshot ads offered a more everyday sort of glamour that resonated with the middle-class "good life."

More generally, as Elspeth Brown argues in her history of modeling, midcentury modeling agencies and fashion photography for advertisements emphasized "models' normative, middle-class femininity" and "sanitized" their sexuality.[14] During wartime, and increasingly in the postwar era, magazines ran stories like *Life*'s "Model Mothers" (1944), which promoted "familiar roles of wife and mother."[15] Although (as Brown details, and as I discuss further on) women of color found ways to articulate glamour in this context, the fashionable ideal emphasized whiteness in the figure of the girlish co-ed and middle-class mom. In 1958, the *Vogue Pattern Book* (aimed at young moms who sewed their own clothes, many of whom were likely unable to afford higher-priced store-bought versions) ran a cover story titled "Casual Clothes for Suburbia U.S.A." It pictured smartly dressed "den mothers" in "relaxed blouse[s]"; pleated skirts "for walking"; "quicky jackets" that women drivers could throw on in a "dash" as they raced to the market; and herringbone knits versatile enough to be worn at a "county pet show" or for city excursions.[16] For the more "mature woman" (whom *Vogue* dubbed "Mrs. Exeter"), the pattern book suggested "shirt-waist dresses with moderate flare"; "neatly stated suits and jacket dresses"; the "feminine graces of full length gowns"; "white, white gloves"; a "flattering hat"; "a delicate shoe"; and "pearls."[17] Although this image of glamour was central to postwar everyday life and can be seen to influence the dress in many of the snapshots, these rigid dictates of the fashion industries is not exactly what I mean by everyday glamour.

Everyday glamour, as I use the term, is grounded in the snapshot's quotidian domestic setting. Everyday glamour is what de Certeau calls a "practice of everyday life," in which women use the language of a fashion system to articulate their own versions.[18] Although social and economic factors are always in play, the point is that women can opt in or out of this system and "make do" with the fashions available to them, some relatively conformist approximations of reigning trends, others more divergent expressions. As time capsules, the snapshots also capture how women mix bits and pieces of fashions from their closets, some this year's models, others last year's. The midcentury snapshots depict women mixing, for example, the Dior-inspired 1950s "new look" fashions (the hourglass flower-like dresses associated with the return to femininity after the war) with 1960s Jackie Kennedy Chanel-style coats. In TV snapshots, women mix fashions in a pastiche of styles that are drawn from different moments of their closets. TV snapshots also exude the stylishness—or out-of-stylishness—of the TV set itself. For example, a mod-looking woman complements her mod-looking portable TV. But other snapshots suggest the "low punctum" of mismatch. A mod 1960s woman poses next to her clunky old 1950s console—a dissonant arrangement that disrupts the staged glamour in fashion magazines or ads for TV sets.

The practice of everyday glamour involves what Elizabeth Wissinger calls "glamour labor," the work that goes into managing appearance. Speaking specifically about online fashion blogs, Wissinger sees glamour labor in relation to other forms of immaterial labor in which "work and play are not clearly defined."[19] Glamour is work, but it also has a ludic dimension. Building on this concept, Felice McDowell considers the glamour labor entailed in the context of 1960s British fashion photography and the work performed by "model girls" of that era. For McDowell, the concept is particularly useful in its application to the production and performance of gendered bodies in photographs.[20] In a related way, Nigel Thrift talks of the work and "calculation" entailed in producing glamour and allure. "Glamour is a constant if fitful quality in consumer spaces, arising out of an environment that mixes human and nonhuman so as to produce captivation." Glamour is an affect produced through "worlding," or the arrangement of objects and humans in space. Glamour achieved through world building signals a transformation of everyday life into a utopian wish that others can also sense and feel. "For all its breathtaking qualities, glamour does not conjure up awe. It operates on a human scale, in the everyday, inviting just enough familiarity to engage the imagination, a glimpse of another life, utopia as a tactile presence."[21] While Wissinger, McDowell, and Thrift discuss glamour mostly in relation to mass culture (fashion photography, blogs, modeling, store design), home-mode snapshots are also products of glamour labor, only a more quotidian sort. Snapshots are the kind of glamour labor historically associated with "women's work," the labor women perform on their bodies, their children's bodies, and on the interior design of their homes.

Thrift's discussion of the world-building dimensions of glamour and the arrangement of object/human environments is especially useful when considering relations between women's bodies and interior décor at midcentury. Magazines and design manuals presented the home as a showcase for women, recommending ways to create glamorous backgrounds on which to enact spectacular scenes. In *The House and the Art of Its Design*, Robert Woods Kennedy claimed that the housewife needed "an effective and glamorous background for her as a sexual being, commensurate with the amount of energy she expends on clothes, make-up, and society."[22] In snapshots, it is not just the woman's clothing or poses but also the objects in and design of her TV setting that compose the world building entailed in glamour labor.

It seems useful to note that the manufacturing and consumer technology industries refer to objects—cars, vacuum cleaners, TV sets—as "models" so that the very language used to discuss objects is the same as applied to the fashion model. Conflating female bodies with television sets was a well-entrenched promotional strategy. Some snapshots resemble 1960s ads for TV sets, the sorts of ads in which smartly dressed young women pose demurely next to the decade's modern-style TV cabinets or new portable and color models.[23] The snapshots show women who appear (like advertising models) to demonstrate their modern-style TVs while simultaneously displaying their own modern style through dress. The glamour labor required for such pictures includes the entire mise-en-scène of the TV setting. For example, one snapshot features a woman in modish ankle-cropped pants as she poses next to her set (figure 3.11). (While slightly longer than the capri style, in 1962 when this snapshot was taken, cropped slacks similarly signified modern womanhood.) The woman's taste in clothes is enhanced by her other object choices that also exude an aura of modern glamour. These include the stylish blonde wood TV set; colorful glass decanters (objects associated with midcentury modernism's penchant for exotica); trendy stacked floor pillows; and an LP collection arranged against the wall. Although this snapshot is cluttered with the mess of everyday life (a dangling TV cord runs to an outlet in the wall), it nevertheless demonstrates calculated world building, an

FIGURE 3.11
1962.

FIGURE 3.12 Woman's TV glamour labor in four different poses.
Top left, 1967; bottom left, 1968; top right, 1968; bottom right, 1970.

arrangement of humans and objects that produce glamour as an *affect* that other people in this period could recognize and feel.

The labor of glamour is especially registered in cases where I have found sets of snapshots depicting the same people in the same room, but on different occasions. These photos show how women reassembled their TV settings over time. For example, a set of four photos presents a middle-aged woman returning to the scene of her TV set to strike a fashionable pose (figure 3.12). In 1967, she poses to the side of her portable TV, which competes for attention with a bird in a midcentury modern cylindrical birdcage (fashionable at the time) that stands in the corner of the wall. Her cranberry slacks are paired with a mix-and-match flowery blouse. Her hair is coiffed, and her makeup is applied, adding to the sense of everyday glamour. One year later, in 1968, this woman poses with a slightly different (and likely newly purchased) portable TV, which sits in the corner of what appears to be a different room. She strikes two dress-up poses, both of which capture her in a black skirt, black nylons, and leopard blouse. In one snapshot, she poses demonstratively, leaning toward and pointing at the set. A sunburst clock hangs on the wall, enhancing the modern feel of the TV setting. In the other snapshot (likely taken on the exact same occasion) she poses in the same attire while seated in a trendy circle chair placed directly in front of the TV, as if she is hoping to show it off for the camera.[24] Finally, in 1970 she returns to the same TV space and models a paisley tunic. As in the other snapshots, her hair is coiffed and her makeup is applied, but in slightly different ways from the previous photos. The décor of the TV setting is also rearranged (the chair is no longer displayed, and objects have been placed on top of the portable). Taken together, the four photos mark the TV space as a ritual place of return. But rather than mere replication, the snapshots indicate that the woman updates her TV setting with a new iteration of glamour for each pose.

More than just indexical evidence of the work entailed in glamour, the snapshots are themselves part of the labor. The snapshot camera is a crucial tool for creating everyday glamour, and women had to learn ways to shoot pictures and to pose, at least if they wanted to achieve optimal effects. Over the course of the twentieth century, women's magazines provided lessons. In a 1946 article, "How to Pose for a Snapshot," *Good Housekeeping* showed women how to arrange angles, stances, and postures to maximize glamour. "Do give the camera a good slant on yourself. Don't face [the camera] squarely . . . because if you are the least bit hippy, the picture will show you big as a barn."[25] In 1958, the girl's fashion magazine *Seventeen* ran an article titled "How to Look Like a *Seventeen* Model." Telling girls to pose "naturally" and "without self-consciousness," the magazine (paradoxically) advised them to "practice in front of a full-length mirror." *Seventeen* also told girls to "use props as models do." "Tilt a pop bottle towards your lips, offer an ice cream cone to the camera!" Despite all the sugary treats, like the *Good Housekeeping* article, *Seventeen* offered tips on "figure focus," giving instructions on "camera trickery" that would enable girls to "cut down the size of your hips."[26]

All these lessons required glamour labor—practicing in mirrors, gathering props, and learning tricks of the camera trade. Everyday glamour in snapshots was a skill to acquire, even if the snapshots were meant to appear like effortless forms of everyday fun. In this regard, the dress-up shots were part of a well-established set of camera protocols for the performance of femininity. Meanwhile, for girls less skilled in the work of glamour, *Seventeen* and other women's magazines advertised mail-order solutions. Photo refinishing and developing companies like Beautitone refinished "your favorite photo to make you look like a 'cover girl,'" while Hollywood Studio Photos turned your snapshot into a movie star pinup.

HOLLYWOOD PICTURES AND SNAPSHOT POSES

Despite the snapshots' quotidian nature, as the above examples suggest, everyday glamour is nevertheless in dialogue with Hollywood and fashion photography, which served as important and mutual influences for the ways in which people posed and arranged their settings in snapshots. As Elspeth Brown argues, Hollywood glamour photographers were influenced by developments in the New York–based fashion world, and "commercial photographers regularly shot movie actresses, working from their end to develop glamour's visual codes in fashion editorials for *Vogue, Town and Country,* and *Harper's Bazaar*."[27] Across the twentieth century, Hollywood and the fashion industry promoted glamour as an everyday practice available to women from all walks of life—or at least to the growing ranks of female consumers whom the industries wanted to court. The Hollywood film studios partnered with stores and fashion houses to create celebrity fashion knockoffs. In 1930, Macy's became the first major department store to open what it called a Cinema Fashion Shop collection, selling ready-to-wear affordable dresses copied from the costumes worn by popular stars like Carole Lombard and Joan Crawford.[28] Pattern companies like Butterick, Vogue, McCall's, and (the aptly named) Hollywood Patterns sold do-it-yourself celebrity fashions worn by screen sirens like Katharine Hepburn, Dolores del Rio, Doris Day, and Audrey Hepburn (to name just a few). By the 1950s, TV fans could sew Desi Arnaz pajamas and buy a seemingly endless array of *I Love Lucy* "Live Like Lucy" merchandise tie-ins, including Lucy bedroom suites, aprons, and baby bassinettes.[29]

Although Hollywood promoted aspirational objects and images, glamour is a complex affair. Richard Dyer observes that stars exude ambivalent values of "extraordinary" and "ordinary," offering ways for average people to identify with screen fantasies and apply them to their own lives.[30] Motion picture and radio-TV fanzines told behind-the-scenes at-home stories with candid photos that made screen idols seem more like average people. *Photoplay*'s column Hollywood at Home (which ran regularly in the late 1930s and 1940s) offered "unique 'living' stories that bring you the personal details of a star's everydays."[31] While it often displayed homes of the rich and famous, the column featured photos of celebrities gardening in yards, knitting near the fireplace, cooking in the kitchen, and so forth—photos that caught people in the ordinary "acts" of everyday life. Radio and television fan magazines similarly negotiated glamour with ordinariness. Stories like *Screenland*'s "All Dressed Up ... to Stay Home" (1954) presented fashion-spreads with TV stars dressed in casual—yet still glamorous—capri pants, hostess jackets, flannel skirts, and elegant loungewear that readers could purchase at department store prices, thereby showing women how to turn their own home lives into a TV-fashion show.[32]

While media historians have demonstrated how fan magazines encourage the reader to cross the boundaries between fiction and life, my interest is more specifically in the ways in which the fan magazines mixed photographic modes of studio glamour photography with candid shots of home life. Some columns displayed pictures in a photo album or scrapbook-style layout, as if the stars had assembled them at home. Photo contests in the magazines encouraged readers to send in their own celebrity look-alike pinups. As with the publicity photo of Desi Arnaz snapping a picture of Lucy and the newborn Desi Jr. in their Beverly Hills home, photo spreads in *Radio TV Mirror* featured star couples taking pictures of each other. A 1956 article describes TV quiz show star Bill Cullen as "an avid shutterbug" and pictures him snapping photos of his wife (a former model) in their glamorous New York apartment. In 1958, the same magazine ran an article on daytime TV host Art Linkletter that offered readers a glimpse at his "precious [photo] album" featuring his wife, kids, and pets. A 1956 story displays TV personality Hal March and his wife leafing through their wedding album.[33] All these "picture-taking" photospreads encouraged readers to imagine their snapshot cameras as tools for staging their own forms of everyday glamour.[34]

Some TV snapshots appear to be modeled (whether consciously or not) on Hollywood glamour photos. Compare, for example, a 1955 studio portrait of Elizabeth Taylor posing with her TV set to a 1960 TV snapshot of an ordinary woman (figures 3.13 and 3.14). Both images are Christmas scenes with a television set toward the right side of the frame and a white Christmas tree toward the left. Just like Taylor, the ordinary poser has jet black hair, ruby red lips, and a white "new look" (pinched at the waist) figure-flattering dress. Nevertheless, the fabric, shade, and cut of Taylor's dress signal custom-made haute couture, and the photo itself is a professional studio shot, with an aesthetic appeal not present, or even possible to attain, in the snapshot. Taylor's white tree is intentionally faded, almost invisible, so that she stands out as the star attraction. Her blonde wood TV console coordinates with the tree and her champagne-hued dress. The Christmas gifts have visible brands on them, giving this studio portrait the look of an advertising tie-in. In distinction, despite the obvious care put into arranging the snapshot, and the fact that it is a Kodacolor print (still a relatively rare thing in 1960), the image is slightly out of focus. The tree, with its green (as opposed to silver) bulbs, has none of the aestheticized ghostly look of the studio portrait; the brown TV set lacks the color coordination of the studio setup; and the woman's black pumps have none of the appeal of Taylor's gold slippers, which she models in a delicate ankle pose. The blur, the bulbs, the pumps, the mousy brown TV set all constitute the "low punctum" of the snapshot, the things that mark its failure to live up to the Hollywood ideal despite its apparent aspirations. Still, the likeness of the two is remarkable (if not uncanny), and it's certainly possible that the woman who posed for the snapshot purposefully staged it as a look-alike. Whatever the intent, the 1960 snapshot draws on the fashion system of Hollywood glamour and advertising images.

Yet, despite their aspirational nature, dress-up snapshots are not mere mimicry. Even while women may have hoped to dress like Hollywood stars, aspiration is not the same as imitation. As Jackie Stacey argues in her ethnographic research on British women's memories of Hollywood stars, women often expressed identification with actors in terms of "similarity and difference."[35] Even while they purchased Doris Day hats or dyed their hair Monroe blonde, women also understood the difference between themselves and celebrities. At times, women viewed stars with envy or felt that they did not measure up. For such reasons, many feminists have critiqued the fashion, beauty, and media industries for encouraging feelings of inadequacy by narrowly defining beauty standards along body type and related issues of race, ethnicity, gender conformity, and class. While not dismissing this important critique, Stacey nevertheless demonstrates that women often understood their acts of imitation in a playful way, and they articulated Hollywood glamour against their actual historical situations, including, for example, class differences.

The difference between imitation and articulation is especially important in snapshots. Glamour and the work entailed in it are embedded in a history

FIGURE 3.13 Publicity photo of Elizabeth Taylor, 1955. Access rights, Getty, Silver Screen Collection.

FIGURE 3.14 Elizabeth Taylor look-alike snapshot, 1960.

of class, ethnicity, race, and other cultural differences that are complex and often difficult to decipher, especially when dealing with highly generic snapshot images. But because TV snapshots portray a range of ethnicities, races, and class orientations, glamour in these photos surely is articulated differently against diverse historical experiences. For example, it seems likely that for many Black women, their TV snapshots resonated with the history of African American glamour and fashion, particularly with images of fashion models and Hollywood stars that appeared in African American magazines and less often on film and TV screens.

By midcentury, there was a well-established discourse on fashion and glamour in the African American press. In *Ladies' Pages*, Noliwe Rooks considers fashion columns in midcentury African American magazines against the longer history of Black women's magazines and etiquette books, and she shows how fashion was, since the late nineteenth century, embedded in the history of struggles around race, gender, skin tone, class, sexuality, and the politics of respectability (particularly insofar as the editors of the magazines were concerned to counteract white stereotypes about Black women's sexuality, stereotypes that revolved around the binary figures of the asexual mammy versus the promiscuous Jezebel).[36] By the 1940s, these issues persisted, but the subject of glamour (especially Hollywood glamour) was increasingly articulated with civil rights. The *Crisis* magazine, the official organ of the NAACP, regularly featured the rising (if small) group of Hollywood stars like Lena Horne and Dorothy Dandridge, who began to appear in major roles on cinema screens. The *Crisis* presented these women as exemplars of racial progress, and while the magazine generally adhered to respectability politics (presenting just headshots of stars), by World War II it included more provocative cheesecake photos created mostly for the pleasure of Black soldiers. Yet, as Megan Williams argues, for Black women, glamour photography and magazine pinups were not just a matter of women's objectification for a male gaze: "By performing respectability through the use of beauty products and etiquette guides . . . African American women could potentially empower themselves to reject stereotypical images of black womanhood and expose race as a construction."[37]

The African American mass-market picture magazines that proliferated after World War II placed an increased focus on celebrity culture and fashion. First published in 1945, the most successful among these, *Ebony*, regularly featured Black fashion models and stars on its covers. It also sponsored traveling fashion shows and reported on these in the magazine.[38] The rise of Black modeling agencies catering to corporate America's increasing focus on Black markets offered new opportunities for Black women who appeared in the Black magazines and ads, chipping away at the hegemony of white glamour.[39] *Ebony* displayed Black models as quintessential success stories for the modern Black woman. According to this logic, glamour labor represented a utopian future.[40] Nevertheless, the postwar magazines also debated the racism in mainstream media. *Jet* magazine lashed out against Hollywood's exclusionary tactics and stereotypes, and to counteract this, it regularly featured pinups of Black women on the cover, typically in bathing suits or low-cut dresses. A 1953 cover (featuring a bathing suit pinup of Etta Rae) promises to tell readers "Why Hollywood Won't Glamorize Negro Girls."[41] Even while sexually provocative cheesecake pinups were a subject of debate in the Black community (many people saw them as detrimental to female respectability and racial uplift), the African American press (and reader letters to the editor) often criticized Hollywood for its failure to glamorize Black women.[42] As *Ebony* put it, "Beauty is skin deep—and that goes for brown as well as white skin. You'd never think it, though, to look at the billboards, magazines, and pinup posters of America." "But," the magazine asserted, "Negro girls are beautiful too."[43] In this sense, the presentation of glamour and pinups functioned as a counter-narrative to reigning stereotypes and exclusions.

Network television was notoriously racist in its presentations of women of color, despite the networks' lip service to integration. During the 1950s and for much of the 1960s, the only program that featured a Black female lead was the short-lived *Beulah*, which revolved around a mammy character. (As I noted earlier, *Beulah* was highly controversial in the Black community.) For most of the 1950s and 1960s, Black female glamour was relegated to the realm of guest star appearances on variety shows (e.g., Lena Horne, Nancy Wilson, the Supremes); bit parts in episodes; or occasional roles in ensemble casts (e.g., Cicely Tyson's Jane Foster in *East Side/West Side* [CBS, 1963–64] and Nichelle Nichols's Lieutenant Uhura on *Star Trek* [NBC, 1966–68]).[44] Similarly, glamorous Latin American performers like Dolores del Río (the Mexican actress, dancer, and singer who came to television from a career in film) or the DeCastro Sisters (singers who hailed from Cuba and were featured on variety shows) were confined to guest star roles in which they often appeared as exotic acts (and sometimes in hypersexualized ways).[45] Apart from Chinese American film star Anna May Wong, who starred in the short-lived series *The Gallery of Madame Liu-Tsong* (DuMont Television Network, 1951), for most of the 1950s and 1960s Asian women appeared primarily as guest stars or in bit parts in variety shows, dramas, and sitcoms. For example, in

1961, the fashionable Japanese American actress/singer Miyoshi Umeki appeared in an episode of *The Donna Reed Show* (ABC, 1958–66).[46] Echoing her role in the 1958 Broadway musical *The Flower Drum Song* (and coinciding with the 1961 film version), the sitcom episode (titled "The Geisha Girl") pictured Umeki as an immigrant, and it included a fashion makeover that visualized her character's assimilation as she trades in her traditional kimono for stylish American clothes.[47] Umeki went on to costar in *The Courtship of Eddie's Father* (ABC, 1969–72), but in this case she was depicted in an updated, if still stereotypical, version of a subservient Japanese housekeeper.[48] More generally, the options for women of color to be glamorous were articulated within the confines of the network star system that featured white women and whiteness as the main attractions.

Diahann Carroll's appearance in the NBC sitcom *Julia* (1968–71) was the first opportunity (since *Beulah*) for viewers to see to a Black woman (or any woman of color) as the lead in a network TV series.[49] But unlike Beulah, Julia was a fashionable modern woman. Not coincidentally, Carroll began her career as a model, and by the time she appeared in *Julia*, she had honed her image as a cosmopolitan fashion queen.[50] In 1962, she starred as the lead in the hit Broadway play *No Strings*, in which she played an expatriate New York girl who becomes a fashion model in Paris. Promoting the play, the 1962 issue of *Ebony* featured Carroll on the cover modeling stylish gowns. (In line with fashion's link to civil rights, the cover also ran headlines about "Black Power" and "segregation.")[51] While Carroll's sitcom character was a middle-class working mom, her costumes spoke to her legacy of glamour. But rather than haute couture, as Julia, Carroll became an icon of a more all-American everyday sort of glamour, with a wardrobe composed of mock turtleneck mini dresses and flair-bottom pantsuits, which must have resonated with women and girls (of all colors) who could imagine themselves slipping into both her costumes and her role.[52] Nevertheless, in its attempt to appeal to mainstream audiences, Julia straddled a difficult line; many critics lashed out at the program's "whitewashing" of Black culture. In a 1968 interview with *TV Guide*, Carroll herself criticized the show in these terms: "At the moment we're presenting the white Negro. . . . Julia, of course, is a product of that."[53] In this regard, as with other postwar images of Black glamour, TV's fashionable Julia resonated with the politics of racism and civil rights.

Given their conventionality, snapshots encode the history of racialized glamour images within a studium of family life that washes over all the photos, making them appear (at least to contemporary eyes) generic, as if they meant the same thing to all posers regardless of race. Nevertheless, when read in the context of discourses on Black glamour and especially the connections between glamour and civil rights, the snapshots suggest something different. The practice of dressing up for poses presented an opportunity for glamour that spoke to African American women, even if Hollywood films, television programs, and mainstream picture magazines like *Life* only sporadically did so and in ways not entirely pleasing. To return to hooks's observation, "Access and mass appeal have historically made photography a powerful location for the construction of an oppositional black aesthetic." She continues, "Photography . . . offered the possibility of immediate intervention, useful in the production of counterhegemonic representations even as it was also an instrument of pleasure. Taking pictures was fun!"[54] Even if the people taking snapshots did not intentionally set out to protest mainstream media, home-mode photography offered a chance to reclaim the pleasures of glamour in the context of everyday life. The snapshots provided African American women (and I would guess other underrepresented and stereotyped women of color) the possibility of self-fashioning their own images through homemade practices of everyday glamour labor that made them the focus of the shot. By placing themselves in front of or next to the TV set and using TV as a backdrop or prop, they drew attention away from the mostly white women on-screen and toward their own stylish displays (figures 3.15 and 3.16).

FIGURE 3.15 (*bottom left*) Circa 1965–69.

FIGURE 3.16 (*bottom right*) Circa 1960–65.

SOCIAL PERFORMANCE

Rather than a mere imitation of a Hollywood ideal, everyday glamour—and the snapshots that stage it—engage women in social relations with each other. Along these lines, Stacey demonstrates that Hollywood glamour provided women with a sense of shared cultural competencies regarding taste and fashion that were central to women's culture and friendships. Distinguishing fabrics and styles, or knowing which hats suited which occasions, are skill sets that women can accrue and that help to form common knowledge—and with that, social ties. From this point of view, the practice of dressing up like stars was not just a rote replication of a shallow ideal, nor was it mere narcissism. It was a way to relate to other women. Moreover, Stacey argues, many women approached glamour as a game of make believe, fully understanding the artifice and masquerade it entailed. Analyzing her own dress-up snapshot that she posed for as a child in the 1970s, Stacey says her "snapshot represents a self-image produced as an imitation of an imagined 1950s Hollywood glamour." While acknowledging that her photo demonstrates her own vulnerability to patriarchal standards of female glamour, she nevertheless argues that her snapshot exceeds the "authority" of the fashion system through the "play of imitation." "The event, the 1950s party, announces imitation in its conception and thus facilitates the denial of the authenticity of the desire to be desirable" so fundamental to femininity.[55] The party snapshot is all about pretense and play, and it acknowledges itself as such.

In a similar way, TV snapshots stage glamour as a form of domestic amusement that drew women together through shared female competencies. Admittedly, the very idea that women had to look good while watching TV is itself a consequence of the constraints of a gendered fashion system that promotes women's view of themselves as objects to be looked at by others. Nevertheless, considering the snapshots, I ultimately return to feminist work like Stacey's that takes women's everyday pleasures seriously as a site of social relations.

Like Stacey, many scholars in contemporary fashion studies consider fashion and fashion photography as tools for women's performative agency and self-conscious pretense or play rather than as just passivity or sexual objectification. In her pathbreaking 1985 book *Adorned in Dreams*, Elizabeth Wilson argues, "fashion is a performance art," noting the folly in attempts to see fashion through binaries of authentic and fake (or to make moral judgments about people or taste based on such binaries).[56] Following Judith Butler, contemporary fashion scholars see performance not just as pretense or make believe, but rather as the very way in which bodies, gender, and sexuality are constructed as sites of meaning.[57] In other words, there is not an authentic material body underneath something staged. Instead, the body and sexuality are produced through the staging. Wilson's book and Butler's paradigm helped shift the direction of fashion studies. As Joanne Entwistle argues in her overview of the field, "What has changed with the rise of fashion studies is the critique of fashion: where once feminists were antagonistic to fashion, certainly in the 'second wave' movement, recent scholars are more likely to see it as a resource for performance and play with identity. . . . This is not to say that fashion is no longer criticized, just that it is not, de facto, always seen as a problem for feminists."[58] It is the social, performative, situated, and playful aspects of the dress-up poses that interest me most.

TV snapshots often feature women posing in fashionable dresswear in social situations with other women (sisters, mothers, grandmothers, or friends). Women line up in a fashion shoot beside the TV (figure 3.17). They sit in the empty space around it at wedding or baby showers, sometimes in candid shots opening presents, but often in posed shots. The people who took these snapshots likely did so as a way of amusing guests and memori-

FIGURE 3.17 1956.

alizing parties. Once again, the people in these photos are not watching TV. Nevertheless, the TV set is a central backdrop in the party scene, sometimes "dressed" for the occasion with flowers or party favors that sit on top.

The sociable and ludic nature of dress-up snapshots is also evident in sets of photos in which people literally take turns (as in a game) modeling their fashions in the TV setting. Often "taking turn" photos present friends or family members dressed for occasions outside the home. An especially striking set of snapshots (all dated August 1972) shows mom, dad, and daughter posing in front of their portable television set placed in the corner of a bright lime green wall, accented with a huge hanging tapestry depicting an elk (figure 3.18). Although the décor is enough to attract one's attention, what especially interests me is the game-like structure of the fashion shoot, as each family member takes turns posing in this same TV setting (sometimes alone, sometimes in couples), always demanding that the domestic gaze be focused on them. Given that these "taking turn" photos were saved as sets, it seems likely that people found them meaningful as family portraits to be documented and remembered as such. These snapshots also suggest the ritual use of the TV space as a place for photographing arrivals and departures.

DRESSING UP AND GOING OUT: TV AS PORTAL OBJECT

When combined with the practice of snapshot photography, everyday glamour is about the *occasion*. It is a special sort of picture taken to document a break with daily routines like cleaning the stove or feeding the baby. It has none of the stains of the apron. Even if glamour is itself a form of labor, the point of glamour work is that it remains invisible and seemingly effortless, as if it is not work at all.

As opposed to the daily flow of morning shows and afternoon soaps that network executives tailored to fit with women's household labor and "rhythms of reception," the snapshots mark the time spent away from daily routines, doing things other than cleaning, cooking, and watching TV.[59] Everyday glamour is somewhere between the linear time of the mother's workday and what Henri Lefebvre (writing in 1950s France) called the "festive time" of everyday life. While Lefebvre dismissed television (along with women's magazines and other forms of women's popular culture) as a commodification of time itself, these snapshots demonstrate something different.[60] They mark the fluctuations between daily labor and the glamour of special occasions. Taking issue with Lefebvre and other theories of everyday life that denigrate domesticity and women's household routines, Rita Felski focuses on the pleasures of domestic habits. In *Doing Time*, she argues against the

FIGURE 3.18 Family takes turns in a TV photo shoot, 1972.

view that women's everyday life in the modern home is characterized by what Lefebvre variously sees as "monotony," "boredom," and the "empty time" of postwar "re-privatization." Instead, "The temporality of everyday life is internally complex; it combines repetition and linearity, recurrence with forward movement."[61] The snapshots are about habits, repetitions, and repertoires of experience, and in their recurring ritual iterations, dress-up snapshots combine recurrence with forward movement, not just across time but also quite literally via spatial movements away from home.

Many of these snapshots appear to be part of a repertoire of going out, pictures taken before leaving or after returning home. In such cases, television serves as a *portal object*, a thing that indicates the passage between the domestic interior and public places. In this regard, I use the term *portal* not just as a symbol or a metaphor, but rather to describe a literal practice in which people use the TV set as a backdrop against which to stage their entrances and exits from the home. Outerwear like fur stoles, shawls, coats, hats, gloves, capes, muffs, and purses indicate leave-taking behavior (figures 3.19–3.22). While some suggest daytime excursions, others mark the time of formal occasions, and some (such as figure 3.18) include husbands or dates.[62] As in figure 3.22, some of these going-out snapshots show rooms with TVs near doors or catch women clutching doorknobs. One little girl even plays dress-up in her mother's mink while standing in front of her TV next to an open door (figure 3.23). Her bare feet give her ruse away.

The placement of TV sets near doors was likely related to the small size of the average home in the postwar period. As many houses lacked a central hallway, putting the set near a door was a practical way to manage a small space. But when depicted next to doors in the snapshots, the TV set functions as a kind of second door, leading to a place that the literal door does not. The going-out snapshots present television as a portal to the imagination— a place that indicates an elsewhere outside the domestic enclosure. Or, to use the parlance of the times, television was a "window on the world" that (imaginatively) transported viewers to places away from the private interior. The snapshots capture and enact this metaphor in quite literal ways as people use TV as a posing place to memorialize journeys away from home.

In some cases, the portal nature of the TV pose is inscribed on the back of the snapshot. Posing in a satin brocade gown, a young woman stands in front of her TV console (figure 3.24). Cursive writing on the back of the snapshot explains: "Ready for Spring Concert at school. To be worn with hoop but due to lack of seating space—no hoop!" The inscription memorializes her exciting public event (figure 3.25). Another snapshot features a father and his young daughter dressed in their Sunday best standing in front of the living room TV (figure 3.26). With her coat buttoned up, the little girl dangles her purse from her arm, indicating an excursion outside the home. The back of the photo reads, "Lu Lee and Daddy on way to Church" (figure 3.27). Like many family photos, this one uses the TV set to mediate the sentimentality of the parent-child relationship. But, as a place to pose before leaving home, the television setting also becomes part of the ritualized activities of leave taking. In the hoop dress and church photos (as well as many other portal snapshots), the pose is anticipatory: it foretells a journey away from home and away from TV. Despite the prominence of the television set in the image, it is the journey that matters, and it is the journey that is recounted in these photos.

In other cases, the journey scenario is integrated with the televised image on-screen. A set of two photos taken in sequence shows a woman in a brown sheath cocktail dress and matching heels. In one of the snapshots, the screen displays what appears to be a newscast (figure 3.28). A second snapshot of the same woman shows her modeling a fur stole draped over the dress, but this time a weatherman is on TV (figure 3.29). While it's hard to say which photo came first in the sequence, they were clearly taken in succession. The attire indicates a special excursion, and the weathercast reinforces the going-out scenario. Here, television's function as a window on the world takes on new meaning. The sequential poses gesture outward, indicating the relation between the metaphorical TV window and the literal living room door. That said, the framed baby picture on top of the TV set ties this going-out scenario to the woman's role as mother, so that the snapshot sequence marks television's double role as a family object and a portal object, imbuing the TV set with ambivalent meanings and functions in images of women and home.

These going-out snapshots contradict dominant assumptions about television's negative effects on the postwar housewife, particularly regarding concerns about women's isolation in the home. During the 1950s and 1960s, sociological studies described women's perceived loneliness, which, at least according to the sociologists, TV helped foster. A 1956 audience study conducted in Southern California reported a range of female complaints. One woman confessed, "All [my husband] wants to do is sit and watch television— I would like to go out more often." Another woman admitted, "I would like to go for a drive in the evening, but my husband has been out all day and would prefer to watch a wrestling match on television." A 1953 nationwide survey found that teenage girls experienced similar dismay. As one girl put it, "Instead of taking us out on date nights, the freeloading fellas park in our homes and stare at the boxing on TV."[63]

FIGURE 3.19
Circa 1955–60.

FIGURE 3.20
Circa 1953–58.

FIGURE 3.21 Circa
1957–62. Printed
with permission
from Mary and
Leigh Block
Museum of Art,
Northwestern
University,
Gift of Peter J.
Cohen, 2019.17.
Photo scan:
Repository and
Digital Curation,
Northwestern
University
Libraries.

FIGURE 3.22 1956.

FIGURE 3.23 Circa 1952–57.

Mar. '62
Ready for Spring
Concert at school.
To be worn with
hoop but due
to lack of seating
space — no hoop!

FIGURES 3.24 & 3.25 Dressed for concert, with inscription on back of photo, 1962.

Lu Lee + daddy on
way to church.

FIGURES 3.26 & 3.27
Dressed for church, with
inscription on back of
photo, circa 1955–60.

The trope of the isolated woman was a constant refrain in popular culture. Women's magazines, television programs, and films of the 1950s and 1960s often told tales of housewives trapped by their TV sets. Among these, Douglas Sirk's maternal melodrama *All That Heaven Allows* (1955) is a particularly enigmatic, and (in feminist TV studies) oft-cited, example.[64] The film tells the story of Cary, a well-to-do middle-aged woman (played by Jane Wyman) who falls for her handsome gardener, Ron (played by Rock Hudson). When her snobbish neighbors and college-aged children roundly disapprove, Cary gives up Ron. On Christmas morning, her son, Ned, gives her a TV set, the ultimate compensation for lost love. Sirk plays the Christmas scene for high melodramatic excess, with an image of Cary reflected—as if imprisoned—in the TV screen. The poignancy of her loneliness is registered contrapuntally

FIGURES 3.28 (*opposite*) & 3.29 Two iterations of going-out pose, 1962.

when the man who delivers the TV set tells Cary, "All you have to do is turn that dial and you have all the company you want, right there on the screen. Drama, comedy, life's parade at your fingertips." The melodramatic dissonance and pathos of the scene dramatizes Cary's dilemma as well as the more general fate of the suburban housewife in the TV age.

In the 1960s, female complaints about television crystallized, particularly in the wake of Betty Friedan's *The Feminine Mystique* (1963), which spoke to the boredom of the "occupation housewife" role.[65] One year after the book's publication, Friedan published a two-part essay in *TV Guide*, "Television and the Feminine Mystique," in which she lashed out at TV's image of woman as a "household drudge who spends her . . . boring days dreaming of love—and plotting revenge fantasies against her husband." Even worse, "the image of woman on television" constitutes an "an eerie Twilight Zone." "Even when the face and body of a woman are there, one feels a strange vagueness, an emptiness, an absence of human identity, a missing sexual aliveness."[66] Similarly, in November 1966 (the year in which the National Organization for Women was formed), *Ladies' Home Journal* ran a story on the "bored housewife," featuring an "American housewife [who] reflects on the monotony of her days." A large photograph shows the woman sitting in front of her television set. The caption explains her only "contact with the world [are the] telephone and TV." Even the career girl was not immune. A 1958 article in *Ebony*, "City of Single Women," presents TV as the last resort for lonely working girls who have problems getting dates. A photograph shows two bachelorettes (one a former beauty queen) spending a "quiet evening in front of [their] TV set"—the compensatory object for the unwed girl. In 1962, *Cosmopolitan* editor Helen Gurley Brown expanded on this logic in her bestselling book *Sex and the Single Girl*. Brown advises, "Have a TV set for quiet little evenings at home . . . but not too *great* a TV set or you'll never get out of your apartment."[67] Screen size somehow translates into women's liberation from domestic doldrums.

Perhaps in response to concerns about loneliness, boredom, sexual frustration, and domestic isolation, advertisers marketed television sets in ads that displayed glamorously dressed couples watching TV. Often published in women's magazines, these ads portrayed women in evening gowns, cocktail dresses, and lavish furs. But unlike the snapshots that show women posing in front of the set, the advertisements depict television as the main visual attraction for social occasions. (Obviously, watching TV is what an advertiser would want to promote.) In the advertising scenarios—even ones that feature women dressed for theater dates or ballroom dancing—women are often represented as housewife hostesses, welcoming guests or serving snacks and drinks. A perfect example is General Electric's 1956 ad for its "Hospitality TV," which features a woman in a cocktail dress wheeling the set around on its hostess wagon (figure 3.30). In these sorts of ads, despite the fancy clothes, women are pictured as housewives. Even if consumers identified with the glamorous models, the ads always associated TV with the interior space of the home (in this ad, the furthest the woman gets from inside her home is her patio).

Conversely, TV snapshots stage, document, and memorialize the *romance* of social occasions *outside* the home. Glamour shots that featured women in domestic spaces were likely taken by spouses or romantic partners. The act of taking a TV snapshot can be a flirtatious, even erotic, occasion, as the cam-

Showpiece G-E Hospitality TV has 4-inch non-marking, roll-easy wheels. Rolls any-where for "wherever-you-are" TV fun. Full-View Top-Tuning; "Set-and-Forget" volume control. Famous G-E Aluminized Picture Tube and dark safety glass for "indoor-out-door" picture quality. Pivoted brass handle with durable lacquered finish. Above, in Willow Green and Gray, Model 21C134. Also in Bermuda Bronze finish, Model 21C133.

FIGURE 3.30
Detail, GE
advertisement
for Hospitality
TV, 1956.

era operator focuses their gaze on a loved one. Glamour snapshots were not just images but also activities that couples did together, activities that potentially engaged them in modes of visual and sexual pleasure.

Glamour photography—even the everyday sort I am thinking about here—anticipates seduction. The visual dynamics in these pictures often belie an erotic detail—the sideways glance or a look at the camera, the flash of the camera operator registered on the TV screen, the trace of an intimate relationship among people in the pose, or just the pleasures of looking sexy that glamour poses afford. Although television and snapshot cameras were marketed and often used as the quintessential family media, the dress-up snapshots do more than document the polite presentation of fashion. As companion technologies, cameras and TV sets could be used together as instruments of sexual attraction. Rather than just looking (secondhand) at plunging necklines on *The Dean Martin Show* or at Hollywood hunks on *Route 66*, with snapshot cameras, people could pose in front of their TV screens and make themselves the center of erotic attention.

DRAG AND MASQUERADE

As I am sure is obvious, most snapshots conform to the prevailing photographic studium of middle-class nuclear family life and gendered glamour. But some photos go against the grain. Some snapshots seem entirely unconcerned with glamour or are perhaps even deliberately antiglamour. Even while intentionally posing, some women make a mockery of glamour by, for example, posing in muumuus and old bedroom slippers, perhaps holding up a dish rag or beer can, or engulfed by household mess. One woman (perhaps on her birthday or New Year's Eve) seems to mock glamour with her makeshift hat (fashioned, it appears, from bows and ribbons) while sitting in front of her TV in a baggy nighty and surrounded by groceries and cartons (figure 3.31). These women are far from the June Cleaver ideal of the TV sitcom, choosing instead to ignore the dictates of the glamour pose even while smiling for the camera in front of the living room TV.

Other snapshots more explicitly play with or defy heteronormative sex roles. One snapshot, dated 1966, features a man dressed in typical male attire (a white shirt, black tie, dark pants) who holds hands with and gazes at his same-sex partner, who is dressed in a silky negligee with a matching sheer coverup and carries a large black purse (figure 3.32). Black socks adorn very hairy legs, the telltale signs of makeshift drag. A vinyl LP rests on top of their head, as if a hat. Penned in Spanish, the writing on the back of the photograph refers to the "disco" (or record disk) but otherwise is silent as to the

FIGURE 3.31
Circa 1956–59.

intent or context of the photo. Nevertheless, the same-sex couple and make-shift drag offer an alternative vision to the performance of heterosexuality pictured in so many of the snapshots. Taken at an angle, the photograph is literally not "straight." As both a canted image and a material object (one has to turn it to see the image properly), the photo promotes a "queer" orientation to both TV and snapshot photography in general.

This image is especially interesting when considered in relation to Ahmed's concept of "queer phenomenology" and object orientation. While I have used the concept in a general sense to suggest that snapshots reorient television's dominant modes of spatial/object relations, for Ahmed, a queer orientation to objects is more specifically a relation to things that speaks to queer sexual orientations. "Turning the tables" on Husserl's phenomenology, while also drawing on Merleau-Ponty's work on perception, Ahmed considers object orientation in terms of lesbian sexuality and the normative "straighten-

FIGURE 3.32 1966.

ing" out of sexual orientation versus seeing the world "slantwise." Ahmed argues that a queer orientation positions itself differently to an object world designed for hetero-spatial norms, in ways that traditional phenomenological accounts do not perceive.[68] In snapshots, the TV set and setting around it are typically organized (and framed by cameras) for nuclear family life. But the posers in the drag snapshot turn the TV setting into a theatrical space for queer/trans performance. The photo *reorients* TV; it presents TV "slantwise." Even while I (and likely others looking at this photo) suspect that the canted angle might be a photographic accident, as an image, the snapshot nevertheless gives the viewer a queer orientation through which to perceive the queer subject matter of the shot.

There is a whole subgenre of drag vernacular photographs, so it's not entirely surprising that a TV snapshot would include a poser in drag. On the one hand, as Butler suggests, drag can destabilize gender by revealing its performative, iterative nature, the ways in which gender is rehearsed through repeated bodily gestures, mimicry, and sartorial expressions.[69] On the other hand, drag can also assert normative gender and at times be misogynistic. This, I think, was often the case in early television variety shows in which comics like Milton Berle, Bob Hope, Ed Wynn, and Jerry Lewis dressed as women and yet secured their heteronormativity by poking fun at femininity at the same time. Nevertheless, as Quinlan Miller suggests, both drag and the figure of the "trans gender queer" were crucial to early TV. Miller shows how, rather than a mere "subtext," gender-nonconforming characters and camp performances were regular features of early domestic sitcoms.[70] Augmenting Miller's focus on programs, the drag snapshot provides a way to think about television from the point of view of people who performed gender-nonconforming acts on the other side of the screen.

Another TV snapshot (dated 1954) shows a woman posing in a man's suit topped off with a US Navy cap (figure 3.33). While standing (with a swagger) in front of the set, she holds a cigar in one hand (apparently a prop) while dangling a cigarette and grasping a drink in the other. The photo suggests a party or some sort of gathering at which the poser performs not just for a camera but also for other people in the home. The eBay dealer who sold me this snapshot labeled it as a "lesbian interest," "gender bender" photo. As a sales strategy, eBay dealers often label snapshots in this way to appeal to the market for gay erotica, even if they don't know the actual sexual orientation of the posers.[71] In this case, the framed photographs that decorate the top of the TV set depict (what appear to be) a heterosexual couple, and the poser may well be dressed for Halloween (as opposed to a more explicit drag performance). Nevertheless, the fantasy the snapshot stages defies the heterosexual tele-decorations on the TV set, and even if taken on Halloween, the photo reorients the typical gender performances in TV dress-up photos.

At midcentury, forms of boyish femininity were promoted by the fashion industry itself. In one snapshot, a woman poses in an improvised version of the then-popular western-wear look, wearing jeans, a flowery button-down shirt, and a scarf tied around her neck (figure 3.34). By the time of the snapshot, western wear was a popular trend in women's clothing. In the 1940s, it was associated with glamorous Hollywood starlets like Veronica Lake and Yvonne De Carlo, who posed for pinups in rodeo-style fashions. In the 1950s,

FIGURE 3.33 1954.

Levi Strauss and Company promoted its women's jeans and the western look as part of the casual-wear women's market. Details in figure 3.34—the blond coiffed hair, red lipstick, Mary Jane shoes, and mother-daughter portraits hanging on the wall—all suggest the feminine attitude assumed in so many of the other poses. Still, this snapshot stands out among the others as not quite the same. While jeans designed for women were usually tapered at the legs, these jeans are baggy. The woman does not smile and wears a holster on her belt, giving the pose a menacing aggressive femininity. It's not clear if the outfit is a costume or daywear, but either way, it offers a performance of glamour that goes against the grain. While I can't speak to the woman's exact intentions, the picture suggests the ambiguity and gender fluidity of cross-dressing.

This snapshot resonates with the history of media representations that presented western wear as a mode of female drag and cross-dressing. Laura Horak has analyzed a whole subgenre of frontier films of the 1920s featuring "cross-dressed" action heroines who appear in cowboy garb.[72] This continued in new iterations on midcentury cinema screens, with Doris Day's Davy Crockett tomboy look in *Calamity Jane* (David Butler, dir., 1953) and Joan Crawford's outlaw style in *Johnny Guitar* (Nicholas Ray, dir., 1954), which turned western wear into an aggressive form of what Jack Halberstam calls "female masculinity." (Both films have been subjects of numerous queer readings.)[73] The western-wear TV snapshot can be read as part of this legacy of cross-dressed women and female masculinity.

This reading is even more convincing when we consider a 1956 Levi Strauss advertisement for women's "ranch pants" that are "inspired by the cowboy" (figure 3.35). The full-page color ad shows two women posing in western wear in front of a TV set (with a TV western on-screen). Although the ad copy claims the "figure flattering" jeans are for the "modish young miss," the ad's illustration depicts two mature (thirty- or forty-something) women, one of whom has gray hair. Her "ranch partner" stands in a powerful stance that mimics the stance of the cowboy on the TV screen. But rather than watch the TV, the women look (ambiguously) at each other and a scarf one woman holds. The ad, in other words, offers numerous fairly straightforward cues to gender fluidity if not outright lesbian desire. When read in the context of Levi's gender-fluid TV-fashion ad, the TV snapshot seems part of an alternative vision of glamour that was marketed to women in the 1950s. Taken together, this ad and the snapshot suggest that TV "dress-up" and everyday glamour need not always replicate the "pretty in pink" feminine ideal.

While not always featuring cross-dressing or drag, other snapshots show women striking poses that mock conventional glamour photos, often through costume, props, and gestures. Taken sometime in the mid-1950s to the early 1960s, one snapshot depicts four young women at the Fort McClellan Women's Army Corp (WAC) base in Alabama (figure 3.36).[74] Lined up on either side of the TV set, the women raise long cigarette holders to their mouths, an accessory typically associated with the glamour shot (as in *Life*'s TV-fashion spread). But rather than wear the typical cocktail sheaths, frilly gowns, or high-heeled pumps, the women pose in baggy shorts, crew socks, sneakers, and T-shirts with the WAC insignia on them. In this sartorial context, the long cigarette holders function as comic props rather than fashion accessories. They also recall (whether intentionally or not) the legacy of camp poses and cross-dressed women who used cigarettes and cigarette

FIGURE 3.34
Circa 1955–60.

holders as props (both in life and in photography and cinema).[75] However the posers intend it, the photo's comic attitude turns the glamour shot into a carnivalesque topsy-turvy reversal of gendered modeling conventions.[76] And because the television set is located at the WAC base, the snapshot literally reorients the place of TV from its typical domestic setting to the institutional barracks in which the servicewomen live. The pose speaks to the military careers of the women and their social ties to each other rather than women's place in the home.

Another group shot (apparently taken in the mid-1950s) features three airline stewardesses (as they were called at the time) dressed in a variety of costumes in front of a TV set (the set is barely visible, truly just a backdrop; see figure 3.37).[77] The woman on the right side of the frame wears baggy

Inspired BY THE COWBOY

FIGURE 3.35 Advertisement for women's ranch pants, Levi Strauss and Company, 1956.

worn-out jeans, suspenders, and a cap. (The eBay dealer who sold me the photo likens the costume to the garb of male rube characters in *Li'l Abner*.) The woman on the left side of the frame seems deliberately engaged in a comic send-up of a glamour girl model. Her black picture frame hat, long black gloves, and midriff blouse evoke the pages of *Vogue*, while her short shorts (or a girdle?), garters, and stockings give the photo a sense of irony, as if the woman is mocking risqué poses in men's girlie magazines. Cigarettes dangling from both women's mouths add to the sense of glamour masquerade. Meanwhile, it's hard to know if the woman in the middle intends her makeshift toga-style dress as a goofy glamour getup or if it is actually her ordinary attire. Even if these women do not intend it this way, their pose calls attention to the thin line between costume and clothes, as well as the tenuous

FIGURE 3.36 Circa 1956–62.

binaries of masculinity and femininity. Moreover, given their profession as stewardesses, these women must have been well aware of the hard work of glamour and gender performance. The snapshot indicates the fun women had using the TV pose as an occasion by which to the turn their glamour labor into glamour play.

In such examples, snapshots evoke ironic relations to mass culture, TV, and the fashion industry, and they partake of the queer/camp sensibility that Elspeth Brown attributes to a group of gay interwar fashion photographers and their models, who worked for magazines like *Vogue* and *Harper's Bazaar*. These fashion photographs often used "bad objects" (for example, she notes Cecil Beaton's "doilies," "enormous paper flowers," and "badly carved cupids from junk shops" in magazines like *British Vogue*) that evoke queer and camp tastes.[78] In the 1960s, as TV itself became a "bad object" (or what FCC chair Newton Minow called a "vast wasteland"), a TV set or screen (or tele-decorations like doilies, fake flowers, and cupids on top of the set) could evoke a queer and camp sensibility in a photo, regardless of the sexual identity or sartorial choices of the posers.[79]

By the mid-1960s, several snapshots appear to draw on the period's discourses on camp in rather pointed ways. A 1966 snapshot is a perfect example. By the time this photo appeared, many people would have read Susan Sontag's "Notes on 'Camp'"(1964), and even if they had not, there were other books and articles on the topic. In 1966, camp and related aesthetics of pop art made it to television with the premiere of ABC's *Batman* (1966–68). In other words, camp was becoming a more *mass* sensibility, not necessarily tied to gay subcultures (as Sontag suggested), even if it still expressed queer

FIGURE 3.37 Circa 1955.

sensibilities. Like other glamour snapshots, this 1966 example features a domestic setting with a TV set (figure 3.38). What look to be junk store decorations (a "bad" landscape, a tchotchke hanging on a string, a sketch of a woman's face beside a garish advertising image of a disembodied woman's head floating in a bright orange background) add to a camp/pop/queer sensibility. The TV set is farther in the background, as the poser calls attention to a different mass medium—a fashion magazine. Wearing a fright wig with horror movie makeup on his face, the poser (I am guessing a young man) holds up an issue of *Glamour*.[80] Headshots of models with long silky hair appear on the front and back cover. The poser's otherwise boyish attire (a plain white T-shirt and torn jeans) clash with his grotesque headshot. He is just a regular

FIGURE 3.38 1966.

"guy" save for the fact of his voodoo mask makeup and the issue of *Glamour* magazine. By turning the glamour pose into a creature feature, this snapshot, whether intentionally or not, humorously unmasks the gender performance that runs through so many other TV snapshots.

My final example comes in the form of a series of screenshots created (slightly after my period) between 1978 and 1982, by Tom Wilkins, an American camera enthusiast who snapped Polaroid photos off his television set (figures 3.39 and 3.40). The screenshots capture images of women who are often scantily dressed or sometimes nude (for example, "Jacqueline Bisset topless from behind" or an unknown "hooker on *Starsky and Hutch*"). They also capture images from commercials for feminine products like Playtex bras. Wilkins dated, numbered, and described his roughly nine hundred screenshots on the white border of each Polaroid frame, thereby creating a series that he compiled in albums he called "my TV girls." After Wilkins's death, the French artist Sébastien Girard (who works with found photos) purchased Wilkins's Polaroid collection and recompiled them in his own self-published books, *My TV Girls* (named after Wilkins's albums) and *The Diary of Tom Wilkins*, Girard's own invention.[81] Girard's second book is especially pertinent to my interests. For the most part, *The Diary of Tom Wilkins* reproduces Wilkins's screenshots—many of which feature women's décolletage and bras. But somewhere in the middle of the book, a different Polaroid emerges—a self-portrait of Wilkins, who appears wearing a similar Playtex lace bra and snapping his photo in a mirror. Wilkins's inscription on the snapshot reads: "27 March 81—Me wearing #646-398 *Beige* Playtex Beautiful Ones Lace Bra. Photograph was taken using a dressing mirror and an SX-70 [Polaroid] camera. Tom Wilkins."[82] Although Wilkins likely took these Polaroids for private pleasure (or perhaps to share with friends), Girard's *Diary* restages the entire collection as a queer family album, in which he places Wilkins's TV screenshots of women alongside the self-portrait of Wilkins in the bra. But even while this book is Girard's homage and reappropriation, Wilkins's Polaroids provide insights into the queer and camp home-mode practices that TV and snapshot cameras (as companion technologies) afforded.

The various drag and masquerade photos all speak to the performativity at the heart of scenes of everyday glamour. Masks and masquerade are prominent concerns in photography theory, and they are also concepts used by photographers interested in issues of subjectivity, authenticity, and dissimulation. In *Camera Lucida*, Barthes argues, "Since every photograph is contingent (and thereby outside of meaning), Photography cannot signify (aim at a generality) except by assuming a mask . . . the mask is the

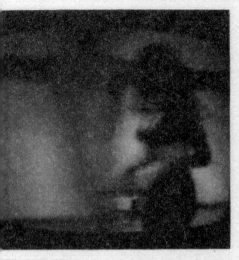

11 SEP 81 #778 OFF T.V. MOVIE - STARCRASH
- GIRL WEARING SKIMPY SPACESUIT

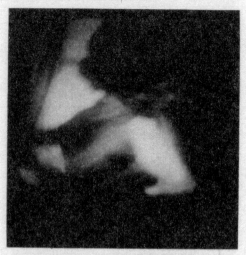

13 SEP 81 #779 OFF T.V. MOVIE - LADY SINGS
THE BLUES
- DIANA ROSS WEARING TEDDY

15 SEP 81 #777 OFF T.V. MOVIE - HANSEL IS
HER VALLEY
- GIRL ON LEFT IS WEARING
SKIRT AND PANTIES, GIRL ON RIGHT IS
WEARING SKIRT.

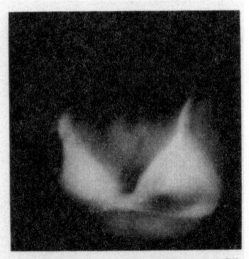

21 SEP 81 #778 OFF T.V. MOVIE - FAME
- HIGH SCHOOL GIRL WEARING BRA.
AND GOLD NECKLACE.

27 MAR 81 - ME WEARING #646-398 BEIGE PLAYTEX BEAUTIFUL ONES LACE BRA. PHOTOGRAPH WAS TAKEN USING A DRESSING MIRROR AND AN 8×70 CAMERA. TOM WILKINS

FIGURES 3.39 (*opposite*) & 3.40 (*left*) Detail from pages in Sébastien Girard, *The Diary of Tom Wilkins*, 2017. Original Polaroid screenshots by Tom Wilkins, photographed in 1978–82. Printed with permission from Sébastien Girard.

meaning."[83] If masks form the very meaning of striking a pose, there is no deeper, more authentic reality behind it. Reflecting on photography as "masks" (or masquerade), Hirsch considers the "masking of the subject" in the photographs of Ralph Eugene Meatyard and Cindy Sherman. For Hirsch, these photographers develop Barthes's concerns. Analyzing Meatyard's photographs in *The Family Album of Lucybelle Crater*, Hirsch argues, "Identity is no longer individual but is defined by the mask of familial relation and of conventions of family photography. . . . When we are photographed in the context of the conventions of family-snapshot photography . . . we wear masks, fabricate ourselves according to certain expectations and are fabricated by them." Considering Cindy Sherman's performative poses (in, for example, her breakthrough series *Untitled Film Stills*, 1977–80), Hirsch claims the photographs are "performances of performances" that acknowledge the dissimulation of self through conventions of glamour and fashion photography.[84] From this point of view, photographs—whether art photography or snapshots—can be understood in relation to Butler's work on gender performance and masquerade (as well as the literature in fashion theory, film and media studies, photography studies, and performance studies that follows in this vein). In all these contexts, masks and masquerade do not cover up deeper meanings or authentic feelings; they construct the photographic subject through poses and performances of self.

While the snapshots of drag poses and campy masquerade are outliers in my collection, they nevertheless remind us that all the dress-up snapshots I've explored in this chapter are gender performances that involve aspects of masking and masquerade. By counter-memory and counter-example, these outlier photos suggest that dress-up snapshots are performances of self and social relations that rely on the glamour labor of makeup, hairstyling, fashion design, poses, settings, props, and gestures. Snapshots of everyday glamour bring these performative aspects of the snapshot to life and raise questions about the visual and sexual pleasures entailed in taking pictures of oneself in front of a TV set. To explore this further I now want to widen my lens of inquiry by moving from dress-up snapshots to photos made specifically for sexual arousal.

4

TV PINUPS

SEX AND THE SINGLE TV

At the dawn of commercial television, pinup model Peggy Corday found a job on the short-lived television program *Photographic Horizons*. Aired on the DuMont Network's New York affiliate station from December 1947 to 1949, the show was hosted by Joe Costa, president of the National Press Photographers Association and supervising editor of the *New York Daily Mirror's* magazine section. Costa offered how-to advice to the growing ranks of mostly male amateur photographers in postwar America, many of whom were readers of photography magazines that featured female pinups on their covers. Meanwhile, Corday alternated roles as Costa's attractive cohost and photographic model. Promoting television as a participatory medium, Costa invited viewers to take "video snapshots" of Corday (as well as other photographic subjects) straight from the screen and enter them into his DuMont Camera Club contest, the winners of which he announced on-air.

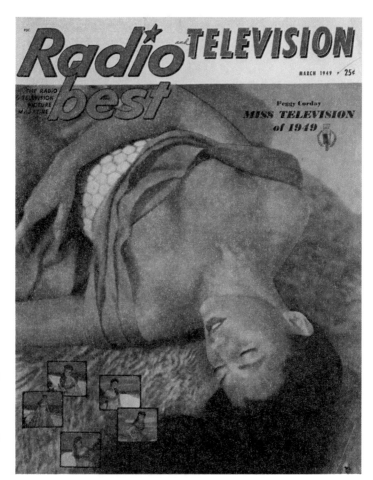

RADIO and TELEVISION
best

MARCH 1949 · 25¢

Peggy Corday
MISS TELEVISION
of 1949

FIGURE 4.1
Cover of *Radio and Television Best*, March 1949, featuring that year's Miss Television, Peggy Corday.

Corday was something of a sensation in the early TV period. By the time she appeared on *Photographic Horizons*, she had launched an acting career that included a role as Venus in Max Reinhardt's 1944 Broadway production of *Helen of Troy*. In that same year, she appeared on the cover of the World War II pinup magazine *Yank*, which featured her posing in high heels and a skimpy nightgown (fringed as if ravaged at the hem). Five years later, *Radio and Television Best* named her Miss Television 1949 in a cover story profiling her achievements and publicizing her appearance on *Photographic Horizons*.[1] The cover art shows her in an overhead shot, lying on a beach in a purple gown with a plunging neckline. Although the image is highly stylized (with color tinting that gives it the look of a painting), the angle of the shot, the plunging purple gown, and her parted red lips invite the viewer to imagine her as a sexual conquest (figure 4.1).

Within the image (cover layout):

Radio ᵀᴱᴸᴱⱽᴵˢᴵᴼᴺ best

Peggy Corday,
Miss Television 1949

FIGURE 4.2
Cover story
in *Radio and
Television Best*,
March 1949.

While the lurid cover art no doubt helped sell this issue, the inside star profile paints a very different picture, demonstrating how a pinup girl could be domesticated for purposes of everyday glamour on TV. The story presents Corday as an innocent farm girl from Maryland who came to New York in search of fame. A full-page photograph shows her riding a bicycle with her hair in a ponytail and a camera hanging from her neck (figure 4.2). A short skirt shows off her legs, but her sweater covers everything else. A smaller image on the lower margin of the layout pictures Corday in her role as co-host on the TV show. Her long hair is now pinned up, and she is dressed in a button-down blouse. In the surviving copies of her appearance on the show, she wears a simple, elegant long-sleeve dress, and her hair is similarly pinned.[2] The sedate outfit and hairdo distract from the bombshell image in her pinups, rendering her both family friendly and mature—a look that conforms to the gold standard of TV's fem-cee decorum. Nevertheless, the fact that a pinup model should appear as a hostess on a TV program offers a way to think about TV snapshots in the context of more explicitly sexy TV pinups that circulated at the time.

Some of these photos were, like Corday's role on *Photographic Horizons*, produced in connection with the television industry itself.[3] In fact, when Corday appeared as Miss Television 1949 on the cover of *Radio and Television Best*, the magazine was drawing on an exploitation tactic common to the broadcasting field since the late 1920s. when Miss Radios began to serve as promotional vehicles for the networks and local stations across the country.[4] By the 1950s, trade journals like *Broadcasting* and *Sponsor* were full of ads for local stations that featured Miss Televisions. In the trade ads, the slippage between signal coverage in a broadcast market and clothing coverage on female bodies was a constant chuckle for the boys at advertising firms and television stations.[5] But Miss Television was also a public figure, a way to woo audiences. There were at least four Miss Televisions at the RCA Pavilion at the 1939 New York World's Fair. In 1950, thirteen Miss Televisions (from local stations around the country) made their way to TV screens in the *Miss U.S. Television* grand finals contest, which was produced in connection with their appearance at the Chicago Fair and aired on the DuMont Network. Framed within the genre of the beauty pageant, the program features the local Miss Televisions competing for the national crown via talent segments (everything from opera to a burlesque-inspired hula act to a bathing suit sequence). Fifteen years later, in 1965, David Wolper (best known today for his 1977 miniseries *Roots*) produced a never-aired pilot for *Miss Television USA*, similarly based on competition among Miss Televisions from across the nation. The Miss Television intrigue fizzled out by the second half of the 1960s, but the sexual associations between TV and female bodies did not.

Here, I want to consider a different group of TV pinups that circulated in the late 1940s through the 1960s. Virtually forgotten in cultural histories of television, these TV pinups used the television set as a background and a prop for the display of women in various stages of undress. Rather than socially acceptable cheesecake shots of Miss Television, most of these were more sexually explicit *borderline* images—photos somewhere between cheesecake and the then-illegal traffic in porn.[6] Borderline photos could be found in men's "girlie magazines," which proliferated in the postwar period. They also circulated in the context of postwar camera clubs, which provided cover for their mostly male members to look at nude women under the guise of hobby art, male bonding, and wholesome comradery. And they were available at stores and through mail-order catalogs, such as "Pinup King" Irving Klaw's New York shop, which sold Hollywood glamour shots as a cover for his large catalog of fetish photos and striptease films, items then subject to obscenity laws outlawing the sale of such materials through the mail. (Klaw, for example, was eventually prosecuted and run out of business.)

Exploring TV pinups in the context of a book on snapshots may seem a curious choice. To be sure, pinups and snapshots were aimed at different publics and circulated in different contexts. The pinups' overt sexual implications and their association with borderline and potentially illicit content seems at first glance fundamentally different from the sentimental images of family life. But as the case of *Photographic Horizons* suggests, home-mode photography was never entirely divorced from pinups, nor are pinups wholly antithetical to the images of everyday glamour—and erotic modes of looking— in the snapshots. Despite their more explicit sexual content, like the snapshots, TV pinups presented women posing with TV sets in domestic settings (either actual living rooms or studio sets made to look like them). In this sense, pinups and snapshots shared a common language.

Just as the early TV industry promoted itself with pinup models, the Kodak company's Kodak Girls fulfilled similar publicity functions. When presenting Corday riding her bicycle, *Radio and Television Best* was borrowing from the long lineage of independent fashionable Kodak Girls, who, like Corday, were often pictured as mobile outdoorsy types with cameras around their necks. While the Kodak Girls of the early twentieth century often posed in long dresses in romanticized nature settings (figure 4.3), by the 1940s they looked more like the modern cheesecake pinups, wearing bathing suits and sometimes even striking provocative pinup poses for cameras (figure 4.4). The promotional photo for the 1964 Kodak Girl (also referred to as the Kodak Model) was shot by Hollywood glamour photographer Peter Gowland, famous for his pinups of stars like Brigitte Bardot and glamour columns for the how-to magazine *Popular Photography*. (His columns were full of pinups and nudes.) Despite their status as wholesome family media, both snapshot cameras and TV depended on sexualized images of women to court consumers.

This chapter traces these overlapping image-making practices. I first explore the historical formations that gave rise to TV pinups. I then analyze the pinups in connection with a group of TV snapshots that borrowed their iconography from the pinup form. While I consider pinups in relation to their objectification of women, I also draw on the work of feminist historians such as Joanne Meyerowitz, Maria Elena Buszek, and Megan E. Williams, who

FIGURE 4.3 Kodak Girl, Kodak advertisement, circa 1913.
Courtesy of the George Eastman Museum.

CONTENTS

Get **Kodak film**

KODAK DEALER NEWS

MAY, 1964

VOLUME 24   NUMBER 1

PUBLISHED BY

**CANADIAN KODAK SALES
LIMITED**

TORONTO 15, ONTARIO

In one package the latest news
about Kodak products, advertising,
sales aids—presented with a view
to helping you make your business
better.

*All prices shown in this Kodak Dealer News are
suggested list and subject to change without notice.*

**Your Girl
for
1964**

She's a girl-watcher's
dream: a lovely
blond lass in a red
swimsuit. Her nationwide
debut will make her
one of the year's most
widely seen models.
She's the Kodak Girl
for 1964. Her name
is Barbara Julian
and her life-size likeness
on the eye-arresting
Kodak Girl Display is
certain to attract
admiring glances. The
picture reflects the skill
that has gained fame for
glamour photographer
Peter Gowland. The
display is being
shipped to all dealers
automatically. Put her
where she'll be
noticed and she'll go
to work for you.

FIGURE 4.4 "Your Girl for 1964" advertisement from the
1964 Kodak dealer circulars. Photograph by Peter Gowland.
Courtesy of Ryerson University Library.

have approached pinups in more complex terms by demonstrating that despite the history of feminist crusades against them, many women embraced pinups and used them as a means of personal or even political empowerment. Buszek, for example, traces women's active negotiation with and political uses of the form, from their audacious poses in burlesque pinups and new women pinups of the suffragette period to pinups in Hollywood fanzines (which at times addressed suffrage) and the "grrrl power" retro pinups that began to appear in the 1980s.[7] TV pinups are likewise a complex cultural form, and they open up questions about exactly what kinds of pleasures they afforded and to whom.

These photos defy received wisdom about early television's family orientations with its prim sitcom housewives and gray flannel dads whose romantic relations (due to censorship concerns) took place in twin beds. On the other side of the screen, in pinup photos, sexy poses are everywhere. Moreover, TV pinups were often shot in family homes, and in the case of the homemade pinups I discuss in the last section of this chapter, they feature ordinary women (as opposed to professional models) posing for snapshot cameras. Taken as whole, the pinups make us rethink the sexual dynamics of family TV.

PINUPS: 1930S–1960S

With their explicitly sexual and burlesque sensibility, TV pinups presented a particular twist on pinup art as it evolved across the twentieth century. Their immediate midcentury predecessors were the painted pinups found in calendar art, magazines, advertising, and related ephemera (such as matchbooks and postcards). Especially popular in the 1930s through the early 1950s, the painted pinups featured young girls, almost always white (at least when in mainstream venues aimed at majority white publics).

When the men's magazine *Esquire* began publication in 1933, it packaged pinups in the context of its more general aura of upper-crust sophistication, first with George Petty's Petty Girls and later in the 1940s with Alberto Vargas's Vargas Girls.[8] Pinups featured young women posing in sultry gowns, bathing suits, negligees, shorts, or even nude (with genitals masked by the angle of the pose or by other objects in the picture). The Vargas Girls were known for their see-through paper-thin dresses and negligees, but despite their sexual content, they were rendered in the fine art tradition of the nude, usually against minimalist backdrops. Other pinups by artists like Gil Elvgren staged simple storytelling scenarios, presenting girls as victims of minor mishaps, and were often humorous, but at the girl's expense. A girl bends over to sweep her rug, and her skirt flies up; a girl gets caught in a gust of wind, and her skirt flies up; a girl reaches for a letter in her mailbox, her hem gets caught on a fence, and her skirt flies up; a girl holds her house cat, the cat's claw snags her skirt, and so on.[9] In such cases, the accidental nature of the "lewd" event maintains the girl's alibi of innocence, although at the same time, she is not altogether lacking in agency. For example, the girl sometimes looks in the mirror and appears self-aware of her sexuality, involved in auto-erotic pleasures or narcissistic display.

Pinups' popularity soared during World War II, when Hollywood stars like Betty Grable, Rita Hayworth, and Jane Russell posed for both painted and photographic versions that soldiers "pinned" to the walls of their barracks. The practice was encouraged by the US Army's *Yank* magazine, a monthly publication that published pinups as "strategic support material" for soldiers, giving them a reason for "why we fight."[10] Pinups were painted onto the wings and noses of fighter planes; an image of Rita Hayworth was affixed to one of the first atomic bombs (it was nicknamed the Gilda bomb, after her famous movie).[11] Meanwhile, on the home front, the pinup girl was a role model for women. Magazines like *Life*, *Look*, and the NAACP's *Crisis* presented pinups as part of women's patriotic contributions to the war effort.[12] The reigning Hollywood pinup model, Betty Grable, appeared in advertisements and in films like the aptly titled *Pinup Girl* (H. B. Humberstone, dir., 1944), in which she played an entertainer at a military canteen.[13] These patriotic connotations continued after the war in magazines, films, and ads (for both women's and men's products). But, during the 1940s, and especially in the 1950s, the pinup genre expanded to include the much more sexually explicit photographs that appeared in the proliferating set of borderline girlie magazines like *Bachelor*, *VUE*, *Modern Man*, *Rascal*, *Spree*, and *Wink*. Featuring photos of women in various stages of undress (often with bare breasts, sometimes almost entirely naked), such magazines drew on burlesque traditions of striptease and exoticism, and they echoed hardcore and stag film scenarios. (To get around obscenity laws, the magazines often used props, costumes, lighting, angles, or posing positions to hide what courts would construe as pornographic photos of body parts.)

The debut of Hugh Hefner's *Playboy* magazine in 1953 was a watershed moment. *Playboy* mimicked *Esquire*'s aesthete disposition, publishing articles on jazz, modern art, men's fashions, and the like, and it even offered a new home to *Esquire*'s Vargas Girls.[14] At the same time, *Playboy* also drew its inspiration from the girlie magazines by featuring nude photographs of women. But while previous girlie magazines were often cheaply published and used black-and-white prints, *Playboy*'s pinups were shot in color by some of the period's leading glamour photographers, including Gowland, Bruno Bernard, Ron Vogel, and Bunny Yeager. Separating their work from cheesecake pinups, these photographers typically used the word *glamour* (and related terms like *figure photography* and *nude*) to signify their class sensibility, a distinction in line with what Hefner perceived to be sophisticated tastes. When *Playboy* first hit the stands in December 1953, its full-color pinup of Marilyn Monroe was a decidedly new twist on the men's magazine.[15] Even more inventive were the full-color Playmate centerfolds, which began in 1954. Given the indexical nature of the photographs—the fact that these were real woman posing nude—Hefner went to great lengths to distinguish the Playmates from the "bad girl" floozie (or worse, prostitute) image often associated with artists' models. As Hefner recalled in 2003, "For models we chose the girl-next-door, not just professional models."[16] Nevertheless, the *Playboy* centerfold allowed readers to manhandle the girl by opening the pages and turning her into a fantasy sex mate.[17]

As this brief historical sketch suggests, by the postwar period, pinups generated a potent mix of ambivalent meanings in which female sexuality was exposed and concealed, spectacularized but contained within discourses of girl-next-door innocence and American patriotism.[18] In this respect, pinups resonated with the contradictory tensions inherent in postwar discourses on sexuality.

Examining these tensions, Meyerowitz argues that postwar pinups generated mixed reactions among women. On the one hand, women's groups (most notably, the General Federation of Women's Clubs) launched campaigns against the girlie magazines, and some female antiporn crusaders testified before the House of Representatives Select Committee on Current Pornographic Materials, which initiated hearings on the subject in 1952.[19] Later in the 1960s and 1970s, in the context of the second-wave women's movements, feminists protested men's magazines (especially *Playboy*), beauty pageants, pinups and related materials for their objectification of women's bodies. On the other hand, some women battled against government censorship on First Amendment grounds, and some read and enjoyed the men's magazines. Examining women's letters to the editors of *Playboy*, Meyerowitz claims that of the fifty letters published between 1953 and 1959, "around four fifths lavished praise."[20] One woman thought *Playboy* was "a refreshing change from the whipped-cream pap of the so-called women's magazines."[21] Another woman enthused, "I . . . am a young housewife . . . and I enjoy [*Playboy*] as much as any man! I am sure a lot of other women do too!"[22] Analyzing reader letters to *Esquire*, Buszek reports that "one-fourth of Vargas' fan mail was from women who wrote not just in support of his work" but also "for advice on how they could emulate the Vargas Girl's style."[23] And the tamer sorts of cheesecake pinups in magazines like *Crisis*, *Ebony*, and *Jet* generated mixed responses among African American readers (regarding respectability politics, Hollywood stereotypes, and civil rights).[24] In his essay on the short-lived Black men's magazine *Duke* (published in 1957 and modeled on *Playboy*), Kinohi Nishikawa finds divided reactions to the magazine's sexually provocative "Duchess of the Month."[25] (The first *Playboy* centerfold featuring a Black model came later in 1965.) By midcentury, then, pinups circulated in a highly contradictory field of culture. The responses to them were never uniform nor entirely predictable by gender, race, class, or any other demographic means of calculation.

Even the labor practices around pinups were not easy to predict. Certainly, many of the female models were poorly paid and sexually exploited. Nevertheless, the lucrative commercial trade in pinups did offer some women opportunities that many other "pink collar" career paths would not. Even though men like Petty and Vargas are typically considered the "fathers" of the form, women artists such as Pearl Frush, Joyce Ballantyne, Zoë Mozert, and Ruth Deckard found gainful employment creating glamour portraits and pinups for film studios, magazines, and calendar art. In the postwar period, some women photographers secured positions in the trade. Most notably, Bunny Yeager was one of the top glamour and pinup photographers of her time (male or female), and she frequently freelanced for *Playboy* and other men's magazines.[26] That said, just because a woman is behind a camera does not mean the images she produces are any less fetishistic than the ones made by men. But the fact that some women prospered in the business does suggest that the work world of pinups was not as rigidly exclusive as is often assumed. Moreover, during and after World War II, women posed for their own homemade pinups made with ordinary snapshot cameras, often sending these pictures to boyfriends or husbands stationed overseas. In other words, making pinups was not just a professional goal; it was also part of women's everyday life—a point I return to later in this chapter.

What I find most interesting about pinups in connection with TV snapshots is their link to women's culture and especially their imagination of sex as a domestic affair. Pinups often depicted domestic interiors, showing women in erotic poses on furniture (modern chairs were a favorite), and they often presented household things (bubble baths, mailboxes, house cats, etc.) as props for sex. The common and the everyday were defamiliarized in pinups that turned even objects of drudgery—brooms, vacuum cleaners, wash buckets—into erotic opportunities. The TV set joined this collection of sexy household things. But its place here is not a simple addition. Rather, TV's appearance in pinups is the result of a parallel historical trajectory that is more specifically a history of erotic images of telecommunications.

TELE-PINUPS

Communications media—especially the telephone—often appeared in the painted pinups of the 1930s–1950s. Telephones implied the titillating possibility of eavesdropping on a conversation—which made them especially tantalizing props for sexual arousal. When visually rendered in pinups, the telephone evoked voyeuristic pleasures, placing the spectator in the role of a Peeping Tom.[27] After leaving *Esquire* in the late 1930s, Petty produced a whole cycle of Petty Girl telephone pinups, which circulated in magazines, in ads, on calendars, and on postcards. One was even used as nose art for the World War II B-17 bomber *Memphis Belle*. In telephone pinups, a woman typically holds a receiver to her ear while the wire dangles across her body (highlighting her curves but also vaguely suggesting the bondage whip).

It is here, in connection with the telephone, where the TV pinup finds its lineage—one that goes back to nineteenth-century fantasies about new media. In Albert Robida's illustrated books *Le vingtième siècle* (1883) and *La vie electrique* (1890), the French futurist imagined "telephonoscope" devices that would allow people to watch and interact with distant events taking place in real time. Illustrations show people using the device as a kind of primitive picture phone, speaking back to the image, and some portray domestic settings with male voyeurs looking at young girls. Titled *La théâtre chez soi par le téléphonoscope* (The home theater of the telephonoscope), an illustration in *Le vingtième siècle* features a potbellied, cigar-smoking bourgeois gentleman lounging at home as he gazes at a Parisian dancing girl transmitted on the telephonoscope's huge mirror-like screen (figure 4.5).[28] A glass monocle (indicated by a small black circle) emphasizes the visual lust afforded by the telephonoscope's larger glass screen. Printed in the same book, *Une erreur du téléphonoscope* (A telephonoscope error), depicts four old gentlemen ogling a girl pulling down her stockings and undressing in her bedroom. The Peeping Tom aspect of the scene is once again highlighted by the spectacles worn by two of the men, one of whom adjusts his glasses as if trying to get a better look.

Robida's drawings appear now as science fiction, but the telephonoscope did have a practical afterlife. As William Uricchio argues, the inven-

FIGURE 4.5 Albert Robida, *La théâtre chez soi par le téléphonoscope* (The home theater of the telephonoscope), illustration in *Le vingtième siècle*, 1883.

tion of the telephone and television were intertwined, and the devices should be considered for their "intermedial" connections. While Uricchio focuses mostly on the technical and aesthetic affordances of the two communication devices (and their similar temporalities of simultaneity), the telephone and television were also connected as "intermedial" doubles in the erotic imagination way past the time of Robida.[29] At the dawn of television's commercial innovation after World War II, TV and telephones (and sometimes radios) were often combined in pinups. As a new technology, the TV set no doubt enhanced the novelty of the pinup; and even more powerfully than the telephone before it, TV evoked the Peeping Tom intrigue of looking at someone who could not look back.

Painted by *Esquire* pinup artist Al Moore, the cover art to the magazine's November 1950 special "TV issue" presents a sultry redhead reclining while holding a telephone receiver to her ear (figure 4.6). The layout positions the redhead in the center of the page inside a yellow circle, which is set inside a blue background designed to look like a TV test pattern. *Esquire*'s mascot, Esky (a cartoon rendering of a bald, mustached, bug-eyed gentleman), floats in this test-pattern background. Dressed in a smoking gown, he reclines on a modern-style lounge chair and ogles the TV screen, which contains a diminutive rendering of the redheaded woman and her telephone. Esky's eyes are drawn off scale, much too large for his face—a drafting choice that emphasizes the Peeping Tom scenario in the image. The cartoon recalls Robida's sedentary male viewers, whose eyes are graphically exaggerated with spectacles and riveted on the women on screens. Taken as a whole, the *Esquire* layout is itself an eye: the blue TV test pattern in the background forms an iris for the yellow circle "pupil" in which the pinup girl appears.[30]

The telephone-television imagery extended to photography. Earl Moran's 1949 pinup of Marilyn Monroe (then model and aspiring actress Norma Jeane Baker) is a striking example (figure 4.7). One of the best-known pinup artists, Moran features Marilyn posing with a telephone at her ear and a TV set to her right. The telephone wire seductively drapes across Marilyn's body but is frazzled at the end (suggesting that Monroe's electrical magnetism has burned through the cord). Emerging from a shower, Marilyn stands on her tiptoes in fluff-trimmed slippers whose peekaboo toes contribute to the Peeping Tom visual dynamics of the photo, teasing the viewer, who sees only so much. Continuing the tease, Marilyn holds a towel around her waist that exposes just glimpses of her breasts and casts a shadow between her thighs. The turned-off television set (with a pinup portrait hung above it and Marilyn looking down at it) offers another kind of visual tease, especially for

FIGURE 4.6 Cover of *Esquire* magazine, November 1950.

FIGURE 4.7 Marilyn Monroe (a.k.a. Norma Jeane Baker).
Photograph by Earl Moran, 1949. Printed with permission
from Peter Koster.

people in 1949, who would be eager to see images on-screen. The blank glow of the screen both attracts and denies the viewer's gaze with its oblique presence.[31] In calendar art of the same period, Moran presents a more sedate version of the tele-pinup, but the blank screen functions similarly as a TV tease (figure 4.8).

The use of television and telephones as partners in sexual intrigue spilled over into other realms of popular culture. On TV itself, the television-telephone pinup materialized in the late-night show *Voluptua*, which aired on the Los Angeles local station KABC in 1954–55. Voluptua (a.k.a. Gloria Pall—one-time *Esquire* centerfold, showgirl, and Miss Flatbush 1947) introduced romantic-themed movies while sitting in her studio set "boudoir" cradling a telephone (trimmed in mink) and wearing negligees or just a man's pajama top. Rather than ring, the telephone moans "Voluptu-ah-ah-ah" to introduce the sexy host, who fields calls from the home audience. The program outraged Christian groups and the local Parent Teacher Association, which called Pall's character Corruptua and pressured KABC to cancel the show. The station did so after just seven weeks. Nevertheless, *Voluptua* drew national attention, for example, in *Life* and *Playboy*.[32]

As the 1950s progressed, the telephone disappeared from the TV pinups. While once a transitional object for thinking about the newer TV medium, the telephone was no longer needed to remind people of the eavesdropping (and sexually titillating) affordances of television. Although telephones continued to be featured as fetish props in pinups (for example, there were many telephone pinups in *Playboy*), the TV set could just as well imply sexual intrigue on its own.

THE "CLASSIC" TV PINUP: DEFAMILIARIZING DOMESTICITY

In the 1950s, TV pinups began to solidify as a genre. They spanned the range of glamour photography, cheesecake, and borderline materials. While many were shot in studio settings for commercial publication and trade, others appear to have been made by amateurs, who sold them or kept them for their own amusement and shot them in motel rooms and homes. Most were the sorts of photos that circulated in men's girlie magazines.

As opposed to women's magazines of the period that depicted TV as a family medium, men's magazines distanced TV from children, wives, and suburban settings. *Playboy*'s depictions of television are especially interesting in this respect. Hefner built the magazine not just by presenting lush color centerfolds with female nudes, but also by promoting a new postwar bachelor lifestyle that was specifically distinct from nuclear family life. As Barbara

FIGURE 4.8 Calendar art created by Earl Moran for Brown and Bigelow Publishing Company, circa 1948–50.

Ehrenreich puts it, Hefner set out to "reclaim the indoors for men," offering how-to lifestyle lessons that focused on the well-appointed urban bachelor pad as the privileged space of masculinity and promiscuous heterosexuality.[33] *Playboy* emphatically distanced the bachelor pad from what the magazine perceived to be the controlling influence of wives. In his first editorial, Hefner wrote: "We want to make it clear from the very start, we aren't a 'family magazine.' If you're somebody's sister, wife or mother-in-law and picked us up by mistake, please pass us along to the man in your life and get back to your *Ladies' Home Companion*."[34]

As the quintessential suburban family medium, television had a particularly vexed relation to *Playboy*'s bachelor lifestyle. While *Playboy* regularly reviewed movies, theater, records, and books, with some notable exceptions (for example, "hip" late-night hosts like Steve Allen or the sexy Voluptua), the magazine ignored TV programs or mocked them as "lowbrow" women's culture. As Ethan Thompson puts it, *Playboy*'s "model was clear: women watched TV, men watched women."[35] Nevertheless, as Thompson also suggests, Hefner used television to extend his magazine's prominence. His nationally syndicated late-night television program *Playboy's Penthouse* (1959–61) took place in a studio set version of his Chicago bachelor pad, filled with bunnies and a racially integrated cast of hip guest stars, including, for example, Sarah Vaughan, Lenny Bruce, Ella Fitzgerald, and George Carlin.[36] More generally, even if the magazine was cool toward most other TV shows, Hefner courted TV manufacturers with trade ads that promised that the average *Playboy* reader was also a TV watcher. One ad shows a handsome Don Draper–type executive (with a woman on his arm) in a furniture store shopping for a color TV (then a luxury good). The copy reads, "Facts: Color TV ownership among *Playboy* households is three times that of the national average. And a higher percentage of *Playboy* households purchased new TV sets within the last twelve months than any other magazine surveyed."[37] In his own aptly named Playboy House (which he purchased in 1959), Hefner installed a rotating bed with a control panel (embedded in the headboard) from which to operate a TV set and other media devices. (A television camera on a tripod pointed at the bed allowed Hefner to record his own sexual exploits.) Although *Playboy* and other men's magazines depicted the hi-fi stereo cabinet—rather than the TV set—as the ultimate bachelor machine, in the 1950s, men's magazines did make many notable attempts to turn the TV set into an erotic object for readers.[38]

Playboy's first erotic foray into television came in its March 1956 issue, when Hefner introduced the three-page centerfold (before this, the centerfolds were two pages).³⁹ This centerfold presented *Playboy*'s first "TV Play-mate," Marian Stafford. These two firsts likely sparked viewer intrigue, as the newness of the TV girl and the newness of the three-page centerfold mutu-ally created new reasons for readers to buy *Playboy*. The cover art immedi-ately announces *Playboy*'s male orientation to television with a whimsical illustration featuring the *Playboy* Rabbit (the male chaser of bunnies) in a TV studio. Pictured from the back (just his head and ears), he sits in front of the TV *switcher* (a device that allows a TV director to choose between shots). The Rabbit chooses between two different images (a closeup and an extreme closeup) of a model's face, which appear in black-and-white on the switcher's small TV screens. Meanwhile, in full color, a "live" model poses in the stu-dio, so that the reader sees her—as the Rabbit does—through the window of the TV control room. Everything is organized around the voyeuristic plea-sure not just of looking at the woman, but also of controlling her image and transforming it from the mundane black-and-white headshot of a tiny TV screen into the vibrant color pinup that the *Playboy* centerfolds promise. The inside copy continues with the theme of masculine control over the techno-logical/video reproduction of a woman's image, explaining Stafford's job as a "human TV test pattern" for the then new color TV cameras used in NBC TV "spectaculars." In this sense, the white female model serves as the "standard" for color technology, making color TV—just like the *Playboy* centerfolds of this period—a specifically racialized image of white beauty.⁴⁰ More generally, according to the logic of this cover, the technologies of TV control—both its switchers and color tests—underscore man's power to view, select, and cap-ture his ideal playmate.

The TV Playmate centerfold, however, presents a more complex picture of bachelor pad TV. While still organized around voyeuristic pleasure, the centerfold paradoxically maintains some of the central features of family TV iconography (as featured in ads for TV sets and in TV snapshots), while de-familiarizing TV's suburban family connotations. The centerfold (most likely shot by female photographer Ruth Sondak) pictures Stafford standing in her baby blue slippers on a white fluffy rug (a classic pinup prop).⁴¹ Stafford poses directly in front of the TV set, holding open her sheer pinkish white robe and partially exposing her breasts and "nightie" panties (figure 4.9). A decorative statue of a Chinese warrior horse sits on top of the set, giving it a masculine touch and framing Stafford's seductive pinup pose by evoking male conquest. Imbuing this television setting with the requisite sophistica-tion of Hefner's tastes, a semiabstract landscape painting hangs on the wall behind the TV, and a low bookshelf rests just beside it.⁴² The focus of the

FIGURE 4.9
Marian Stafford, first
TV Playmate, *Playboy*
centerfold, March 1956.

shot, of course, is Stafford, who obviously is nothing like an ordinary female TV viewer, a point underscored by the fact that she is holding an issue of TV Guide upside down—in other words, not reading it. Instead, the TV Guide functions as an erotic prop that she holds in her hands just above her panties. Not only is it upside down, but Stafford also pulls it wide open and splits it in half, so that it mimics the logic of the centerfold. As she opens it, her pulling gesture also appears to tug on and open her sheer robe. Yet, despite the centerfold's attempt to present TV in this sexy bachelor pad context, it is in some ways consistent with the scenes of everyday glamour in the TV snapshots. As in the snapshots, Stafford stands in front of the TV screen, drawing attention away from it and toward her. And in this sense, the centerfold subverts the logic of the issue's cover art. While the Rabbit on the cover controls the female body on his studio switcher, in the centerfold's domestic mise-en-scène, Stafford calls the "shots," blocking the TV set and demanding that the male reader focus only on her.[43]

In November 1958, *Playboy* featured its second and last TV Playmate, aspiring actress Joan Staley, who appears (almost nude) emerging from her dressing room at CBS Television City studios where she acted in bit roles on CBS productions.[44] But even while the TV Playmate was short-lived, other men's magazines presented similar TV pinups, often copying Hefner's sensibility.[45] A 1964 issue of *Bachelor* features a "full color profile" of "Bachelorette of the Month" Suzanne Morton, who strikes a sultry pose in front of a TV set in a bachelor's tastefully appointed den.[46] (figure 4.10). In other variations, TV pinups appear in bachelor party scenarios. A 1960 issue of *Spree* ran a full-color spread of a "Hollywood Pajama Party," in which three women, in various stages of undress, tune in the set at a bachelor pad and pass out in front of it.[47] A 1965 issue of *Modern Man* presents a hipster hanging out in his handsomely appointed pad with three women (in panties, garter belts, and the like) grouped around a modern TV/hi-fi console. The caption reads, "Adjusting television, guy at gal-filled gala [appears] thunderstruck over high-voltage display."[48] (The pun follows a whole history of discourses on technology that equated male control over electrical currents with their sexual power.)[49]

While *Playboy* and its ilk presented aestheticized TV pinups set in high-end bachelor decor, other TV pinups were more basic black-and-white "nudie" shots photographed in bare-bones studios, photographers' homes, or motels. They present women in traditional sorts of pinup and burlesque or fetish poses but now positioned on top of, beside, or in front of a TV set. Models wear an assortment of high-heel pumps, boots, garter belts, night-

FIGURE 4.10
"Bachelorette of the
Month" Suzanne
Morton in *Bachelor*,
December 1964.

gowns, sheer or fishnet hose, black corsets, long black gloves, and push-up
bras to create intrigue (figures 4.11 and 4.12). Nevertheless, the photographs
(especially the ones shot in homes) show telltale signs of domesticity (as with
the candy dish tele-decoration on top of the TV in figure 4.12).

Despite their less aesthete disposition, like those in *Playboy*, these sorts of
pinups defamiliarized the normative domestic associations of the TV set by
restaging TV's nuclear family iconography through scenes of sexual play and
foreplay. Many pictured women posing in front of run-of-the mill TV sets in
what appear to be middle-class or working-class living room settings. But
the models strike poses associated with public forms of nonmarital sex and
what the antiobscenity crusades of the era considered to be indecent expo-
sures. Some of these appear to have been shot by professionals, while others

FIGURE 4.11
Pinup model
turning on TV
in motel room,
circa 1962–67.

look like the work of aspiring amateurs hoping to sell their photos to men's magazines. Many were likely distributed through mail-order catalogs.

The most famous of the pinup models, Bettie Page, appeared in several examples. Given the abundance of Page's photos (she was the most photographed pinup model of her time), it is not surprising that she would appear in TV pinups. One photo (likely produced and/or sold in the mid-1950s by the Klaws) features Page in a leopard bikini, black nylons (rolled down on her thighs), and high-heel pumps (figure 4.13). She sits on a living room chair, the TV set beside her, with her leg resting on a hassock.[50] (It serves the same beautifying function as the TV hassocks did in *Life* but is used for greater erotic effect.) The setting is homey: the cushiony club chair is upholstered for comfort; a vase of flowers sits on top of the TV; the stone wall of a fireplace is partially visible; daytime light and foliage gleam through the win-

FIGURE 4.12
TV pinup with
candy dish on
top of set, circa
1955–60.

dow next to the TV. Everything follows the décor of a midcentury TV home that could be found in a snapshot. But the decorum is strikingly "off," as Page refuses to play the role of the 1950s housewife, opting instead for the pinup queen. In another TV pinup, this one a more explicit version, Page appears in an unbuttoned shirt, black nylons (again, rolled down on her thighs), and pinup shoes but otherwise is naked, with her legs spread wide in front of the TV.

Some pinups hark back to burlesque comedy acts and the related humor of the painted pinups.[51] One photo features three women gathered around a TV set, all dressed in provocative "short shorts" (as they were called at the time). The humor arises via a trick shot, as a man (who appears to be inside the TV) reaches through the screen and grasps the thigh of a model who seems to be "turning him on" by turning on the TV set. The photograph is titled *Feel-a-*

FIGURE 4.13 Bettie Page, circa 1955.

vision' TV!' A less ambitious but more explicitly borderline comedy shot shows topless models scampering around a TV repair shop (figure 4.14).

The TV pinup even extended to exploitation cinema. *Suburbia Confidential* (Stephen C. Apostolof, dir., 1966) features the lonely sex-starved housewife Helena Fox, who seduces a TV repairman when her traveling salesman husband is on the road. Opening the door in her baby-doll see-through negligee, Helena welcomes the repairman, offering him a cocktail and a place next to her on the couch. In the tradition of the telephone pinup, she receives a phone call from her estranged husband. But the joke is on him. Rather than play the lovesick housewife, Helena takes revenge on her man through telecommunications—first lying to him on the telephone, then pouncing on his TV repairman rival. One thing leads to another—very quickly—and she has her way with the TV repairmen in full soft-core exposure (her breasts are the major visual attraction). Never actually fixing the TV, the repairman takes his leave, and upon his departure, the happy Helena kisses her TV. But Helena isn't alone for long. In the next sequence, an unsuspecting milkman knocks at her door.

Suburbia Confidential looks like a soft-core answer to Sirk's *All That Heaven Allows*. As opposed to Cary, whose Christmas TV is a tragic symbol of her unfilled sexual desire, Helena uses TV to her sexual benefit. Nevertheless, to avoid censorship, *Suburbia Confidential* is packaged in the socially redemptive framing device of a morality play. The film is an example of exploitation cinema's attempt to legitimate sex via a "pedagogical" ruse. The Helena plot is framed by a psychiatrist (actually an actor playing a psychiatrist) who analyzes the reasons for her naughty behavior. A common tactic, the pedagogical frame in such films served as legal cover for the scandalous

FIGURE 4.14 TV repair shop as setting for TV pinup, 1959.

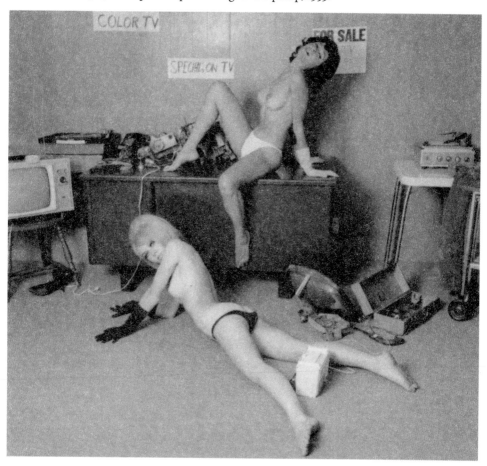

imagery.[52] While purporting to cure sex-mad housewives, this film was targeted at men and distributed on the grindhouse theater circuit located in postwar red-light districts.

Seen alongside the more buttoned-up snapshots of everyday glamour, TV pinups (and related films and ephemera) are at first glance the antithesis of the middle-class decorum and performative normality of the snapshot poses. But rather than view them as opposites, it seems more useful to think of the two sorts of pictures on a sliding scale. For one thing, as is already obvious, the TV pinups are often staged in domestic spaces with everyday things. Like the snapshots, they use the TV set as a backdrop for the woman's pose. Even more pervasively, like television's *Photographic Horizons*, the photography magazines aimed at male readers skirted the lines between domesticity and sexual intrigue. Magazines such as *Popular Photography* and *U.S. Camera* ran family-friendly articles like "Portrait of a Home," "How to Photograph Your Aquarium," and "Filming the Family Candidly," and they engaged readers in competitions like the "Better Living Beautiful Baby" contest.[53] These family-oriented subjects appeared alongside how-to columns about pinup photography and nudes so that readers would have seen them mixed. The aura of domesticity went hand in hand with the bikini-clad and nude models pictured on covers and throughout these publications.

More generally, TV pinups were often a family affair. In Gowland's *Popular Photography* column, he told readers to use wives as models for glamour shots, figure photography, and/or nudes or to scout out ordinary girls (waitresses, teachers, even dental assistants) who might work for little compensation. Addressing the pitfalls of the untrained model, Gowland gave posing advice, telling readers to engage wives and girlfriends in interesting activities to ensure that they would not look bored or stiff in front of the camera.[54] Speaking directly to the problem of the bored wife, in 1953, *Popular Photography* ran an article (by a lesser-known author) titled "How to Shoot Your Wife." Framed in "wife joke" humor, the article presents glamour shots as an occasion for "a good deal of fun" for both men and women. Photos feature housewives posing in ostrich feather stoles and black gloves, or in pinup costumes that humorously clash with their kitchen props. One woman wears a bikini top while holding a frying pan. The article concludes, "You'll both get a kick out of working this out together!"[55] Despite the marital comradery, the lesson was no doubt aimed at the male amateur's aspiration to make pictures that could mimic, or ideally be sold to, the girlie magazines.

Although all of this confirms the sexual exploitation at the heart of the genre, the women photographers and models who made pinups sometimes took matters into their hands and inflected the form with specifically female concerns. In a 1965 TV news profile, the (by then) well-known pinup photographer Bunny Yeager talked specifically about her perspective as a postwar housewife. The male interviewer begins: "You are one of the world's foremost photographers of women. . . . Do you make a good living at it?" Yeager responds, "Well, I make a nice living. But the big thing about it for me is I'm married and I have two children, and I can make my own hours and still indulge in having a career."[56] At a time when Friedan's *Feminine Mystique* derided women's containment in the home and the objectification of women's bodies in mass media, Yeager saw pinups as a means of juggling motherhood with entrepreneurial self-fulfillment. Despite her work as a pinup photographer, her perspective is oddly in line with second-wave feminism's career woman spirit. And, perhaps for this reason, in recent years, feminist critics and museum curators have reclaimed her photos as a prelude to "grrrl power."[57] In her own time, Yeager was a savvy businesswoman, and she used TV to promote her career, not only in the local news show but also on network TV, including a guest appearance on NBC's *The Tonight Show Starring Johnny Carson*.[58]

Yeager's mass-market how-to books on glamour photography discuss her female experience as a midcentury homemaker. While Hefner's *Playboy* privileged the bachelor pad as the mise-en-scène for sex, Yaeger, who lived in a suburban home in Miami Shores, often photographed models in her suburban ranch-style interior and its tropical patio surroundings. Many of her early photos, shot in collaboration with model Bettie Page, take place in her home. Her 1962 book, *Bunny Yeager's Art of Glamour Photography*, begins with a chapter titled "Using the Home as a Studio." In it, Yeager speaks in the language of women's how-to manuals, offering handy household tips. She recommends the use of common supermarket products like dishwashing detergent for erotic bubble bath photos.[59] She tells readers how to make their own costumes on a budget by sewing a bikini themselves. (Pinup models often made their own bikinis and thought of them as costumes. They did this not only for thrift but also to avoid the pitfalls of off-the-rack loose-fitting suits that drooped and sagged.) Yeager's book expands on the "sew it yourself" concept, showing readers how to make do with mundane items in the closet. As an example, one photo depicts Page looking ravishing in a leopard garment draped around her body, revealing only cleavage and legs. The caption reads, "Who would dream that this exotic costume was only a rayon housecoat?"[60] Unlike the endless techy tips of the male-authored photography magazines, Yeager interweaves tech talk with feminine knowledge.

Yeager produced several TV pinups (I have found three). Two are 1960s black-and-white photos shot in the heyday of the men's magazines. One of these features a model wearing what is likely one of Yeager's homemade costumes (a bustier attached to a sheer flowing skirt) while posing in front of a TV/hi-fi shelving credenza filled with LPs (figure 4.15). Flowers, a modern-style lamp, and a woman's purse are on top. While the stereo and LPs suggest a bachelor pad, the flowers and purse evoke a woman's space, giving the photograph an ambiguity of gender and place. The second pinup (or, rather, series of pinups) are part of Yeager's photoshoot for an issue of *Modern Man*.[61] The contact sheet shows a nude model lying in various poses on the floor of what appears to be a suburban living room (not a bachelor pad) next to a French provincial console. The ornate if elegant décor once again suggests a woman's space. In one pose, she pretends to watch TV; in others she looks toward the camera, sometimes gesturing with her hand over her mouth as if shushing the viewer of the photo who is disrupting her TV pleasures. The third photo (a color pinup, taken later in the cycle, likely the early 1970s) uses direct address more aggressively, even threateningly. Sitting on top of a TV set, the model squeezes her breasts together (thrusting them toward the camera), and licking her lips, she appears to stick out her tongue at the viewer. The photo ambiguously affords the female poser agency (the model seems to direct the gaze and even intimidate the viewer), yet at the same time, it is squarely within the pinup genre's "come on" appeal to male readers. It shares a sensibility with more sexually explicit photographs that began to appear in magazines like *Penthouse* and *Hustler* in the 1970s—photos that Yeager (in the 1990s) said were "no longer beautiful" and called "demeaning to women."[62]

Yeager's practice suggests the contradictory sexual politics entailed in pinups. Although Yeager's photographs were squarely within the pinup genre, in her own time, Yeager would have bristled at the term. Instead, Yeager used the terms *glamour* and *figure photography* to describe her images of women and related presentation of sumptuous women's spaces in domestic interiors. Yeager's meticulously staged indoor photographs are consistent with (and perhaps influenced by?) architectural photos in design magazines as well as the photos in women's home magazines that taught female readers to look at and lust after household décor. In fact, Yeager published some of her tamer glamour photographs in magazines like *Redbook* and *Women's Wear Daily*. In this respect, Yeager's photos provide a bridge between what Hefner defined as the supposedly all-male culture of the *Playboy* pinup and the glamour and fashion photos that circulated in women's venues. Given Yeager's

FIGURE 4.15 Photograph by Bunny Yeager, circa 1960–65.
© Lynn Spigel, author's collection.

status as a mother/photographer/homemaker/model, her feminine point of view on pinups is also a bridge back to snapshots.

SNAPSHOT EROTICA

While obviously aimed at separate audiences and used in different ways, pinups and snapshots are both manifestations of the same postwar photographic *dispositif*, a social-technical-cultural apparatus through which gender and sex were rendered visible. With their overtly sexual content, the TV pinups offer a more exaggerated version of the gendered logics of visual pleasure than the snapshots do. But the absurd staging of women's bodies and TV sets in the pinups calls attention to the equally contrived elements of the dress-up snapshots discussed in my previous chapter. Frankly, when looking at the snapshots and pinups as a set of photographic options for postwar women, I often feel that the housewife and the pinup girl were foils for each other's dilemmas and pleasures. Taken together, these two sorts of photos reveal how fashion and striptease operate as the flipsides of a historical record through which to trace the intimate history of sex, gender, and TV.

In pinups, the TV screen harks back to the bedroom dressing screens in bourgeois homes—a place for dressing but also, in nineteenth-century studio photography and early twentieth-century films, a vehicle for risqué scenes, where women took off slips, stockings, shoes, and the like.[63] In other words, when used in early photos and films, the dressing screen was often an "undressing screen." Similarly, in snapshots the TV screen could swing both ways—it could be used as a backdrop for dress-up poses, but it could also easily become an "undressing screen," where women engaged in various forms of striptease and bodily display.

In case my proposal seems the stuff of overinterpretation, there is some evidence for the connection between pinups and family snapshots. Some TV snapshots cross the line over into the pinup and cheesecake or borderline modes, and some are explicitly pornographic. As opposed to prom gowns, cocktail sheaths, and luncheon suits, the women in these photos appear in the pinup attire of short shorts, bathing suits, sheer nighties, ruffled panties, and push-up bras, and sometimes they are partially or entirely nude. While the professional pinup models are shot with high-end cameras and film stock, the homemade versions bear the marks of the low-end snapshot camera with its limited technical affordances. It is, of course, difficult to know with certainty who operated the camera, but since the women in these snapshots are not pinup models, and since they pose in ordinary homes, my sense is that, in most cases, these are pictures that husbands took of wives, much as the photo magazines recommended. Finally, while the professional TV pinup models were exclusively young and white, the homemade pinups have wider demographics, and they were made in different international contexts (I have seen ones from the USSR, England, Chile, Serbia, and France).

These snapshots are part of the history of homemade pinups. Exploring World War II examples, Buszek argues that the women who made homemade pinups were not just imitating stars like Grable or fulfilling their wartime obligation by sending pictures of themselves to boyfriends or husbands at war. While this may have been part of the practice, Buszek instead emphasizes the "apparent and subversive pleasure that women seemed to take in their own pin-up imagery."[64] She explains, "Examples of homemade cheesecake from the World War II era show women displaying a sense of humor, fun, and creativity." The women pose "with sass" and seem amused at their "own audacity."[65] Moreover, Buszek argues, "not all homemade pin-ups . . . were destined for a heterosexual male recipient." Many "appear to have been created for the delectation and amusement of exclusively female audiences."[66] (For example, Buszek cites pinups taken at an all-girl picnic.) In this sense, homemade pinups are consistent with the TV dress-up snapshots I explore in chapter 3. Although they may at times be complicit with self-objectification performed for men, they are much more than that. Their erotic playfulness demands attention.

As they circulate today on the secondhand market, homemade pinups are rare commodities that go for high prices. As a select subgenre of the homemade pinup, the TV versions are especially pricey and hard to find. (I have lost many bidding wars on eBay!) While I have seen at least forty online and off, I have collected roughly fifteen. I have decided not to publish some of the more explicit ones, as the posers in these snapshots were likely not interested in having strangers see them. (The compromise, I admit, is imperfect insofar as the women in the more modest poses I illustrate here could not have imagined that they would wind up in a book.)

Pinup poses range from sedate cheesecake to full-frontal nudes. On the sedate end of the spectrum, women are fully clothed, but the camera focuses on body parts (especially legs or cleavage). Like *Life*'s "floor viewers," the women in these snapshots often lie on carpets or rugs (figure 4.16). Some are action shots taken in the empty space around the TV, as in a photo of two woman pulling up skirts and showcasing their legs in a pose reminiscent of wartime pinups (figure 4.17).

Other snapshots depict women in bathing suits or bras. Some women strike the "sassy" poses that Buszek describes in World War II homemade pinups. One snapshot shows a young woman in a bathing suit playfully adopting a beauty pageant pose, as she stands close to the TV (figure 4.18). But despite her confident pose, there is something off in the picture (at least when compared to the professional pinup). Her busy floral drapes (a no-no among glamour photographers like Yeager and Gowland) suggest the homemade nature of the shot, even as she dons the posture of the pinup girl and smiles wide for the camera. Other snapshots present women in less confident stances, yet still enacting the pinup pose. A woman in a black bra and shorts

strikes a three-quarter pose, perhaps attempting to approximate a model's pose in figure photography (figure 4.19). Standing in front of busy drapes, she is almost lost in the floral fabric that dominates the picture. In this case, a cord from a portable radio on top of the TV runs across the wall toward the woman, revealing the mess of media that, for example, a *Playboy* pinup would not show. On the left, a telephone sits on a television stand—but this time the telephone-TV combination lacks the titillating Peeping Tom appeal of the TV-telephone pinups. Instead, a doily under the telephone suggests women's crafts. Another snapshot presents a less cluttered mise-en-scène. A woman in a one-piece suit stands next to her TV set, her hand resting on it (figure 4.20). The wall behind her is blank (it appears as if the photographer put a sheet up on it to simulate a studio portrait). Nevertheless, an oddball object on top the TV set (is it a large straw hat or a bowl?) distracts attention away from the woman and is, at any rate, incongruous with the sorts of things typically in professional pinups. It is a detail of everyday life, not a prop.

The women in these pinup poses don't exhibit the sort of glamour labor required of the professional model. Their hair is not teased, some wear glasses, and their bathing suits look like they came off the rack, perhaps several years back. In other words, they are bathing suits—not the carefully

FIGURE 4.16 (*opposite*)
Circa 1962–65.

FIGURE 4.17 (*left*)
Circa 1955–57.

customized costume bikinis that photographers and models like Yeager and Page sewed for their poses. And rather than the classic peekaboo slippers or high-heel pumps, they wear flats or are barefoot, or (even worse) the photographer cuts their feet out of the shot. The woman in figure 4.19 is almost frozen, wears flats, and does not smile. The woman in figure 4.20 smiles and looks a bit more relaxed, but her standing pose with one arm almost dead at her side lacks the "natural" allure required of the professional figure model. Yet, even if the photos don't achieve the picture-ready pinup ideal, they display a sort of informal knowledge about a pinup pose and how to enact it.

These bathing suit snapshots resonate with the evolution of the Kodak Girl and her Polaroid sister. As I noted early on, by the 1960s the Kodak Girl looked increasingly like a pinup model, and while her costumes were never as revealing as the ones worn by models in girlie magazines, she nevertheless wore bathing suits (both one-piece suits and bikinis). Store displays pictured her in life-size cardboard cutouts, and Kodak packaging featured an 8-by-10 pinup insert (the first thing a consumer would see when opening the box). Polaroid was even more explicit in its appeal to erotic modes of looking. As opposed to Kodak's *Ozzie and Harriet* commercials, Polaroid often advertised on the more risqué late-night talk shows, with hosts like Jerry Lewis, Garry Moore, Jack Paar, and Steve Allen. In line with Polaroid's prom-

FIGURE 4.18
Circa 1955–60.

AUG 1962

FIGURE 4.19
1962.

FIGURE 4.20
Circa 1953–58.

ise that its cameras would make men the "life of the party," some late-night hosts invited pinup models on stage to pose for snapshots that developed in an instant on the TV screen. By 1965, in an aggressive attempt to corner the youth market and to cash in on the ascendant culture of sexual liberation, Polaroid introduced its affordable ($19.95) Swinger model. Commercials featured young people at parties or on the beach dressed in bikinis.[67] But while they wore the classic pinup costume, the girls in these ads did not adopt the pinup pose. Instead, the commercials and print ads showed them in action poses that implied an ambiguous mix of youth culture sexual liberation and wholesome fun.

During the 1950s and 1960s, many outdoor and vacation snapshots featured women in bathing suits (sometimes bikinis) near pools or beaches. But bathing suits functioned differently in the family snapshots taken in domestic interiors. Once the bathing suit pose is taken indoors and enacted with a TV set, the snapshots no longer resonate as images of active leisure or wholesome merriment. When located inside the home, and shot in a glamour pose, the women modeling bathing suits look much more like the provocative TV pinup girls.

In this regard, a set of photos taken by the same woman is especially interesting for what it suggests about the status of television in the bathing suit pose. One snapshot shows the woman posing proudly in a bathing suit next to her TV (figure 4.21). While striking a similar pose to the one in figure 4.20, this woman's body is more relaxed, with her elbow bent at her waist, legs together, and one knee slightly in front of the other (as if attempting to achieve the grace required of standing pose in figure photography). Although her bathing suit is still unlike the pinup girl's costume, and while she stands barefoot, the woman does dress up for the part, wearing pearls around her

FIGURES 4.21 (*below*) & 4.22 (*opposite*) Different style poses in front of TV and fridge. Both shot in 1952.

neck and matching earrings. This snapshot is one among several of the same woman, who poses with various objects in her house (for example, a refrigerator). But in those cases, she is not in the bathing suit, nor is she striking a figure pose (figure 4.22). In that sense, there seems to be something about posing with the television set that encourages the homemade pinup. Perhaps the posers and camera operators had seen similar photos in men's magazines or were familiar with the TV girls at fairs and beauty pageants. Whatever the reasons, the TV set became a setting for pinup performances at home.

Some women assume postures that closely resemble the burlesque or even borderline modes of pinup expression and embodiment. They bend, rear first, with their backsides to the TV set, similar to the classic Bettie Page pose.

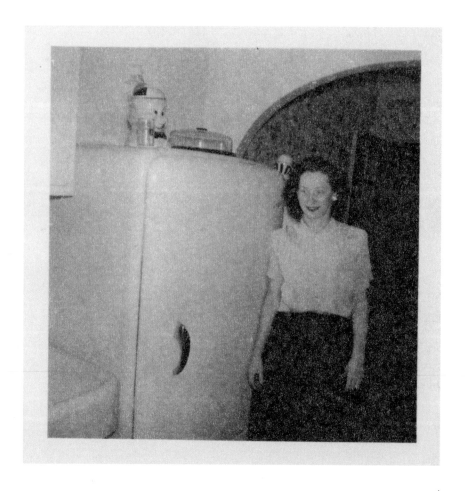

One woman poses rear first in frilly underwear, and she smiles at the camera with an over-the-shoulder flirtatious grin. Another woman poses in the same rear-first mode, but with no underwear. Several snapshots show women in sheer nighties and lingerie (like the *Playboy* example). A color photo (likely taken some time in the early 1960s) presents a glamorous woman standing in front of her modern blonde wood TV set in a white bra, lace bikini panties, and red lace see-through lingerie, revealing her undergarments (figure 4.23). Her white high-heeled pumps, teased upsweep hairdo, makeup, and bangle

FIGURE 4.23 Circa 1960–65.

bracelets, as well as her demure standing pose, all indicate her familiarity with the pinup genre. But—as is so often the case—the mise-en-scène says something else. The room is cluttered with the signs of domesticity—a huge flower arrangement on top of the TV; family photos behind it; wires and boxes on the floor; and clothes strewn across the couch. Other women pose with their negligees left open so that they appear bare chested in front of the TV, or else they pose entirely nude, sometimes with backs to the cameras. In the nudes, the poser is often ambiguously a young wife or a hired model, but the mise-en-scène of home (for example, flowers and children's photos on the TV set), or a flash of camera in the screen, suggest the homemade nature of the photo (figure 4.24).

FIGURE 4.24
Circa 1965–70.

One of the most explicit snapshots (dated January 1970) pictures a young woman (entirely naked) sitting on top of a large walnut stereo-TV console, her legs splayed in a full-frontal shot, much like Bettie Page's hardcore TV pinup. Her head slightly tilted, she smiles at the camera operator but not with the knowing, joyful, and flirtatious look that Page performed. Instead, some homemade pinups register the failed attempt or reluctance to play the role required by the professional pinup. Like the awkward bathing suit posers, some women look stiff and uncomfortable; they appear more as alienated objects of a camera gaze than as proud performers. It is not just that ordinary women are older than pinup girls or lack the ideal dimensions of the figure type. Instead, there is a low punctum to these shots. The details are somehow just off. A sour look, a baggy swimsuit, a rigid arm, sagging stockings, a house cat peeking around the corner, a baby picture on the TV set, or a view of a messy bedroom break the frame of the pinup's allure. These photos (especially when women don't smile and seem rigid) evoke the affective realm of everydayness where things are never just so. They often exude sexism more than sexiness. At least for me, the photos are often poignant reminders of the ways in which women often participated as only partially willing subjects in their own sexual objectification.

That said, at other times, the women who posed for homemade pinups seem more like the 1950s housewives in Meyerowitz's research who read and liked *Playboy*. They also recall women in Buszek's wartime snapshots, who enjoyed making pinups and assumed sexual agency through their pose. In TV snapshots, some women look—and perhaps were—happy to play the role of the pinup girl. Rather than objectification (or perhaps in addition to it), there is a ludic aspect to some of these photos that suggests a break with routine. Like the picture-ready woman in her red lace lingerie, and the more relaxed women in the bathing beauty pinups, some of the posers appear to enjoy the chance to be a pinup girl at home. In these snapshots, the TV set may well have served as a backdrop for sexual flirtations between posers and camera operators. So, too, it's possible, given women's pleasure in looking at men's magazines, that at least for some women, the pinups appealed to lesbian desire and same-sex fantasies. In any case, whatever transpired at the time of the snapshot's creation and reception, TV was pictured as an erotic zone in the home.

These pinup poses should be viewed in the context of the period's changing sexual mores and discourses on sex. John D'Emilio and Estelle Freedman argue that by midcentury, America had become a "sexualized society" where *both men and women* valued sexuality as a road to personal happiness.[68] The pinups resonate with this sexualized society and the broad transitions in attitudes toward female sexuality triggered largely by the 1953 Kinsey Report on female sexuality and Masters and Johnson's subsequent research on female orgasm and sexual pleasure. Both studies were widely discussed in the mass media.[69] At the same time, marital sex manuals advised women to develop their sexual know-how and take more responsibility for arousing their man, warning against the pitfalls of the frigid woman whose husband might look elsewhere to fulfill his desire or just lose it entirely. Increasingly, however female sexual pleasure was no longer necessarily tied to marriage.[70] The dissemination of the birth control pill, which first hit the market in 1960, made it easier for women to view sex apart from motherhood and marriage. Helen Gurley Brown's 1962 *Sex and the Single Girl* drew (loosely) on 1950s sexology to make sex before marriage a goal for career-minded young women rather than a prohibition.

In the context of the burgeoning discourse on female sexual pleasure and the emphasis placed on women's sexual know-how, some women might have felt more comfortable striking sexy or even nude poses at home. As the "How to Shoot Your Wife" article in *Popular Photography* suggests, camera experts tried to show husbands how to turn posing for pinups into marital fun. And even if this was ultimately meant for the benefit of the male shutterbug, some women may have enjoyed the pinup pose. Given the fact that female photographers like Yaeger and Sondak made photos for men's magazines, the pursuit of the pinup was not just a male affair. And, as Buszek argues, even before World War II, ordinary young girls wrote to *Esquire* asking Vargas "for advice on how they could get into a career as pinup illustrators."[71]

More broadly, the midcentury risqué adult market was in many ways a mainstream heterosocial affair. Burlesque and comedy LPs offered sexy soundtracks for parties and intimate marital pleasures. In 1963, Roulette Records' "How to Strip for Your Husband" tied striptease directly to TV. The cover illustration shows a woman stripping for her husband, who lies in bed in his pajamas and gazes at his wife as she removes her long black glove. The "instructional insert," written by "America's most famous strip-teaser" Ann Corio, told women, "You listen to me, and I guarantee, the next time your husband wants to go to bed before eleven, it won't be because he's already seen the movie on the late show!"[72] A woman could, according to this logic, easily arouse her husband and distract him from his bedroom TV. The record hit the market the same year that Betty Friedan's *Feminine Mystique* challenged the patriarchal culture that led to women's degradation. But even while second-wave feminists like Friedan and Gloria Steinem condemned women's objectification in mass media, they nevertheless presumed sexual pleasure to be a feminist right. As I observed in the previous chapter, Friedan's concerns with television were not just with the way TV objectified women but also with its presentation of women as "empty," "Twilight Zone" voids, "missing a sexual aliveness."[73] The homemade pinups depict television in a different light—as a means of erotic play for women. Rather than a just a bad object voiding out women's sexual pleasure, the snapshots suggest that television offered women a much wider set of possibilities.

While the scarcity of homemade TV pinups makes it difficult to draw conclusions, the fact that they are hard to come by raises important questions about sexuality and the photo archive. Their rarity likely has to do with the more general self-censorship entailed in snapshot photography, particularly those cameras (like Kodaks) that required people to send their film to developers, who might look at, or even keep or sell, other people's photos.[74] Even if more people did take sexy pictures, they might not have saved them in family albums, which were subject to the modesty (and internal censors) of their owners.

Censorship and the McCarthy-era homophobic lavender scare may also account for why I have found just a few photos of men posing with TV sets. Still, at midcentury, there was an emerging consumer culture around *physique* photos and magazines made by and aimed at the gay market, a market that, as Thomas Waugh suggests, helped to create and solidify gay men's sense of community and identity.[75] Some of these photos include TV sets. I found one on eBay labeled by a dealer as "gay exotica." This physique portrait appears to have been shot by a skilled amateur and presents a naked man with an erection posing next to a portable TV in what appears to be a bedroom or motel. Its explicit nature suggests that it likely circulated on the underground market at the time. Another eBay seller posts a more soft-core snapshot she labels "Nude Sailors Watch TV in a Motel Room Gay Interest." But this is likely misleading. While eBay sellers of "gay interest" photos typically know little about the sexual orientation or lives of posers, they often spin stories about them that "queer" the archive (sometimes in productive ways, sometimes in ways that obscure historical contexts or even engage homophobic stereotypes and tropes).[76] In this case, there is no reason to believe that the posers are sailors or in a motel; instead, the space looks to me to be a basement, an "underground" place apart from the family spaces of the house. The snapshot is a physique portrait of male models posing nude (but just torso up) looking in the direction of a TV, which appears as just a sliver on the right side of the frame. While the posers seem to watch TV, the photo (with its barely visible TV set) asks us to "watch" the men, thereby rendering TV spectatorship not as a family activity but as a home-mode homoerotic gaze.

Along these lines, another photo even more pointedly suggests the ways in which a midcentury TV home could become a space for gay practices of looking and queer orientations. Created by Grenville Michael Scott (a postwar amateur photographer who specialized in male models), the photo is composed in the tradition of the painterly nude but takes on more (intentionally?) humorous appeals.[77] Shot in Grenville's California home, the photograph features a man lying seductively with a 1963 issue of *TV Guide*, which forms a "fig leaf" over his penis (figure 4.25). Like *Playboy*'s TV Playmate Marian Stafford, who holds a *TV Guide* in her centerfold portrait, this male model simultaneously uses the magazine to hide and to call attention to his genitals. In this case, however, the issue of *TV Guide* has special significance for gay men: an illustration of gay icon Judy Garland is on the cover.

FIGURE 4.25 Male nude with a *TV Guide* "fig leaf." Photograph by Grenville Michael Scott, circa 1963. Printed with permission from David Chapman.

The final two photographs are the subject of David Chapman and Thomas Waugh's book *Comin' at Ya! The Homoerotic 3-D Photographs of Denny Denfield.*[78] In the 1950s and 1960s Denfield specialized in the rare art of 3D photography with his *stereo-realist* camera, using the technique to photograph muscular young male models on California beaches and at parties inside his mother's home (although his mother was not aware). Denfield's photos "redecorate" his mother's middle-class interiors with male nudes doing "queer" things with her everyday things. One of the *stereo-view* photos presents a male model in a standing pose next to a TV set. The second pinup aligns itself with the TV trick shots, here enacted by a male model holding up the frame of a TV screen in front of his head while posing in a full-frontal nude against living room drapes. Denfield's photos offer a markedly queer orientation, not only to TV but also to the glossy TV pinups that appeared in the girlie magazines. As Waugh's introductory essay suggests, these stereo-realist and (at the time) highly illicit photographs depict "outlaw artistry" and lives lived at the margins.[79]

In a sense, all the pinups exist at the margins of the family album. When looked at together, the professional and homemade TV pinups open an area of inquiry that has at best been muted in TV studies. While numerous books and articles consider gender and sexuality on television programs and in relation to theories of TV spectatorship, sex in TV homes is relatively uncharted territory—even though so many people watch TV in bed. While media ethnographers have considered television with respect to family viewing habits, daily routines, and gender dynamics, sex remains a neglected (if not entirely absent) topic. Broadcast television's legacy of sexual taboos and family-friendly rhetoric may in part account for the general lack of scholarship, at least in the US context.

Nevertheless, the history of commercial broadcast TV is in many ways an exception to the rule. When visual media are new, pornography usually proliferates on them. The early appearance of porn on the internet is a prime example. This was also true of nineteenth-century visual toys and of early cinema. Speaking of the latter, Linda Williams argues that the history of cinema ushered in a new discursive proliferation of sexuality, what she calls a "frenzy of the visible," which she traces from Eadweard Muybridge's nineteenth-century photographic motion studies through to hardcore pornographic films.[80] The analog to this in television goes back to Robida's drawings of men ogling at women with the imaginary telephonoscope. But unlike cinema, which quickly developed pornographic genres (for example, in the form of silent stag films), early US broadcast TV did not move in this direction. Unlike the publics for film or digital media, television's first audiences could not produce or screen the medium outside the government-regulated broadcast stations on which TV programs aired. Videotape, and especially the camcorder, offered new ways for media publics to engage with sex, particularly as the camcorder's innovation intersected with the simultaneous rise of cable TV in the 1970s and 1980s. It was at this moment that pornography took hold in TV culture (videotape, VCRs, and cable were new outlets for soft and even hardcore porn, for example, in hotel rooms or on some of the first cable-access stations).[81] But at midcentury, the broadcast industry designed TV with family viewing practices in mind, and programs were often heavily censored by network continuity departments. *Fringe-time* late-night fare like *Playboy's Penthouse* and the short-lived *Voluptua* are exceptions. But even these were tame compared with the borderline TV pinups that circulated in men's magazines and some of the more explicit homemade pinups. As a 1966 promotional ad for *Bachelor* magazine put it, "Television is fun, but you'll find elements in *Bachelor* you'll never find on TV."[82]

Rather than *on* TV, in the early decades of commercial television, sex took place *around* it. As a companion technology to the TV set, the snapshot camera allowed midcentury publics to engage in the "frenzy of the visible," even if early broadcast television did not. TV pinups (both professional and homemade) presented the television set as something quite different from the electronic family hearth. With the aid of a snapshot camera, even a novice photographer could turn TV into an erotic encounter. At least in the case of these midcentury photos, the television set was not just an "all in the family" affair. TV could also be sexy.

5

TV MEMORIES

SNAPSHOTS IN DIGITAL TIMES

By the second decade of the twenty-first century, analog snapshots and analog television were officially things of the past. In 2009, US broadcasters transitioned to digital TV, and three years later, in 2012, Kodak announced plans for bankruptcy. By then, these companion technologies of midcentury family life were already piling up in garbage heaps and landfills. Rising from the ruins, a luckier set of objects found new homes in vintage stores and online. Television sets and snapshots of them are now part of a widespread analog nostalgia for nonnetworked media things—things that came inside walnut cabinets, record sleeves, film cans—timeworn objects with noisy scratches, missing inserts, faded colors, flashed flashbulbs, and bent antennas searching for signals no longer in the air.

It seems appropriate to end this book where it started—in the digital graveyard of analog things where I first encountered most of my archive. As leftovers from an ephemeral past, TV snapshots have found new purpose in contemporary digital times. Online sellers (especially on eBay) and photo-share sites like Flickr and Pinterest have amassed a new archive for media history that is seductive in its quantity and ease of access but that also poses its own historical enigmas—most obviously, as I said at the outset, the problem of context. As found objects, the snapshots tell us little about their origins or the paths they traveled. Yet, the new digital archives at our disposal are an opportunity to think about how and why invisible histories of everyday life are made visible now, at a time when TV is no longer a box in the living room or even primarily a family medium. Ironically, the snapshots and the TV sets they picture have become visible today primarily because of the digital media that displaced them.

In their viral travels online, TV snapshots return today as what Charles Acland calls "residual media," media that find new life in contemporary times.[1] Applying Raymond Williams's concept of "dominant, residual, and emergent" cultures, Acland recognizes how old media objects and practices find new uses, even as they are no longer dominant cultural forms or even material things.[2] One of Acland's chief interests is to trouble the entire concept of *new media*, which was a buzz term in 2007 when his anthology appeared. Rather than theorize newness, Acland offered a way to understand the layering of old and new, drawing on Jay David Bolter and Richard Grusin's concept of "remediation."[3] In addition, Acland draws on Walter Benjamin's concept of the "ruin" to consider how modernity is experienced as a confrontation of past, present, and dreams of the future.[4] Obsolescence, waste, recycling, and trash are part of contemporary media formations, but more than that, the concept of residual media is about the whole sensorium of mediated experience that collapses moments in time. The term pertains to all things trashed, recycled, re-collected, remediated, and yet reinvigorated and reused for new purposes, turned into what Acland calls "living dead" media. Residual media span the gamut of old radios rewired and turned into digital sound machines to the vintage markets for vinyl records or greeting cards—or in my case, old snapshots of TV sets.

In this chapter, I consider the digital media ecologies in which TV snapshots now circulate. I focus on photo-share sites, where people upload, store, display, discuss, and creatively reappropriate TV snapshots. The proliferating scholarship on digital photography and photo-share sites offers ways to think about the sites as forms of commerce, social networking, cultural (user-generated) production, memory making, and archiving.[5] On share sites, the archival impulse is less about acquiring the "real" thing (as on eBay) than it is a mode of sharing as possession, even self-possession. People share photos but also save them on their personal photo streams, turning them into their own archives, sometimes establishing reputations as online curators. In a related practice, photographers post what I call TV snapshot *remakes*, new digital TV photos that hark back to the midcentury TV snapshots through strategies of creative reappropriation. Through their interface design, user protocols, and archival logics, photo-share sites facilitate ways of seeing, remembering, and saving the snapshots for present-day uses and concerns.

In *The Culture of Connectivity*, José van Dijck argues, "Digital personal photography gives rise to new social practices in which pictures are considered visual resources in the microcultures of everyday life. In these microcultures, memory does not so much disappear from the spectrum of social use as it takes on a different meaning."[6] Like most theorists of photo sharing, van Dijck focuses on the new forms of online memory making among people who upload contemporary selfies, pictures of food, vacations, pets, and so forth. But her argument regarding memory and "microcultures" points to the small-scale cultural formations and practices that form around photos in their everyday viral circulation. In online "microcultures," TV snapshots are reappropriated and digitally remediated, consigned to new archives, contexts, functions, and value. This is an everyday practice where history and memory collide.

What happens when snapshots move from the private albums of their original picture takers to digital networks that circulate across the globe? How do snapshots accrue value as objects of memory or counter-memory online? How do people participate in their recirculation, curation, and creative *remaking*? By what archival logics are they saved? And what is not in these archives—in other words, what histories do these share sites and their digital archives forget? This chapter addresses these questions, and I end with some general observations on the archive, memory, and TV history.

PHOTO SHARING THE TV PAST:
MEMORY WORK AND NOSTALGIA

People engage in photo sharing for numerous reasons that typically have little to do with the preservation of photographs or archiving in the traditional sense. Photo sharing is both a mode of social communication and a big data business governed by corporate logics of viral marketing and the visual content industry. (Getty Images, for example, manages rights to photos on Flickr, which angers many photographers who post original artwork on the site.) While some people upload their own TV snapshots to photo-share sites, in other cases they poach them from other regions of the web, including eBay. In this sense, the archive dynamics of selling and sharing are tangled together in everyday online memory practices.

Flickr and Pinterest (the sites I found most useful in my research) have different brand identities, user bases, and technological affordances. Launched in 2004, Flickr began as a desktop site, originally formed as a commons through which photographers could share and sell their work. The site went through numerous corporate takeovers, starting with its acquisition by Yahoo in 2005; Verizon's takeover in 2017 (via Verizon's umbrella company Oath); and most recently in 2018, its acquisition by SmugMug. As mobile social media apps (especially Instagram) came to dominate the market, Flickr's fortunes faded, and it changed its identity numerous times, recently adding a mobile app.[7] Flickr allows people to upload, title, tag, and comment on photos and sort them into themed groups that they can "administer" or curate and that are shared by other people online. Even while it remains a niche space for photographers, as with other user-generated platforms, Flickr includes a vast repertoire of visual materials (for example, digital scans or photos of vintage ads, posters, and paintings, as well as short video clips) that are archived on the site. Pinterest was launched in 2010 as a social media platform and amassed a robust following (as of 2019, it had an estimated 300 million monthly users). It especially appeals to women (who in 2019 made up 70 percent of its user base). It now brands itself as a "visual discovery engine for finding ideas like recipes, home and style inspiration, and more."[8] It also promotes itself as "a tool for collecting and organizing things you love" that allows people to "pin" visual materials (often pulled from the web) onto "pin boards" and described in captions written by the "pinners." By establishing social networks around the pins, the site has become a platform for influencers and entrepreneurs who use visual materials as attention-seeking devices. On Pinterest, people sometimes pin TV snapshots to attract people to a product or service. For instance, I have found TV snapshots pinned by women who design and sell midcentury faux-vintage jewelry and fashions. In this regard, the people who post TV snapshots do not necessarily or even primarily do so as photography collectors, nor are they always interested in TV.

On Flickr and Pinterest, TV snapshots appear in searchable databases with titles that range from "Vintage TV" to "Midcentury Kitsch" to "Prom Dresses." They are also archived in art historical ways, for example, in collections titled "Surrealism" or "Pop Art." Photo-share sites break down traditional distinctions between home-mode and art historical concepts of photography. On the one hand, as Martin Hand argues, "Digitization allows for a reinvigoration or remediation of what is essentially a form of album-making, which can co-exist with other forms of memory-making."[9] On the other hand, the sites also function as gallery-like exhibition spaces. Quite literally combining the two, Flickr encourages users to organize their own photos in "albums" and to move other people's photos on the site into their own personally curated "galleries," so that a TV snapshot can appear in both at once. As the album and the gallery merge, memory is not just personal; it becomes part of an archive of feelings, where people remake the past and affectively engage it.

On Flickr, people tell family stories about their TV snapshots, and they also post found photos that generate stories about other people's midcentury TV homes. One snapshot shows a little girl posing in her plaid dress. Standing between a Christmas tree and console TV, she holds a doll close to her chest: "Christmas—Aunty Carol with doll by tree and TV."[10] Another post features a girl and her little brother all dressed up and posing with their console TV: "My Brother Gregg and I—Easter 1950s—Houston Texas. Aren't we just too cool? I love my brother's bow tie and especially his 'debonair' pose! Our first TV in the background, complete with rabbit ears and TV lamp."[11] Another woman uploads a family snapshot of herself as a little girl near a large TV console. In response, someone comments, "Back in 1948 or '49 we had the first television on our block. Dad would open the windows and door on the front of our house so the neighbors could look in. The living room was always full." The person who posted the snapshot responds, "Having a TV was a big thing back then. I remember that test pattern and the hum that went with it. How different it was from today." In a separate post, a person uploads a 1957 found photo of a baby sitting in a highchair in front of his TV. All fifteen comments that follow share memories of TV sets. For example, "Oh, man, what a blast from the past. We had a TV pretty much like that"; "Folks were so proud of their television sets in those days. I can think of many family pictures where people are posing by the TV!"; "Does anyone remember that when one tube went out, Dad had to take all the tubes out to test them?"; "Ha ha, I remember the controls on back of the TV!"[12] Such dialogues recall practices I've analyzed throughout this book: the TV parties, the messy wires and tubes, the tele-decorations, and people's poses in front of the set. History and memory are intertwined.

TV memories are sometimes recounted in intergenerational dialogues. A snapshot on Flickr titled "Dad by the TV at 60 Turner Place" shows a man in a suit and tie posing in front of his walnut TV cabinet, which has a stylish turquoise glass decanter on top. The commentary (which I will present partially here) tracks a conversation between mother and child:

MOM: This is Daddy at a TV. This was the "in" thing—a Magnavox cabinet.

ME: It's funny that we have a bunch of photos with TVs in cabinets, but none of them are open.

MOM: Well, that was [the] thing in those days. It was very sophisticated in those days to have the TVs hidden. Remember, you're talking about those ugly tubes. . . .

ME: What happened to it?

MOM: It came to Bellmore. We had it in Bellmore for years, and I guess it finally broke.

ME: I don't remember the TV.

MOM: Well, by the time you came along, it was nearly ten years old. We probably got a new one by then.[13]

The TV snapshot marks a family itinerary as they move from home to home. It serves as a form of family heritage and evokes what Marianne Hirsch calls a "postmemory," a secondhand memory acquired from an older generation (a past the child in this conversation never directly experienced).[14] Like my grandmother's practice of stacking one TV on top of another, in online chats people recall not just a TV set, but also missing loved ones or prior selves, the people who once posed in the ritual space of the TV setting. The process of digital *remediation* turns into acts of *reanimation*. As people post and chat about snapshots, they vivify the image with stories that literally *move* them.

Barthes called photographs "clocks for seeing." Photographs make the passing of time visible. But beyond a clever metaphor, Barthes intended this in a literal sense, recalling that historically "photographic implements were related to techniques of cabinetmaking and the machinery of precision." The sound of the camera, Barthes argues, is the "noise of time" and "perhaps in me someone very old still hears in the photographic mechanism the living sound of the wood."[15] The old TV sets, with their wood-grained cabinets, are part of this history of photographic implements; the old linear broadcast schedule (like a train schedule) was itself a "machinery of precision" encased in a decorative box. Even when dormant, the noise of time registers in the tuning dials and, more figuratively, in people's memories of the broadcasts that emanated from TV (the hum of the test pattern or favorite programs). As they circulate online today, the snapshots recall these analog, material ways of clocking time, even as they are now stored in the dematerialized clouds and on-demand temporalities of digital platforms.

Scholars associated with the fields of media archaeology and digital memory studies have explored how digital platforms and archives have changed the temporalities of the past and what scholars variously call collective memory, social memory, and cultural memory.[16] Much of this work considers the present tenseness of digital memory and archives. Putting the issue most succinctly, Wolfgang Ernst writes, "Digital communication is a system that is permanently archiving presence."[17] Speaking specifically about Flickr, Susan Murray argues that even if photo sharing is engaged with memory, it no longer foregrounds the photograph's relation to death and mourning in the way that Benjamin, Bazin, Sontag, and Barthes theorized. Instead, she claims, on share sites, "photography becomes a more alive, immediate, and often transitory practice/form, as the digital camera has become an essential tool in the navigation and documentation of daily life."[18] Murray's main concern is with contemporary digital photos on the site. But she also considers how Flickr operates as a transitory archive: "The photo-stream moves old pictures out of the way to make room for the new ones, which creates a sense of temporariness for the photos."[19] From that point of view, it makes little difference if you upload a selfie taken with an iPhone or a midcentury snapshot torn from a family album.

Although I agree that photo sharing foregrounds transience, presence, and immediacy, in my view, the photograph's relation to death and mourning is not easily erased. As material objects, TV snapshots bear traces of their use and quotidian storage in basements, attics, and dresser drawers. They are faded, moldy, torn. These fades and rips often appear in digitized scans and speak to the snapshots' (and posers') aging through time. In this sense, midcentury family photos on share sites exist ambivalently in multiple temporalities between transience and the "that-has-been." They are part of the transience and immediacy of digital archives, but as images they still conjure up what Bazin called the "charm of the family album": the "disturbing presence of lives halted at a set moment in their duration, freed from their destiny."[20] Part of that "halting" has to do with the passing of analog photography itself. TV snapshots are stuck in the time of their cameras and the types of image making that snapshot cameras afforded. In other words, even while (or perhaps because) they appear on digital screens, TV snapshots look old. The comments that accompany them on photo-share sites express a sense of loss and even at times melancholia for the passing of analog devices and culture. As I poached from online archives for this book, it became increasingly obvious that the comments posted on share sites alongside the snapshots are not just "extras" or surplus value; rather, the commentary inscribes the snapshots with voices and affects that turn them into memory texts.

That said, online memories are performative as the people who post them or comment on them typically do so to attract followers and "likes." Online, the once intimate discourse networks of analog snapshot photography become part of the networked world. Rather than collective memory, which suggests a group affiliation (like national heritage), share sites generate what Andrew Hoskins calls the "memory of the multitude," which circulates on social media ubiquitously. He argues that the "connective turn" is defined by two main cultural shifts. The first is the rise of a participatory networked culture in which people "constantly snap, post, record, edit, link, forward and chat in a digital ecology of media. The second—a direct consequence of the first—is that the memory of the multitude is all over the place, scattered yet simultaneous and searching: connected, networked, archived." Social media create and store "unpredictable and often invisible and unimaginable trails and connectivities."[21]

One of my favorite photos—a picture of a boy and his TV set—has generated 52,488 views and fifty-three comments. The person who posted the picture describes it as an image of himself at home in Eugene, Oregon, "probably in 1952 or 1953," when his family first purchased the TV set (figure 5.1). He discusses the bad reception in his town and the fuzzy pictures on-screen. Other people respond with comments about the photo and their own memories of TV. A few people ask for permission to share the picture, including someone from Norway who writes, "I found this since it is used in a blog post in the blog of the Norwegian Broadcast Corporation (NRK)." Unaware of his international fame, John Atherton (the man who uploaded the photo) thanks him for the information. Atherton also told me how surprised he was that his photo generated so much attention.[22] As in this case, digital snapshots travel across space and time in ways that can't be predicted by their owners.

The global travels of this TV snapshot raise questions about the image itself—what made so many people pick out this photo among the multitudes? Was it just a function of the algorithmic logics of virality? Or is there something about *this* picture of *this* little boy and his TV set that "pierces" strangers across the globe? Perhaps it is the low punctum of the boy's not

FIGURE 5.1
John Atherton,
snapshot, circa
1952–53. Printed
with permission
from John
Atherton.

quite picture-ready pose—his disheveled slouch and his slouchy TV tilting off a table too small for it—that provokes an affective engagement. Whatever the reasons for its popularity, this ordinary photo becomes a conversation piece for memory making online.

In their ability to stimulate international and intergenerational dialogues, photo-share sites facilitate what Annette Kuhn calls "memory work," an interpretative strategy that ties personal memories in snapshots to public histories and images in mass media. For Kuhn (who wrote about family snapshots before the rise of digital photo culture), memory work offers ways to investigate a shared past, despite the photograph's personal nature. Via memory work, the photograph can "extend far beyond the personal" and "spread into an extended network of meanings that bring together the personal within the familial, the cultural, the economic, the social, the historical. Memory work makes it possible to explore connections between 'public' historical events, structures of feeling, family dramas, relations of class, national identity and gender, and 'personal' memory." Considering its political stakes, she adds, "Memory work is a method and practice of unearthing and making public untold stories. . . . These are the lives of those whose ways of knowing and ways of seeing the world are rarely acknowledged, let alone celebrated, in the expressions of hegemonic culture."[23]

As I've argued throughout this book, even if snapshots are highly generic, they can provide counter-memories and alternative histories of television. The photos I've amassed picture "untold stories" of ordinary people "whose ways of seeing the world"—and seeing TV—are rarely acknowledged in history books. As with photos of TV mess, glamour and drag photos, and homemade pinups, TV snapshots chart the practices of everyday people in ways that at times defy the production of picture-ready families that Kodak encouraged.

That said, the nature of online memory work varies. It is difficult to know whether the share sites and photo blogs are a form of what Svetlana Boym calls "restorative nostalgia" that encourages a sentimental longing to "return to . . . original stasis" (or what she also calls a "perfect snapshot") versus the degree to which they critique the past, or what Boym might endorse as "reflective nostalgia" that "cherishes fragments of memory," recognizes historical contradiction and ambivalence, and can often be "ironic and humorous."[24] My point here is not to judge the cultural politics of other people's memories, but rather to question the uses of TV snapshots in the present. As I noted early on, the nostalgia mode was inscribed in Kodak's marketing campaigns before and during the midcentury period. But it is also central to the history of digital photography. Instagram's first designers fashioned the app to look like a Polaroid camera, and the square frame and filters it supplied for users promoted the vintage look. Even while the company revamped its app and added support tools for nonsquare images and videos, the Instagram icon is still a rendering of a snapshot camera eye (although now the image is more abstract). Theorizing the app's vintage appeal, Nathan Jurgenson asks, "Why was the rise of everyday social photography . . . so defined by an aesthetic saturated with nostalgia?" Jurgenson argues that vintage filters make "contemporary photos seem more important, substantial, and real" and "endow the powerful feelings associated with nostalgia to our lives in the present."[25] But to what end are these powerful feelings directed?

On photo-share sites, the nostalgia mode can be used toward conservative *restorative* ends. It can paint the past in rosy hues, preserve troubling political ideologies, or turn the present into a "future perfect." The sites at times engage what Arjun Appadurai calls "ersatz nostalgia," or "nostalgia without lived experience or collective historical memory." Ersatz nostalgia is often deployed in advertisements that create desire for products by making them appear to embody "a way of living [that] is now gone forever."[26] Considering contemporary techno-culture in these terms, Boym writes, "Technology and nostalgia have become co-dependent: new technology and advanced marketing stimulate ersatz nostalgia—for the things you never thought you had lost—and anticipatory nostalgia—for the present that flees with the speed of a click."[27] Yet, despite its conservative and commercial uses, Boym and other scholars have reclaimed nostalgia's potential as a means of critical reflection and reappropriation. Nancy West, speaking specifically of snapshots in her history of Kodak, argues, "Nostalgia exemplified by the uses of photography does not necessarily entail retreat; it can equally function as retrieval, as a means of reclaiming the past and even of shaping the future."[28] In similar ways, film and television scholars such as Amy Holdsworth, Pam Cook, Paul Grainge, Alison Landsberg, Kate Darian-Smith and Sue Turnbull, and Alex Bevan show how nostalgia can provide tools for thinking about the present.[29] As Holdsworth observes, "This revisionist work on nostalgia seeks to rescue nostalgia and its potential from more pejorative, conservative and simplistic applications of the term, and to complicate the notion of nostalgia as being essentially inauthentic, ahistorical, sentimentalizing, regressive and exploitative."[30] Her book *Television, Memory and Nostalgia* explores the uses of nostalgia in British television dramas but also in memory cultures around TV (such as British TV programs that present clips of vintage television shows or galleries that exhibit TV-themed installation art). For Holdsworth, these varieties of TV memory generate a history of the present. "What is central to the textual re-encounters with past television is not the recovery of the original broadcast or viewing experience but its positioning within new frames and contexts that hold the past at a distance and reframe it in relation to the present."[31] The same can be said for the memory cultures around TV snapshots.

TV SNAPSHOTS FOR THE PRESENT:
RETRO-AESTHETICS AND REMAKES

Even if they are not directly critical of the past, the people who post and chat about TV snapshots online often reappropriate them in terms of present-day concerns and sensibilities. Rather than family sentimentality, people writing on discussion boards often observe the "cracks in the picture window" of the postwar home.[32] On Flickr, a snapshot of a 1960s family sitting in front of their fireplace and TV set generates a string of comments that variously dispel the myth of family integration staged in the photo. One man who calls himself "Tattoo Dave" remarks on the relative state of mind of each family member. Pointing out that they variously look "annoyed," "happy," or "barely happy," he concludes, "They don't look like a very cohesive family." But, he adds, "I DO like that TV and transistor radio" on top of the TV console. Another man commenting on the same snapshot adds, "I'm a big fan of the John Waters movie 'Polyester.' And the first thing I thought when I saw this picture was 'Get off me Francine!'" (referring to the suburban housewife in the film played by drag superstar Divine).[33] As in this case, TV snapshots often generate comments that express an ironic, parodic, or camp sensibility that punctures the myth of TV family bliss performed in many of these pictures.

On Flickr, one man posts a midcentury snapshot of a woman posing by her Zenith TV console (figure 5.2). Commenting on the photo, people discuss the TV set while also weaving a dark tale around the woman in the photo, whom they decide to name Violet (the color of the walls in the room). One person writes, "Movie idea: a bunch of stoners take over the house for a short time because they like the violet walls and antique television. Violet is so stoned herself on booze and prescription drugs that she thinks it's [her] family visiting her. Yes, it's the Manson family, but the furniture is so damn appealing." Another person (who decides Violet is a nurse because of the blue dress and three-cornered white hat she wears) conjures up a different scenario, this time in the voice of the woman in the picture: "Harold! I'll be late getting home. I'll be assisting Dr. Reaper over at Angeles of Mercy. There's a casserole in the oven." Responding to both posts, a third person praises their stories and "clever captions."[34] In other cases, people upload TV snapshots with titles like "Retro-Christmas" or "Retro-Families," and some are colorized with bright magenta or turquoise hues, the palette of the digital present.[35]

The storytelling comments and photoshopping techniques accompanying these snapshots echo the promos on nostalgia networks like Nick at Nite and TV Land that edit together vintage sitcom clips with a campy wink as they repackage old TV for contemporary viewers and taste cultures.[36] Similar strategies are found in popular retro novelties (like greeting cards and cocktail napkins) with campy captions and colorized tones. More broadly, the photo-share sites draw on the captioning, cut-and-paste, and color-tinting techniques of the scrapbook, the historical genre (associated especially with nineteenth- and twentieth-century women's culture) from which these popular novelties themselves borrow. Like scrapbooks, photo-share sites juxtapose and rearrange found photos and turn them into stories. Analyzing Pinterest, Julie Wilson and Emily Chivers Yochim show how the site

FIGURE 5.2
A Woman at her Zenith, undated. Printed with permission from Cardboard America.

conjoins scrapbooking with social networking as women use Pinterest to swap photos of the "happy objects" of domesticity (like cakes they baked or clothing they sewed).[37] While Wilson and Yochim focus on women's affective labor (and Pinterest's use of their free labor for its own commercial success), photo sharing also turns scrapbooking into an entrepreneurial activity in which people establish reputations. Katie Day Good argues that Facebook (which owns Instagram) borrows from scrapbooking and encourages users to make "personal media assemblage[s]" through which they form friendship networks but also tap into like-minded taste cultures and accumulate "cultural capital" via their curating activities online.[38]

Some online curators have specialties and develop online reputations as archivist auteurs with distinct cultural capital. One woman who calls herself Tackijulie (a name that speaks to her ironic sensibility) specializes in snapshots of little Christmas trees on top of TV sets. In one post, she talks about where she finds them. In another, collector/archivist Eartha Kitsch (whose name also speaks to her ironic sensibility) praises Tackijulie for her curating talents. The work of online curators like Tackijulie and Eartha Kitsch is particularly interesting in light of the way they use scrapbooking and craft practices to imbue the TV snapshots with retro aesthetics that reappropriate the scenes of domesticity around which midcentury TV snapshots were organized.

The kitsch, camp, and retro sensibilities people apply to TV photos suggest a critical perspective on TV and the midcentury culture of domesticity around it. Admittedly, kitsch sensibilities and ironic commentary may at times enforce a sense of present-day superiority over the past that can make us forget contemporary troubles and can wind up validating the present as a "better" place and time.[39] But people who post TV snapshots are often self-reflexive about their memory work, and their posts are more in keeping with the irony and humor of Boym's reflective nostalgia than with the restorative mode.

Retro aesthetics are also central to photographs made by contemporary photographers who post TV snapshot remakes on the sites, especially on Flickr. Restaging the formal features of TV snapshots in newly rendered versions, these contemporary photos rework TV memory for the present. One artist (who goes by the company name of TimelessPhotos) posts a series of pinups titled *Vivian*, in which a model poses in retro clothing with a vintage TV set in a midcentury living room setting (figure 5.3). Her Bettie Page hairdo, capri pants, short shorts, and bright red lipstick recall the dress-up snapshots and homemade pinups of the past. At the same time, her images draw on traditions of art photography—especially the glamour poses of Cindy Sherman—and the thriving retro culture around pinup art.[40]

Reclaimed since the 1990s as a form of "grrrl power" (and often reappropriated for its subversive potential by feminist and queer artists like Annie Sprinkle, Marlene McCarty, Lutz Bacher, and Shonagh Adelman), the pinup has been elevated to the walls of museums.[41] For example, in 2014 the Warhol held a retrospective of Bunny Yeager's work, and Berlin's Bunny Lounge gallery is devoted to her photos. Pinterest's name is itself a call back to pinups. Pinterest is both an archive (as in "put a pin in it," or save it for later) and a repertoire in which people cite and reiterate the actions entailed in pinning

FIGURE 5.3
JRG/Timeless
Photoworks,
Vivian, 2012.
Printed with
permission from
JRG/Timeless
Photoworks.

photos to virtual pin boards (much as the soldier pinned photos of women
to the walls of his barracks). But on share sites, the pinning activity is often
performed by women, who share pinups with each other or establish reputations as pinup artists or models.[42] As in the case of Vivian, many of these
photos specifically recall TV pinups.

   One of the earliest uploaded versions was created by Chilean photo blogger Natalia Quiroz, who skirts the boundaries between everyday glamour

and pinup with a photo that places a woman (with bare legs and shoulders) in a sultry pose sitting on top of a TV set.[43] Even more directly quoting the pinup genre, studio photographer and photo blogger Chip York presents a photoshoot (2017) of his self-proclaimed "muse," Anna-Marie, in a cherry print dress, pinup heels, and red lipstick (figure 5.4). In several photos, she lifts her skirt at her hip while posing in front of a portable TV, while others show her (in a different costume) on top of the TV set.[44] Theresa S. Thompson creates a retro Polaroid snapshot (complete with the faux date "Aug 58" stamped on the deckled edge) that shows a woman (in peekaboo pinup heels) standing on a retro household pull-out ladder placed next to a TV console (a vintage lamp and sunburst clock accent the period style; figure 5.5). Thompson captions it with an ironic reference to *Leave It to Beaver* (ABC, 1957–63): "June, don't you think this . . . is setting a bad example for the Beaver?"[45] More pointedly part of the "grrrl power" genre, Kelly McCarthy's *TV Land II* (2017) presents a pinup of a woman with red pigtails, tattoos, red lips, and black stiletto pinup heels (figure 5.6). Posing rear first on top of a baby blue painted TV, she holds a bunch of baby pink balloons. The photograph self-consciously plays with the mix of innocence and explosive sexuality found in classic Depression-era and wartime pinups, but the tattoos and black stilettos give the woman a dominatrix look.[46] Similarly, Spanish fashion photographer Eva Mañez presents *Pola TV* (2009), a photo of a model posing on top of her TV in a polka-dot camisole, black panties, red lips, and strappy black stiletto sandals.[47] German artist Christine von Diepenbroek offers a more contemplative, self-proclaimed "surreal" interpretation of the TV pinups with *The Show Must Go On . . .* (ca. 2019), which depicts a woman in her corset dancing with a pelican in a pink polka-dot room, which has a tiny 1960s console TV collaged into the corner.[48]

Certainly, not all pinups are created equal. Some—like *TV Land II* or the portrait of Vivian (with her fist on the set and her scowl)—are in dialogue with the retro-feminist pinups, while others seem more enmeshed in the kitschy nature of both TV sets and 1950s femininity. Some are exemplary of the vexed mix of self-surveillance, "subjectification," empowerment, and irony that Rosalind Gill (writing in 2007) saw as central to postfeminist media.[49] But regardless of their differences, on photo-share sites, the retro pinups are often placed directly next to the midcentury TV snapshots. For example, on Pinterest, a group administrator for retro pinups invites someone to share a 1950s TV snapshot in their retro-pinup gallery so that the historical photographs are reappropriated as part of the contemporary retro mode.

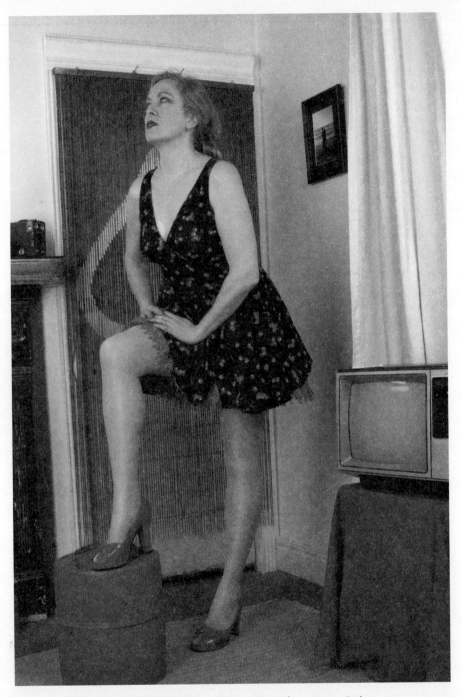

FIGURE 5.4 Chip York, untitled, pinup of Anna-Marie (one in a series), 2010.
Printed with permission from Chip York.

FIGURE 5.5 Theresa S. Thompson, untitled, 2009. Printed with permission from Theresa S. Thompson, Hoosier Photos Inc.

FIGURE 5.6 Kelly McCarthy, *TV Land II*, 2017.
Printed with permission from Kelly McCarthy.

In this sense, the logic of display on the photo sites is the logic of the collection where, as Susan Stewart argues, "The collection replaces history with *classification*, with order beyond the realm of temporality." "In the collection," she claims, "time is not something to be restored to an origin; rather, all time is made simultaneous or synchronous within the collection's world." For Stewart, the collection operates through metaphor, where each part is meant to stand for a whole rather than its unique historical meaning. Moreover, Stewart stresses the use value of the collection for the present. "The collection is a form of art as play, a form involving the reframing of objects . . . and manipulation of context. Like other forms of art, its function is not the restoration of context of origin but rather the creation of a new context."[50]

Still, even if the photo-share sites are not about history per se, by scrapbooking the midcentury snapshots alongside the retro versions, these collections do allow for memory work on the part of people who share them, comment on them, and, to use Stewart's term, engage with them as a "form of art as play." Notably, Stewart distinguishes the scrapbook from the collection, arguing that the scrapbook is more like a souvenir. Rather than metaphor, the souvenir is about the metonymy of parts, where each item tells a story about its past. In my view, the photo-share sites present a hybrid of collection and scrapbook, mixing present/past, metaphor/metonymy, and the data classification afforded by computers with the storytelling function of the souvenir.

In addition to pinups, artists post photographs that recall TV screenshots, still lifes, and trick shots.[51] Yet, at the same time, these photos evoke the history of artworks and museum exhibitions inspired by television and produced by a range of artists, from midcentury pop painters like Richard Hamilton, Tom Wesselmann, and Andy Warhol; and photographers like Lee Friedlander and Stephen Shore; to pioneering video and installation artists like Nam June Paik and Dan Graham; as well as feminist photographer/filmmaker/installation artist Lynn Hershman Leeson (whose *TV Legs #1* [1987], *Seduction* [1986], and related photographs show women's bodies, often in pin-up-type poses, with their faces encased in TV screens). These TV-inspired artworks continued in the 2000s with, for example, the exhibitions Maeve Connolly discusses in her book *TV Museum* and with the more recent work of contemporary artists like Nicholas Galanin (whose conceptual tapestry *White Noise, American Prayer Rug* [2018] weaves a TV screen filled with static into a devotional Indigenous American prayer rug).[52]

In the tradition of Paik's series *Video Fish* (1975/1997), in which video monitors are placed alongside fish tanks with real fish that seem to be swimming inside the TVs, Sara-Lusa Menina uploads a photo of a goldfish swimming inside a TV screen (untitled, 2009). The screen is a bright turquoise blue, and digitally enhanced fluffs of lime green grass float around it. The TV set itself is a run-of-the-mill faux walnut 1980s portable set, so the colorful processed image forms a sharp contrast and surreal setting for it.[53] Harking back to midcentury snapshots, but also to the disturbing interiors of Friedlander's *Little Screens*, Chrissie White's *A Peculiar Sort of Thing* (2008) features a darkly lit room with a woman sitting on an antique wing-backed chair with a Raggedy Andy doll resting on its arm (figure 5.7). A Victorian-style mannequin "poses" next to a large 1990s-era TV set, giving the photo a time-out-of-joint sensibility. A still life arrangement of bowls, flowers, and an orange are on top of the TV, but the screen is all static.[54] My point here is not that Menina deliberately imitates Paik or that White copies from Friedlander. It could, after all, be argued that Paik's *TV Fish* and his decorative *Prepared TVs* borrowed from domestic practices of tele-decoration and TV still lifes—for example, the placement of aquariums on top of the set. And Friedlander's photographs were created at a time when many people made still life snapshots with their TV sets. In any case, it seems useful to think about the recursive loops between digital photography, gallery art practices, and midcentury TV snapshots.

Other photographs use aesthetics of debris art and ruin porn to turn TV into a markedly "unhappy object." Circulating on Pinterest and Flickr in groups with names like "Abandoned—Art of Decay" and "Ruins and Rust," these photos retain some of the formal characteristics of the midcentury Kodak print but present TV sets in rooms that have rotted with years of neglect. The poignant melancholy of declination, devolution, and technological obsolescence reframe the TV snapshot as a sad relic of lives once lived and broadcasts once "live." A photographer who calls himself Darko portrays a TV wasteland with a 1960s faded wood console on a gloomy carpet soiled with debris and old newspapers strewn around it (figure 5.8). Peeling wallpaper and gold curtain sheers (the only thing that seems to have survived the wreckage) flank the wall behind the TV set. A partially drawn window shade provides a gleam of light that illuminates the room with an eerie glow. The ghost of Rod Serling smokes a cigarette on a faded black and white TV screen. Recalling the *Twilight Zone*'s famous tagline, the photo is titled *Imagine If You Will . . .* (2014).[55] Riddim Ryder's *As If You Never Existed* (2014) features an abandoned house with a rusted vacuum cleaner, a closet filled with rumpled clothes and sheets, and a tarnished gold frame hanging pictureless on a dingy wall (figure 5.9). A timeworn TV set recedes in the corner. About

FIGURE 5.7 Chrissie White, *A Peculiar Sort of Thing*, 2008.
Printed with permission from Chrissie White.

FIGURE 5.8 Darkophoto, *Imagine If You Will . . .* , 2014.
Printed with permission from Darkophoto.

to fall off the edge of the console, a lonely lamp with a crooked lampshade casts dark shadows on the wall, turning the scene into a *TV snapshot noir*, an apt ending for the genre.[56]

The photographs on share sites take multiple forms and circulate virally in unpredictable ways. The share sites juxtapose old and new, memory and history, art and artifact. Whether or not they intend it this way, the people who share TV photos online are historians and artists of the everyday who create an image bank for the TV past.

The digital labor people perform online can be understood in relation to what Abigail De Kosnik calls "rogue archives."[57] Looking at people who build nonprofit online archives, De Kosnik emphasizes the social and political interventions they make as they create alternative ways to preserve and conceptualize often forgotten or devalued pasts (one of her main case studies is digital archives for fan fiction). Drawing on Diana Taylor's *The Archive and the Repertoire*, she argues that digital archives are not just created through logics of computer storage but also via "repertoires" of cultural memory

FIGURE 5.9 Riddim Ryder, *As If You Never Existed*, 2014. Printed with permission from Riddim Rider, www.riddimryder.com.

and the performances of human actors who engage in collective history and memory work online. Although De Kosnik reserves the term *rogue archives* for nonprofit sites, in my estimation, her argument is still valuable for thinking about the digital labor and memory work that take place on commercial sites like Flickr and Pinterest. My point here is not that photo-share sites are radical (at times, they can be quite conservative or restorative in Boym's sense). Rather, the photo-share sites afford people opportunities for knowledge sharing, storytelling, and the various modes of creative reappropriation I have presented. The memory work, art practices, and curatorial labor that people perform on share sites and the archives that they build have become *my* archive; and I am very conscious of the fact that *they* and *I* fall apart very easily, as many scholars—like me—are also collectors and regularly use digital photo archives.

Like the photographs posted online, the history I've crafted in this book is one of rearrangements, reappropriations, and new archival consignations. I've taken scraps from the past and compiled them in ways their picture takers did not imagine. Using online archives makes the cut and paste, match and fit scrapbooking aspects of history writing more visceral, more material. It can also make us rethink exactly what is not in the archive and why.

MISSING PERSONS

While writing this book, I searched for one especially historically significant TV snapshot, which nevertheless does not circulate on the share sites that picture families and their TV sets. I already knew of this photo but could not find it in the search terms I usually use in online searches (for example, terms like *TV snapshot, vintage TV, 50s TV,* or *TV rooms*). Taken in 1955, the snapshot is just like many others. It shows a boy dressed in what appears to be his Sunday best, standing next to and leaning on his console TV. He is smiling and looks happy. A feeling of hominess and hospitality pervades the picture. A leaf-patterned rug is beneath him; a decorative curtain flanks a wall that separates a bedroom from a parlor where the TV stands. The subtle ghost of the CBS eye trademark is visible in the blurry picture on-screen. Everything is in place. Yet, I am not sure where to place this picture in my archive. It both fits and disrupts, and at any rate (to the best of my knowledge) has not been discussed in histories or memories of TV.

This is one of several pictures of Emmett Till, the fourteen-year-old boy who was murdered by white men in Mississippi in 1955. In an act of resistance against the white killers and the justice system that enabled the violent attack, his mother, Mamie Till, turned to the press. She gave newspaper and magazine publishers photographs of Emmett before and after the brutal beating to elicit national outrage and build her court case. The most famous photograph pictures Emmett's face distorted beyond recognition—an image that helped spark the civil rights movement and has since been the subject of much attention in histories of the movement and histories of photography. His mother demanded his body be shown in an open casket for all the world to see. There were also photos placed in the casket, including the snapshot of Till posing with his TV set. While the photo of Till's bludgeoned face arouses shock and horror, the TV snapshot of Emmett Till provokes affect in its ordinariness. He, like so many other boys, poses with his TV set, the ultimate aspirational family object of the period. The punctum here is not just in the details of the image but also in its incongruous appearance in Till's casket, where it signifies the violation of the ordinary life and childhood memory that it depicts.

Today, this snapshot is part of an archive of national trauma—the long and seemingly unending history of American racism, violence, and social injustice. Rather than circulating in online archives of family snapshots, this photograph is consigned elsewhere to a national story of brutality and shame. In 2009, when the National Museum of African American History and Culture acquired Till's exhumed casket and placed it on display, the photographs—including this one—were exhibited alongside it. The official memory of the snapshot places it in a proper history of civil rights. This is clearly its most important archive, and the one to which his mother consigned it. As Mamie Till intended it, this is foremost a photograph of Till's humanity, which she hoped to honor and use in her struggle for justice. Recovering this snapshot for the purposes of my history here risks the sort of secondary violence that Saidiya Hartman cautions against in her study of the archive of slavery and her speculative histories about silenced Black subjects of violent pasts.[58] Nevertheless, I think this photograph should also be considered as part of the history and memory of television. Given Mamie Till's desire to bring the photos of her son to public attention through mass media, it seems appropriate to archive it in the context of TV history and allow it to disrupt any sense of racial innocence that TV snapshots, and family snapshots as a genre, may otherwise convey.[59]

Even while many of the photos I've found on eBay are racially diverse, the online memory culture around TV does not typically discuss race. And even while the digital archives contain photographs from various parts of the world, the share sites flatten out distinctions among cultural contexts and say little about specific national experiences. The "missing persons" in my photo searches are especially hard to imagine because the digital archive fills absence with abundant presence; it's easy to think you've seen it all.

Online archives can be deceptive in their speed and volume. The vast amount of material that circulates on them encourages fantasies of encyclopedic mastery. Speaking of such issues in the mid-1990s (at the dawn of digital culture), Derrida claimed, "Today we can pretend (at least in a dream) to archive everything, or almost everything. . . . But because it is not possible to preserve everything, choices, and therefore interpretations, structurations, become necessary." And for this reason, "whoever is in a position to access this past or to use the archive should know concretely that there was a politics of memory, a particular politics, that this politics is in transformation, that it is a *politics*."[60] For Derrida, archives (whether digital or material) are not just places of recovery. Instead, as he argues in *Archive Fever*, they are riddled with loss, absence, trauma, and even a "radical evil" that erases histories, such as the histories of people forced from their homelands.[61] (Derrida's book was first delivered as a lecture at the Freud Museum in London, which is also the home in exile to which Freud escaped in the Nazi era.) The archive is not just an empirical holding place but also a *spectral* space never fully present or absent in material terms.

In a more materialist fashion, Foucault approaches the archive as a technical apparatus (or "dispositif") that stores the "positivities" of the past—things that are said and recorded, as opposed to everything or everyone. While archives may indulge the historian's positivist dream of completion (the desire to find every artifact), in a counterintuitive move, Foucault argues that the archive exposes the "rarity" of statements it was possible to speak in the discursive formations of their times.[62] In that sense, even if we were able to find every single television recording or TV snapshot ever made (the ideal TV archive), that archive would still be founded on the principle of rarity. As discursive systems, TV and its archives give voice only to what is *speakable*— and, I would add, only what is *recordable* and *savable*—in the context of their social, industrial, technological, political, historiographical, and institutional parameters. Paradoxically, in this respect, the archive preserves absence.

While Derrida and Foucault wrote prior to the contemporary explosion of digital archives, the questions of presence, absence, and rarity they variously engage are profoundly relevant to online storage. Like other digital files, snapshots persist online in a precarious way, through what Wendy Hui Kyong Chun calls the "enduring ephemeral." Even while digital media leaves trails and personal data we can't erase, "Digital media is not always there. We suffer daily frustration with digital sources that just disappear. Digital media is degenerative, forgetful, erasable."[63] This is often the case on commercial sites. In 2018, when Flickr introduced its premium subscription service Flickr Pro, it announced new restrictions on users, allowing nonpaying users to upload only one thousand files free of charge; by 2019 it began deleting the oldest files (until the one thousand limit was met). While Flickr made its computer logic explicit, more typically, as Chun suggests, the operations of digital media and archives are not apparent. Speaking specifically about photo archives, Nina Lager Vestberg observes: "The analog era produced materialist critiques of the ways photography supported and reinforced existing power structures through the institutional apparatus of the archive. This apparatus consisted of technical installations such as filing cabinets and working practices such as classificatory editing; however, its workings were for the most part hidden in plain sight, that is to say, obscured by the visual impact of its contents. Today, the digital machinery that enables browsing and searching through online picture archives has become imperceptible to its users in much the same way."[64]

The missing picture of Emmett Till speaks to this complex relationship between visibility and invisibility in online archives. Digital platforms like Flickr and Pinterest encourage new forms of memory making and creative reappropriation, but at the same time, the archival search leads to lost footprints that encourage me to track different trails.

THE ARCHIVE REFRAMED:
COUNTER-MEMORIES AND TELE-MEMOIRS

Rather than end my book with a *telos* of photography, in which digital photo archives present the ultimate new media resource for historians, I want to pause here to think about how the "old media" of books and films have used family snapshots as an *archive of feelings* for counter-memories of the TV past. Snapshots have been a central feature in some of the most insightful histories of race and television, work created by filmmakers, scholars, and novelists who've challenged the white privilege of seeing yourself on TV.

In his 1992 documentary *Color Adjustment*, Marlon Riggs grapples with the "possessive investment in whiteness" that sustained twentieth-century television.[65] The film traces the history of African Americans on television from *Amos 'n' Andy* and *Beulah* to *The Cosby Show*. By 1992, the history of race on US TV was a familiar subject, a story told not just by historians but also by television producers (most of them white) who often lauded themselves as masters of TV's racial progress. But Riggs deals with this history from a critical race perspective, questioning the story of progress and TV's *telos* through an archival filmmaking practice. Oral histories featuring Black actors, producers, and scholars are edited together with clips of TV programs, vintage ads, commercials, and other ephemera. I find the film especially interesting in the context of my book because it foregrounds the family snapshot and its intimate connection to television's depictions of race and family life.

Riggs's opening sequence begins with a quotation from James Baldwin: "The country's image of the Negro, which hasn't very much to do with the Negro, has never failed to reflect, with a kind of frightening accuracy, the state of mind of the country." This is followed by the voice of Ruby Dee: "This is a picture of the American Dream." Riggs cuts to a clip from the opening sequence of early television's most famous Kodak family, Ozzie, Harriet, David, and Ricky Nelson. As in the TV credit sequence, in Riggs's film, the moving image of the Nelsons transforms into a still Kodak snapshot. Using a graphic mask, Riggs inserts the *Ozzie and Harriet* credit sequence into the frame of a screen on an old TV console. Off screen, Dee explains, "This is a picture of what the Dream once was." Riggs then cuts to a clip from *The Cosby Show*'s opening sequence, showing the fictional Huxtable family dancing joyously together. But this clip also appears inside Riggs's mock TV frame. Dee says: "This is a picture of what the dream has become." Riggs goes on to montage footage from vintage commercials and sitcoms (like *Leave It to Beaver, Beulah*, and *Julia*) with archival footage of white people watching TV.

In this opening sequence, Riggs provokes a historical counter-narrative that investigates the whiteness of early television and introduces the topic of his film—namely, ongoing questions about myths of progress and racial inclusion on TV. By creating a double frame in which *Ozzie and Harriet*'s Kodak snapshot appears within the contours of a TV screen, Riggs calls attention to how cameras—both TV cameras and snapshot cameras—operate as machines for the production of myths about race and family life. He also shows how to repurpose these myths by literally reframing archival footage to create counter-narratives of the TV past. For Riggs, the Kodak picture frame becomes a filmic device and metaphor for this endeavor. Moreover, the film (whether intentionally or not) follows practices of African American scrapbooking that came before it. In her book *Writing with Scissors*, Ellen Gruber Garvey shows how African Americans of the nineteenth and early twentieth centuries used scrapbooking as an oppositional practice, snipping clips from newspapers (mostly written by whites) in ways that rearranged them (sometimes alongside other ephemera) and thereby critiqued the stories told in the white press. The scrapbooks served as "alternative records" that voiced what one Black journalist called "unwritten histories."[66] Riggs's documentary montage similarly "snips" from television history to provide a counter-narrative and memory of the medium. And in this way, as I am sure readers will recognize, Riggs's scrapbooking practice predates the scrapbooking on photo-share sites, using scrapbooking in the context of a different political history and trajectory.

This tactic of scrapbooking is even more central to Ann duCille's book, *Technicolored: Reflections on Race in the Time of TV* (2018). The book tracks television history through the lens of duCille's autobiographical memories of growing up with TV. Throughout, duCille's tele-memoir retrieves the textures of her experience with TV as an African American girl. "My family was one of if not the first in our blue-collar community to own a TV."[67] She recalls the sunny California sitcom homes she wished she lived in and eventually purchased. She discusses her pleasure in watching Black guest stars on variety shows and her anger or disidentification when watching recycled Shirley Temple movies on TV. While *Technicolored* is not about TV snapshots, duCille includes numerous snapshots of herself and her family. Her photos provide a counter-memory for television history, showing families that TV did not typically portray. The snapshots (and related ephemera like classroom pictures and letters) are interspersed with publicity stills of television programs and performers.

Across the book, duCille's scrapbooking tactics offer implicit and explicit parallels between her life and the images on TV. On one page, she juxtaposes a snapshot of her family at the Thanksgiving dinner table with a frame grab of Cicely Tyson in the 1974 CBS made-for-TV movie *The Autobiography of Miss Jane Pittman*. Archival news photos (of, for example, the 1963 March on Washington or Donald Trump's 1989 newspaper announcement calling for the death penalty for the Central Park Five) place duCille's tele-memoir in the context of the broader history of civil rights and white supremacy—a story she tells throughout the book. The scrapbooking aesthetic in *Technicolored* carries through to the cover art, which features a childhood snapshot of duCille and her siblings that is photoshopped into the screen of an old wood-grained TV cabinet. By repurposing her family photo album, duCille asks the reader to experience television not just as programs but also as the ambient backdrop of her family's daily life as it intersects with the life of the nation.

Significantly, even while *Technicolored* compiles family snapshots and other material ephemera, duCille reflects on her use of digital archives to write her book. Admitting that her exposure to blogs, tweets, and Facebook was minimal before she began this project, duCille says she discovered the "oddly wonderful" aspects of being able "to sit at my desk at home and watch on YouTube a sitcom I saw on television sixty years ago."[68] She nevertheless observes, "There is something else the virtual world offers that is, as my Jamaican father would say, 'beautiful ugly'—beautiful for the ease of access, ugly for what one may discover when one looks." For duCille, it's not just the historical racism of the old broadcast TV shows that is ugly. As she searched online for source material, she also encountered the Twitterverse of racial slurs and white backlash. As duCille puts it, "If you want to know what evil lurks in the hearts of men, turn to the Internet."[69] In this sense, the book warns against teleological notions of racial and media progress. Rather than move from unenlightened old TV to a more progressive digital world, duCille frames her tele-memoir as a confrontation between past and present.

In a somewhat different strategy of memory work, poet, experimental novelist, filmmaker, and artist Tan Lin offers a fictionalized tele-memoir in his "ambient novel" *Insomnia and the Aunt* (2011). Described on the book's cover as a "scrapbook," the thirty-two-page novel pieces together ephemeral memories of a Chinese American family. The unnamed first-person narrator (who may or may not be Tan Lin), reflects on his boyhood past and takes the reader on a journey to his aunt's motel in the Seattle wilderness, the site of his yearly childhood vacations. As the epitome of a temporary home, offering only the most conditional forms of hospitality, the roadside motel becomes a metaphor for the Chinese American diaspora. For Lin, the motel is a transient space where memory melts easily into forgetting. As one of the motel's major attractions, television becomes a central figure of diasporic identity—the process of learning to be American through the (ambivalent) forgetting of home.

Throughout the book, the insomnia-afflicted aunt fills her waking hours with late-night TV. The narrator recalls bonding with his aunt as they watch together in loops of nightly experience: "We like to see things about sharks, any form of mental illness, psychological studies of sex in humans (as if they were primates), dating shows of people my age or just a little bit older, strange sporting events—like women spitting kidney beans into tin cups—and commercials during peak broadcast moments. These are all extremely soothing to my aunt and me."[70] The list of favorites goes on until the narrator reflects:

> For an immigrant like my aunt, America is not the images on a TV, it basically is the TV, which is why she decorates it with paper doilies, vanilla incense sticks and stuffed Garfields. This is also why my aunt thinks all

TV, even live TV, is canned, and she thinks America is basically not a place or even an image, but furniture. For my aunt, the live broadcast of the Vietnam War of my youth and her early middle age resembled a re-run. My aunt accordingly has very few memories of violence or even racism in America. TV made her forget all these things. Likewise, it is very hard for me to remember her even though I miss her immensely. The more I miss her the more she becomes furniture or a TV commercial for Tide detergent.[71]

Known for his poetic recombinations of everyday ephemera, Lin inter-weaves these "memories of forgetting" with family photos, motel postcards, and TV and film stills. A photo of a boy and a woman appears in postage-stamp size on the front cover and cover page, and is also featured in a full-page photoshopped (pixelated) version on the back cover. But it's unclear if this family photo has anything to do with the fictional narrator and his aunt. In fact, toward the end of the novel the narrator claims he removed "the last of my aunt's photographs from this scrapbook." "In this way," he says, "what you are reading no longer contains some of the things I have been telling you about."[72] As with Barthes's photograph of his deceased mother (which he no-toriously chose not to publish in *Camera Lucida*), the book denies the reader the photographic reveal. In a similar way, Lin also frustrates the reader with dead-end notations. His footnotes are often searches for wiki links that don't exist or don't relate to the subject at hand. They are searches for nothing but the act of searching itself—an apt metaphor for diasporic memory and look-ing for home through a TV screen. At the end of the ambient novel, the nar-rator observes, "People like my aunt don't need to be remembered; they need to be forgotten inside a TV set. The era of forgetting isn't over, it just needs to be reinvented by databases."[73]

Although in different ways, for both Lin and duCille, a mix of personal keepsakes and digital archives is central to their processes of recollection, as they interweave material things (snapshots, postcards, letters) with digital searches in ways that produce hybrids of memory and history. Their scrap-book aesthetics are less about recovering lost pasts than about reframing the present. For Lin, the search winds up in a nowhere land of media diaspora, where it's not even clear if his aunt was an actual person or just an ethereal emanation from the TV screen (his "screen memory").

Even while digital archives are an important tool for historians, they are not a straightforward repository of "lost" histories or restored pasts. The dig-ital archive is a memory apparatus based on computational memory whose relation to human memory and history is complex. Following the work of Friedrich Kittler and his concepts of memory and "discourse networks," Ernst suggests that the computer replaces human memory with digital operations of storage.[74] Ernst is interested in the nonhuman nature of recording technologies—beginning with photography and continuing through to digital media. He writes, "With the emergence of photography, the idea of the theatrical gaze literally staging the past is displaced by the cold mechanical eye, a technologically neutral code rather than a subjective discourse."[75] In his work on digital archives, Ernst continues to explore how computers register the past coldly.[76] But for people like duCille and Lin, whose stories are not typically saved or told, the digital archive is not neutral code, and human memory remains a major resource. That said, rather than a simple triumph of inclusion in history, for duCille and Tan, the digital archive becomes an ("ugly beautiful") resource and an (often deceptive) link through which questions about TV, memory, identity, and everyday experience can be posed (if not entirely answered).

As old things (of all sorts) migrate to the web, the digital archives at our disposal pose new questions about how to frame them and what historical frameworks (if any) to use. Midcentury family photos, with their little white frames, call attention to devices of contextualization and boundary marking that make images into artifacts, artifacts into memories, and memories into histories. In this book, I've tried to cross these boundaries, though not as an experimental novelist (like Lin) or an autobiographical historian (like duCille), but rather as a collector of other people's things, the Kodak moments they left behind. I turn now to some brief final thoughts that reflect on my book and the archive I've amassed.

CONCLUSION

———————

HARD STOP

HARD STOP (plural hard stops): A mechanical device that limits the travel of a mechanism. A definite time when someone must end a task in order to meet another time commitment.—"HARD STOP," https://en.wiktionary.org

Given the generative nature of online archives, it has been difficult for me to know exactly when to stop collecting photos and finish this book. Ends are arbitrary. TV snapshots pile up, find new routes of circulation, show up in places and in ways I hadn't imagined when I first discovered these photos some eight years ago. By then, the end of TV (at least as an analog box) was well underway. Television's reinvention as a digital platform with streaming content has been an ongoing process as I've written this book. Collecting the past is often a way to negotiate the alien mutations of the present. In any case, ending this book is a hard stop, a conscious effort to shut off the mechanisms of my digital devices and personal obsessions.

In the postwar period, the snapshot camera was a companion technology for television. Rather than think of media devices as a procession of new things replacing old ones, we should think about how old and new media merge to form hybrid cultural practices. Histories of new media usually focus on one object (typically, an emergent thing like TV in the 1950s and 1960s or personal computers in the 1970s and 1980s) without considering how people assemble social life by combining and recombining media devices in ways not imagined by the media industries. Even actor-network theory, with its focus on the shared agency of people and things, rarely considers more than one thing (or one device) at a time. The concept of *companion technologies* accounts for parallel trajectories of devices that are both *in use*—or, perhaps, *misuse*—at the same time.

Why did people—in so many places of the world—take pictures of themselves with their TV sets? How can we account for the ubiquity of this practice and its persistence through time? This book didn't really attempt to answer what is fundamentally a psychological question. While the practice seems virtually everywhere, I hesitate to call it *universal*. Instead, as I've argued throughout these chapters, TV snapshots are best read in their historical and material contexts, as a practice, a thing people did by pairing two media devices in unexpected ways. Those unexpected assemblages and encounters demonstrate the myriad things people did with TV other than watch TV programs. Snapshots show how people organized their (often disorganized) media homes; used TV sets as backdrops for the performance of self and gender; turned TV sets into settings for ritualized picture taking and everyday glamour; and used TV as an erotic plaything. They demonstrate how television's first audiences transformed TV from a spectator amusement into a craft practice, with still lifes, trick shots, screenshots, fashion shoots, and pinups—pictures of people's own making.

With this book, I hope to have rekindled and redirected interests in the everydayness of media, specifically television, at a time when everyday practices around TV have markedly changed. In the era of digital television, with its streaming services, interactive apps, multiple platforms, time shifting, and place shifting, television and TV viewing have changed considerably. Not surprisingly, scholarship has also changed direction toward issues of digital TV production cultures, transmedia franchises, user-generated content, online fandoms, and narrative analysis of the vast amount of programs streaming in television's new "golden age." But there is value in relocating these present-day concerns in the context of theories of everyday life and in earlier scholarship on broadcast TV's everydayness, such as the early work on everyday TV in British cultural studies and in the early feminist scholarship on soaps.[1]

Understanding the history of everyday life poses challenges, in relation to both source materials and methods of analysis. While scholarship on vernacular photography is a growing field, snapshots nevertheless remain a largely neglected historical resource in television studies and studies of media and everyday life more generally. Although family snapshots are always particular to the people who pose in them, when collected in groups and approached as an archive, snapshots offer ways to see, or at least hypothesize about, general cultural practices, aesthetics choices, and recurring themes. As pictures of intimacy, snapshots demand a conjectural approach to history. They provide ways to speculate on aspects of daily life that are not documented in official archives. TV snapshots offer clues into the history of media, domesticity, and family life, and the snapshot can even expose counter-memories and historical practices that don't conform to midcentury gender ideals and sexualities. At times, snapshots offer counter-narratives to the images of family life (especially the hegemonic whiteness) on midcentury TV screens.

As both a popular image-making practice and as textual forms, snapshots literally frame experience, but they also ask us to imagine what is out of the frame. Snapshots are both archives and repertoires that allow us to see iterations of actions and to feel the "low punctum" of affects that loop through daily experiences. Snapshots are sociable. As I have argued across this book, TV snapshots provide a sense of what was happening on the other side of the screen where people gathered to pose or engage in a range of activities (such as game play or ritual activities like performing a wedding ceremony). Snapshots are useful for anyone interested in the space and place-making functions of media devices and screens in the domestic interior. They also open up new ways to think about media temporalities (as with the screenshots, which arrest moving images and freeze the flow of media events, or with the contemporary photo-share sites that make old snapshots relevant for the present). My historical approach to everyday TV is conducted through a search not only for archives but also for new ways of thinking about the uses—and residual reuses—of media technologies in the often invisible cultural practices of home, where gender, generation, and what I call the "sex life of TV" play a central role.

As the snapshots return in digital culture, analog TV and snapshot cameras are now residual media simultaneously, remediated by computers (but also through material practices in physical sites like vintage stores). By the last two decades of the twentieth century, the pairing of TV and snapshot cameras itself became a residual practice as new devices performed their function. In the 1980s, video cameras offered families a new tool for performing and imaging family life. The TV industry figured out a way to combine technologies of TV and cameras into one technological operation and practice that could be sold back to consumers. Based on the celluloid home-movie camera, home-video camcorders (when paired with a VCR) could be directly connected to a TV set. Now, rather than play accordions or pose in tutus in front of the set, people could watch themselves perform *on the screen in motion* and *with sound*. Not surprisingly, as with Kodak's still cameras before it, home video was marketed as a family medium. Family rituals and pleasures—weddings, birthdays, vacations, cute pet tricks—were the recommended repertoire.[2]

Nevertheless, as with the craft practices of snapshot photography, the home-video camera gave way to inventive uses. As Henry Jenkins demonstrates in his pathbreaking book *Textual Poachers* (1992), people used VCRs to make their own media, taping and reediting broadcast programs to create *slash* fiction. (Jenkins's book largely initiated fan studies, showing how fans, for example, recut TV's *Star Trek* to make Spock and Kirk into a homoerotic couple.) His later book, *Convergence Culture* (2006), explores relations between television, film, video, digital media, and other media platforms, focusing on the *transmedial* forms, popular practices, and user-generated content that spread virally across the internet.[3] By now, the field of convergence studies deals with a wide range of questions about industry, culture, technology, textuality, social media, and user-generated content. But it does not quite grasp the historical practices I have in mind here, which are centered around pairing devices (cameras and TV sets) that are not already designed to be connected or to afford such connection. For example, fans who made slash videotapes were using devices—the VCR and TV set—that the industry had already designed to be paired as component parts, even if the fans found novel ways to combine them. Similarly, people who make music videos or web series and post them online are taking advantage of, and often innovating on, the possibilities for media production, distribution, and reception that computers, digital cameras, and social media apps afford—and are often intentionally designed to afford—in concert with each other.

Today, in the context of digital photography, analog home-video cameras and VCRs have joined the stockpile of dinosaur technologies that give way to affective longing.[4] Some people post their home videos on YouTube, recalling their family video-making practices and the cameras and cassettes they used.[5] Early video games are now also memory objects on photo-share sites. As Alison Gazzard demonstrates, Flickr hosts a retro memory culture for gamers, who upload old snapshots of video games like *Pac-Man* as well as of themselves and their friends playing now defunct games in video arcades.[6]

As I tried to think of other versions of companion technologies, I considered, for example, how people used reel-to-reel audiotape recorders to record programs off TV (before the VCR) or how they paired TV sets with telephones (one of my father's favorite tinkering activities) to receive TV broadcast signals through a purely audio medium (effectively, turning TV back into a radio). But it seems to me that contemporary media industries have entirely colonized the companion technology concept, taking it from everyday practice and turning it into the logic of smart design. Now, mobile devices like iPhones and iPads turn telephones, video cameras, snapshot cameras, writing pads, typewriters, radios, TVs, and celluloid films (in the form of streamed media) into portable media ensembles. The Internet of Everything networks mobile technologies with home security systems, smart fridges, flat screen TVs, and more (much more!), while personal assistants like Alexa now promise to administer (or "housekeep") all these devices so that humans won't need to sort out the mess of their multiplying digital things. In this present-day configuration, companion technologies are orchestrated according to preprogrammed scenarios that predict protocols and repertoires of use. This does not mean that people can't hack or otherwise reimagine their devices, but it does suggest that *companion technologies* is a historical concept, more pertinent to the cultures of mechanical reproduction than to everyday life in smart times.

While home video, games, iPhone cameras, and selfies may be more familiar to today's digital natives, they did not entirely usurp the TV snapshot. People posed with their TV sets well into the 1990s. In 2014, Dutch curator Erik Kessels unearthed TV snapshots from the People's Republic of China (PRC) taken in the 1980s, when television became widely available in the PRC and a major feature of domestic space.[7] (Examples that appear on his blog show a woman using her TV set as a ritual backdrop for displaying her outfits.) Meanwhile, in the United States over the past few years, TV snapshots from the 1980s and 1990s have begun to accrue "vintage value" online, at flea markets, and in thrift stores. In these later iterations, the domestic décor and TV sets may have changed, but the practice of posing with TV continues. Even today, people post pictures of themselves in front of flat screens and computers. Many of these contemporary photos conform to genres of the past—dress-up poses, performance poses, baby pictures, and even a few trick shots, pinups, and porn shots.

Nevertheless, the photos don't just repeat the past. Many are performative reiterations that suggest historical twists and discontinuities across time. For example, photos on Pinterest collected on pin boards titled "My Messy Room" feature selfies of homes in disarray. Many depict television sets, computers, and mobile devices lost in piles of clothes, cheese doodles, empty pizza boxes, rumpled bedsheets, half-full makeup bottles, and other everyday things. They also picture media devices like TV sets and computers stacked on top of each other with wires dangled and exposed. While some of these photos are tagged as "before and after" pictures with tips for home improvement, others show people proudly posing with their media mess. In other words, unlike the midcentury snapshot, in contemporary selfies, media mess is no longer the low punctum, evoking the failure to live up to an ideal. Instead, the contemporary messy room photos revel in the hoard. While a handful of midcentury snapshots photographed mess around the TV in what appear to be carnivalesque portraits of things gone awry, now media clutter is a widespread meme and quotidian aesthetic articulated in the context of performative self-presentation online. In this sense, even if the practice of taking photos with a TV set (or other media devices) continues, the historical associations have changed.

As leftovers of a time once lived, TV snapshots offer new ways to explore everyday life in media homes. But as documents, snapshots are unreliable narrators. Despite their multitudes, the five thousand or so images I've collected are not a repository of all things done or all things felt. Snapshots present only that which was *speakable* with the postwar visual machines on which they were produced. As an archive of the everyday, TV snapshots remind us of the uncanny pursuit of media history itself—a history that, as Lisa Gitelman observes, is based on records of its own recording.[8] Still, archives are more than records. In the process of arranging my collection, the snapshots have become part of my inner life, my own archive of feelings. And perhaps this is why ending this book is such a *hard stop*.

Last night, after hours of working on my final chapter, I fell asleep and had a nightmare. In the dream, my friend stole one of my TV snapshots and said she planned to publish it in her own book. This enraged me. I told her I owned the photo, and she would have to delete it. But she said the photo could not be removed. This dream is no doubt related to the anxiety that comes when you are about to end a book and (at least in my case) the fear of having other people read it, as well as my sense that the entire thing has been a mistake. At the end of *Camera Lucida*, Barthes writes, "Photography is simple, banal; no depth: 'that has been.' I know our critics: What, a book (even a short one) to discover something I know at first glance?"[9] While I don't mean to compare my book to that brilliant text, I do take comfort in the anxiety of others.

On second thought, maybe my dream is about a troubled friendship (which I think it is). And maybe it is also about my relationships with the snapshots, and the people in them who have come to be my "friends." I am sad to finish because I am also ending these snapshot friendships (another meaning for *companion technologies*!). In any case, the emotion I attached to the dream was excessive, and I woke up feeling bad about myself. Why do I think I possess the photos? How do I own someone else's past? Was I a bad friend to the people posing in the snapshots? Did I say things they did not think or want me to say? And why couldn't the image/friend be deleted? Will the photos/friends I did not publish forgive me for consigning them to absence? Dreams, as Freud taught us, are always about remembering and forgetting via processes of displacement and condensation, as well as secondary revisions upon waking.[10] In digital archives, forgetting is built into the storage logics of computers, their means of rotating and deleting data to make room for the new. So, my anxiety dream may also be a dream about the archive—a fever dream—or as Derrida put it, "archive fever."

Inevitably, snapshots evoke the death of the people who posed for them. Midcentury snapshots are often sold at estate sales, where dealers buy them in lots for resale on the vintage market. At flea markets and in thrift stores, snapshots are tossed together in boxes and bins as if in mass graves with no tombstones. Carolyn Steedman argues that the archive is a place where historians form "intimacies" with the dead and fill in their stories. Intimacies may develop in all archival work, but when the dead are ordinary people who did not write or do things meant to be witnessed by others, these intimacies are fraught with complex questions regarding the relationship of the historian to her research subjects and the pursuit of speaking for the dead. Steedman is concerned with British archives, where she traces, for example, the largely unrecorded lives of domestic servants.[11] But my homemade do-it-yourself archive of TV snapshots raises similar questions of intimacy, memory, and death. Snapshots of smiling fathers, frilly prom gowns, stuffed sofas, and decorated TVs have an inherent melancholy to them. They picture other people's parents and other people's things to mourn by proxy. In a sense, the studium of the TV snapshot paradoxically becomes its punctum—it is the outworn fashions, habits of life, and clunky TVs that stir my emotion, that "pierce" me.

TV snapshots remind us of the end of a particular way of living with TV in midcentury culture. They mark the "that-has-been" of broadcast television. They track television's passage through time. In the contemporary moment of mobile technologies, multichannel networks, and streaming content, the antiquated objects and people in these snapshots attest to the accelerating decrepitude of a twentieth-century design for living that was organized around nuclear families and their living room TVs.

Even while I (and I would guess most readers) do not want to return to the past they picture, TV snapshots are haunting reminders of endings. But as found images made by anonymous picture takers, they ultimately haunt someone else's house. As I work with these snapshots, I often find myself angry at them for failing to tell me a truth I hope to find. Snapshots are confounding, annoying, and disruptive, and they usually refuse to respond to the questions I have. They are always promising to tell me something I want to know. But, in the end, they are also about the things they don't say; the stories they can't tell; the sounds they evoke but don't make. Even my own TV snapshot denies me. "Listening to images," as Tina Campt claims, is a way to hear the photograph's affective resonances, to make use of its silence.[12] Maybe it is partly because of their silence that TV snapshots have become a point of fascination for me and for others who share them, curate them, reappropriate them, and remake them. In their silence and stillness, the photographs offer ways to think about TV through alternative perspectives and orientations. As an archive of everyday life, TV snapshots make us look through the lens of someone else's camera and, thereby, see TV anew.

NOTES

INTRODUCTION

1 For cultural histories of media and technological innovation, see Marvin, *When Old Technologies Were New*; Gitelman, *Always Already New*; and S. J. Douglas, *Inventing American Broadcasting*. For early television at exhibitions, see Wheatley, *Spectacular Television*, 23–55; A.-K. Weber, "Television before TV"; and Bird, "From Fair to Family." For oral histories and memory, see O'Sullivan, "Television Memories and Cultures of Viewing"; Darian-Smith and Hamilton, "Part of the Family"; Penati, "Remembering Our First TV Set"; Swaim, "'Our Ticket to 1950s Culture'"; and Swaim, "When Television Entered the Iowa Household." Swaim's essays are oral histories, and the second essay includes snapshots of Iowa homes, hospitals, and rest homes featuring TV sets, all of which she found in the State Historical Society of Iowa collections.

2 Spigel, *Make Room for TV*.

3 The Bell and Howell studies are cited in Zimmermann, "Hollywood, Home Movies, and Common Sense," 28. See also Zimmermann, *Reel Families*. Richard Chalfen reports that by 1973 US households took 6.23 billion still pictures, and that in 1971 US households snapped an average of 77 pictures each. Chalfen, *Snapshot Versions of Life*, 13–14.

4 N. West, *Kodak through the Lens of Nostalgia*.

5 Goc, "Snapshot Photography," 41.

6 Bourdieu, *Photography*, 19.

7 Chalfen, *Snapshot Versions of Life*, 19.

8 TV snapshots fall into four broad, although not always exclusive, catego-

ries: (1) demonstrative shots where TV is the specific subject of the image; (2) poses where people use TV sets as a theatrical backdrop and a ritual setting for picture taking; (3) shots in which the TV set is not necessarily the focus of attention; and (4) hobby art photos (as with TV trick shots or screenshots).

9   Barthes, *Camera Lucida*. Barthes argues against the scientific study of "amateur photographs, dealt with by a team of sociologists; nothing but the trace of a social protocol of integration intended to reassure the Family" (7). Although he does not name Pierre Bourdieu, Barthes is likely referring to him.

10 See, Barthes's discussion in *Camera Lucida*, 76–80, 92–96.

11 Barthes, *Camera Lucida*, 26.

12 Barthes, *Camera Lucida*, 27.

13 Spence and Holland, *Family Snaps*; Kuhn, *Family Secrets*; Hirsch, *Family Frames*.

14 Butler, *Gender Trouble*.

15 Brown and Davidmann, "'Queering the Trans* Family Album,'" 188.

16 For a recent anthology that brings together some of the best scholarship on vernacular photos and gives a sense of the history of this scholarship and its archives, see Campt et al., *Imagining Everyday Life*.

17 Hirsch, "Introduction," xvi.

18 Rose, *Doing Family Photography*, 8. See also Tinkler, "'Picture Me as a Young Woman,'" 279.

19 Advertisement cited in Buse, *Camera Does the Rest*, loc. 1976 of 6829, Kindle. Polaroid initially aimed its cameras at the "well-heeled" consumer (loc. 786 of 6829). This changed, particularly with the introduction of the inexpensive Polaroid Swinger in 1965.

20 Buse, *Camera Does the Rest*, loc. 532 of 6829.

21 Eastman Kodak, *How to Make Good Pictures* (1951–52), 189–94, 214, 200, 209, 211.

22 The contest was promoted and broadcast on a 1949 episode of the DuMont Network's *Photographic Horizons* (I return to this program in chapter 4).

23 For more on the design and logic of the exhibition, see Turner, *Democratic Surround*, 181–212.

24 The CBS documentary was an episode of the public affairs program *Adventure* (broadcast June 19, 1955). The book remains MoMA's most popular publication ever, with more than three hundred thousand copies sold as of 2015. David Gonzalez, "'The Family of Man' Reunion," *Lens* (blog), October 29, 2015, https://lens.blogs.nytimes.com/2015/10/29/a-family-of-man-reunion/. For the book, see Steichen, *Family of Man*.

25 In 1956, Roland Barthes wrote a scathing critique of the Parisian (traveling) version of the exhibition. See Barthes, "Great Family of Man," 100–102. For more critiques (and history of the criticism) of the show, see Sekula, "Traffic in Photographs"; Hirsch, *Family Frames*, 48–69; Turner, *Democratic Surround*, 181–212; and Hurm, Reitz, and Zamir, *Family of Man Revisited*.

26 Willis, *Picturing Us*.

27 Willis, *Picturing Us*; Willis, "Search for Self," 108.

28 hooks, "In Our Glory," 57.

29 hooks, "In Our Glory," 62.

30 Hall, "Reconstruction Work," 156. Originally in *Ten 8*, no. 16 (1984): n.p.

31 Hall outlines the concept of articulation in "Encoding and Decoding in Television Discourse," Centre for Contemporary Cultural Studies (CCCS), paper no. 7, 1973, excerpted and reprinted in Hall et al., *Culture, Media, Language*, 117–27. For more on Hall's concept of articulation, see Slack, "Theory and Method of Articulation in Cultural Studies."

32 DeCarava and Hughes, *Sweet Flypaper of Life*.

33 African American newspapers like the *New York Amsterdam News*, the *Los Angeles Sentinel*, and the *Chicago Defender* often featured articles about photography as well as amateur photography contests (some sponsored by Kodak and Polaroid). Ads for Kodaks and Polaroids in *Ebony* were designed for the African American market, with Black faces and bodies, making picture taking an especially relevant visual medium for Black publics, one that featured them as the subject image. (Polaroid ads in *Ebony* began to appear in the late 1950s. The first Kodak ad I found in *Ebony* appeared in the May 1964 issue.)

34 hooks, "In Our Glory," 59.

35 Berger, *Understanding a Photograph*, 292.

36 As proposed by science and technology studies (STS), especially Bruno Latour, and scholars such as Michel Callon and John Law, actor-network theory explores how social worlds are created through feedback chains between humans and nonhumans. Actor-network theory affords objects nonhuman agency in this equation so that humans are not the sole determining influence over the built or natural environment. The term *affordance* (which I use in this book) suggests that objects allow for (but don't entirely determine) human actions. So, for example, a television set might be watched, but it might also be used as a backdrop for a pose. Latour, *Reassembling the Social*.

37 S. M. Smith, *Photography on the Color Line*.

38 Many photos have dates stamped on borders or backs. In cases where no dates appear, I have used a combination of methods for dating, including the paper types; color versus black-and-white; edges (for example, deckled edges were popular in the 1940s through the early 1960s); and content in the image (such as fashions, décor, TV set models, etc.). I've also relied on people with more expertise in this area for opinions.

39 Note that funny sayings were often highly conventional. Kodak manuals even recommended captions (or "titles to tease your imagination") that people could write in their albums. See Eastman Kodak, *How to Make Good Pictures* (1951–52), 199.

40 See, for example, photographer Oliver Wasow's *Artist Unknown* series, which organizes found snapshots (picturing all kinds of things) into subject matter like "Fights," "Hair," and (most relevant to me) "Go Over There by the TV." See

Artist Unknown, Oliver Wasow website, accessed June 30, 2021, https://oliver
wasow.com/series/138/224/series_works/list?view_a11=1.

41 Hillis, Petit, and Epley, *Everyday eBay*. Also see Michele White, *Buy It Now*.

42 Campt, *Image Matters*.

43 Browne, *Dark Matters*.

44 It is difficult to judge how many TV snapshots were made in the 1970s and
after. Because the snapshots from the 1950s and 1960s are considered *vintage*
(and, therefore, bring in higher prices), most dealers have begun to sell ones
from later decades only recently.

45 Derrida, *Archive Fever*, 3.

46 D. Miller, *Comfort of Things*.

47 Edwards and Hart, *Photographs, Objects, Histories*; Olin, *Touching Photographs*; Pinney, *Camera Indica*.

48 Cvetkovich, *Archive of Feelings*.

49 Cvetkovich, "Photographing Objects as Queer Archival Practice," loc.
5712–6220 of 9316, Kindle.

50 For a range of perspectives, see Gregg and Seigworth, *Affect Theory Reader*.

51 K. Stewart, *Ordinary Affects*, p. 1 of 130, Kindle.

52 K. Stewart, *Ordinary Affects*, p. 2 of 130, Kindle. Stewart places herself between
Williams's materialist concept and the Deleuzian inflections on the term *affect*.

53 K. Stewart, *Ordinary Affects*, p. 3 of 130, Kindle.

54 K. Stewart, *Ordinary Affects*, p. 5 of 130, Kindle.

55 Lefebvre, *Critique of Everyday Life*, vol. 1.

56 de Certeau, *Practice of Everyday Life*; Edwards and Hart, *Photographs, Objects,
Histories*, 6.

57 R. Williams, *Television*.

58 Morley, *Family Television*; Silverstone, *Television and Everyday Life*; Gauntlett
and Hill, *TV Living*. For more, see Gillespie, *Television, Ethnicity, and Cultural
Change*; Lull, *Inside Family Viewing*; Moores, *Satellite Television and Everyday
Life*; and Mankekar, *Screening Culture, Viewing Politics*.

59 Modleski, "Rhythms of Reception"; Brunsdon, *The Feminist, the Housewife,
and the Soap Opera*; Hobson, *Soap Opera*; Geraghty, *Women and Soap Opera*;
Cassidy, *What Women Watched*; Levine, *Her Stories*.

60 Pascucci, "Intimate Televisions," 52–54; Villarejo, *Ethereal Queer*; Q. Miller,
Camp TV; Needham, "Scheduling Normativity"; R. Becker, *Gay TV and
Straight America*; Joyrich, "Epistemology of the Console"; Joyrich, "Queer
Television Studies"; McCarthy, "*Ellen*."

61 Kavka, *Reality Television, Affect, and Intimacy*; Bonner, *Ordinary Television*;
Ouellette, *Lifestyle TV*; Gates, "Activating the Negative Image"; B. R. Weber,
Makeover TV; duCille, *Technicolored*; Mimi White, "'A House Divided'";
Holdsworth and Lury, "Growing Up and Growing Old with Television"; Holds-
worth, *On Living with Television*.

62 Ben Highmore discusses related methodological issues in his edited collection
Everyday Life Reader, 1.

1 N. R. Kleinfield, "The Lonely Death of George Bell," *New York Times*, October 17, 2015. The story was a finalist for the Pulitzer Prize. I am describing the story in the digital version of the *New York Times*; the print version has additional photos.

2 Caption for photo in Kleinfield, "Lonely Death of George Bell," 1.

3 M. Douglas, *Purity and Danger*. Note that metaphors of dirt are often applied to TV. See A. West, "Reality Television and the Power of Dirt."

4 Perich, *Changing Face of Portrait Photography*, 35.

5 Chalfen, *Snapshot Versions of Life*, 89 and 94.

6 Veblen, *Theory of the Leisure Class*.

7 Harry Henderson, "Rugged American Collectivism, *The Mass-Produced Suburbs*, Part II," *Harpers*, December 1953, 80; Riesman, *Lonely Crowd*; Whyte, *Organization Man*.

8 Eastman Kodak, *How to Make Good Pictures* (1951–52), 77.

9 Sylvester L. (Pat) Weaver, "The Task Ahead: Making TV the 'Shining Center of the Home' and Helping Create a New Society of Adults," *Variety*, January 6, 1954, 91.

10 Olofsson, "Revisiting the TV Object"; Roth-Ey, "Finding a Home for Television in the USSR"; Perry, "Healthy for Family Life"; Varela, *La televisión criolla*; Wheatley, *Spectacular Television*, 23–55; O'Sullivan, "Television Memories and Cultures of Viewing"; Silverstone, *Television and Everyday Life*; Rivero, *Broadcasting Modernity*; Kumar, *Gandhi Meets Primetime*, 55–70; Penati, "'Remembering Our First TV Set'"; Yoshimi, "'Made in Japan.'"

11 When analyzing snapshots, it's often hard to know if the set is new. But the types and dates of the snapshots, combined with the models of the TV sets, suggest that TV was a relatively recent addition to the home in the earliest photos. For summaries of statistics on TV's penetration into homes, see Spigel, *Make Room for TV*, 189. For similar reports on portable TV, see Spigel, "Portable TV," 97. For color TV, see Murray, *Bright Signals*, 183.

12 For surveys and popular press accounts, see Spigel, *Make Room for TV*, 127–28.

13 Vanderbilt, *Complete Book of Etiquette*, 294–95.

14 *Kodakery*, April 1915, 18; *Kodakery*, July 1915, 5; *Kodakery*, October 1915, cover; Eastman Kodak, *How to Make Good Pictures* (1922), 22, 71, 75; Eastman Kodak, *How to Make Good Pictures* (1951–52), 17, 78, 142, 144–45.

15 I searched for ads through each issue of *Ebony* from 1946 to 1970. The first ads I found are from 1952. See, for example, advertisements for Motorola TV, May 1952, 31; RCA Victor TV, August 1953, 3; Sylvania TV, May 1954, 21; RCA Victor TV, March 1955, 47; Sony Portable TV, October 1961, 6; and RCA Color TV, October 1963, 33.

16 For local TV, see Forman, *One Night on TV*, 249–72. Polaroid sponsored Howard's program (253).

17 Cab Calloway, "Here's What Cab Thinks About . . . ," *New York Amsterdam News*, July 1, 1950, 26.

18 For histories of African Americans and TV in the 1950s and 1960s, see, for example, Bogle, *Primetime Blues*; Bodroghkozy, *Equal Time*; Acham, *Revolution Televised*; McDonald, *Blacks and White TV*; Torres, *Black, White, and in Color*; and Classen, *Watching Jim Crow*. For a pathbreaking study that considers the later years of the network system (especially the 1980s and 1990s) and "post–civil rights" era TV, see H. Gray, *Reading Race*.

19 For *Amos 'n' Andy*, see Cripps, "*Amos 'n' Andy* and the Debate over American Racial Integration"; and Bogle, *Primetime Blues*, 26–42. For *Beulah*, see Bogle, *Primetime Blues*, 19–26; and Bodroghkozy, *Equal Time*, 25–37.

20 Alvin Chick Webb's "Jim Crow" column ran from November to December 1954.

21 In March 1965, in response to the police brutality at the march in Selma, Alabama, Martin Luther King Jr. told protesters and TV news reporters, "We are here to say to the white man we no longer will let them use clubs on us in the dark corners. We are going to make them do it in the glaring light of television." Quoted in Bodroghkozy, *Equal Time*, 2.

22 For civil rights protests against TV, see especially Bodroghkozy, *Equal Time*; Acham, *Revolution Televised*; Torres, *Black, White, and in Color*; Classen, *Watching Jim Crow*; Tahmahkera, *Tribal Television*; Noriega, *Shot in America*; and Perlman, *Public Interests*. For histories of local television and communities of color, see, for example, Wald, *It's Been Beautiful*; Heitner, *Black Power TV*; and Thompson, Jones, and Hatlen, *Television History, the Peabody Archive, and Cultural Memory*; M. Williams, "Strains of Orientalism in Early Los Angeles Television."

23 Bourdieu, *Distinction*.

24 De Certeau, "Spatial Stories."

25 "A Dissection of Cyclops . . . His Pathology . . . His Habitat . . . Anatomy . . . and Kin," *Interiors*, July 1951, 62. In the same issue, see "Cyclops: The Nature of a New Household Pet," 61; and "How Cyclops Is Domesticated," 74. These articles have no credited authors.

26 Spark, *As Long as It's Pink*; Nelson and Wright, *Tomorrow's House*.

27 Nelson and Wright, *Tomorrow's House*. For my discussion of the storagewall, see Spigel, "Object Lessons for the Media Home."

28 For an example, see *Practical Encyclopedia*, 1:37. For more see Spigel, "Object Lessons for the Media Home," 545–54.

29 Olofsson, "Revisiting the TV Object"; Ureta, "'There Is One in Every Home'"; K. M. Smith, "Domesticating Television"; Wheatley, *Spectacular Television*, 53; Darian-Smith and Hamilton, "Part of the Family," 39.

30 Spigel, "Media Clutter," *Harvard Design Magazine*, Winter 2017, n.p.

31 De Certeau, *Practice of Everyday Life*, 29–42.

32 Motorola created an annual chart that indicated how each year's models would blend with popular furniture styles. See Lavin, "TV Design."

33 Lefebvre, *Production of Space*, 87, 154, 191.

34 Lefebvre, *Production of Space*, 192–93.

35 De Certeau, *Practice of Everyday Life*, especially 91–110 and 114–30.

36 Jenkins, *Textual Poachers*; For video game play, see Newman, *Atari Age*.

37 Goc ("Snapshot Photography") argues that Kodak encouraged mothers to take candid shots with children in soiled pinafores or overalls as well as their Sunday best. But, I would argue, Kodak suggested a system of socially sanctioned, or "cute," dirt for children that was not the same as the disordered mess in some TV snapshots.

38 Cvetkovich, "Photographing Objects as Queer Archival Practice," loc. 5989 of 9316, Kindle.

39 Ahmed, *Queer Phenomenology*, 40–41.

40 Cowan, *More Work for Mother*.

41 Spigel, *Make Room for TV*, chapter 3, "Women's Work," 73–98. Note that industry executives and advertisers worried that daily chores would make it difficult for housewives to watch TV. In response, NBC devised program types with segmented "magazine" formats like the *Today Show* (1952–present) and *Home* (1954–57), which allowed women to watch in discrete intervals while doing their housework. For more, see Cassidy, *What Women Watched*.

42 For more on gender and early home video, see A. Gray, *Video Playtime*.

43 In a few cases, the reverse is true. For example, sometimes new hi-fis seem to displace the old TV that sits in the corner of a room.

44 Leal, "Popular Taste and Erudite Repertoire"; McCarthy, *Ambient Television*, 128; McCarthy, "From Screen to Site."

45 Cartoonist Bradford, "Still Life Photography as an Outlet for Your Artistry," *Kodakery*, March 1922, 11. *Kodakery* was aimed at amateur photographers, and the still life instructions are therefore offered in that context.

46 Eastman Kodak, *How to Make Good Pictures* (1951–52), 184–85.

47 Bryson, *Looking at the Overlooked*, loc. 51 of 3169, Kindle. I am vastly condensing Bryson's genealogy of the modern still life and its development from the xenia. He observes that the theatricality of the form is evident before the seventeenth-century Dutch examples.

48 Walker Evans cited in Jonathan Blaustein, "Lee Friedlander's Photos of 1960s T.V. Sets," *New York Times*, July 3, 2017.

49 Goc, "Snapshot Photography," 27. Chalfen, *Snapshot Versions of Life*, 75–77, claims that the two biggest events that sparked the purchase of a camera were the birth of a baby and taking a vacation.

50 Leslie, introduction to *Walter Benjamin*, loc. 55 of 1844, Kindle. For the essay in which Benjamin discusses this, see Benjamin, *Berlin Childhood around 1900*, 131–32. Benjamin makes a similar analogy in "Small History of Photography," in Leslie, *Walter Benjamin*, loc. 809–1353 of 1844, Kindle.

51 Barthes, *Camera Lucida*, 14.

52 Feminist critics and historians have considered how family photographs

divert from the family romance. See, for example, Spence and Holland, *Family Snaps*; Kuhn, *Family Secrets*; and Hirsch, *Family Frames*.

53 Olin, *Touching Photographs*.

54 Campt, *Image Matters*, loc. 1763 of 4191, Kindle.

55 Rose, "Family Photographs and Domestic Spacings."

56 I am borrowing Bruno Latour's term. See his *Reassembling the Social*.

CHAPTER TWO. TV PERFORMERS

1 Over the years, Kodak partnered with other family-friendly T V performers including Ed Sullivan, Dick Van Dyke, Elizabeth Montgomery, Bill Cosby, and Betty White.

2 Foote, "Family Living as Play," 297, 299.

3 Bateson, "Theory of Play and Fantasy," 185.

4 Goffman, *Presentation of Self in Everyday Life*.

5 For dramaturgical approaches to digital culture, see, for example, Markham, "Dramaturgy of Digital Experience"; and Gottschalk and Whitmer, "Hypermodern Dramaturgy in Online Encounters."

6 See, for example, *Kodakery*, April 1915, 18; *Kodakery*, July 1915, 5; *Kodakery*, October 1915, cover; Eastman Kodak, *How to Make Good Pictures* (1922), 22, 71, 75; Bailey, *Indoor Photography*, 92; and Eastman Kodak, *How to Make Good Pictures* (1951–52), 17, 78, 142, 144–45.

7 Barthes, *Camera Lucida*, 10.

8 For discussions of the "window on the world" metaphor, see Spigel, *Make Room for T V*, 95–132 and 168–69; and Friedberg, *Window Shopping*. For T V as hearth, see Tichi, *Electronic Hearth*, 42–61; Spigel, *Make Room for T V*, 38; K. M. Smith, "Domesticating Television," 30; and (for radio) Frith, "Pleasures of the Hearth."

9 D. Miller, *Stuff*, 50–51.

10 I am applying Miller's language. See D. Miller, *Stuff*, 50–51.

11 *Magic circle* is a term coined by Johan Huizinga in *Homo Ludens*. It is often used in accounts of video games.

12 Foucault, "Of Other Spaces." Foucault distinguishes the unlocatable space of utopia from the actually existing locatable heterotopia, but he sees the mirror as a "mixed experience of both." The mirror "is after all, a utopia, in that it is a place without a place. In it, I see myself where I am not, in an unreal space that opens up potentially beyond its surface; there I am down there where I am not, a sort of shadow that makes my appearance visible to myself, allowing me to look at myself where I do not exist: utopia of the mirror. At the same time, we are dealing with a heterotopia. The mirror really exists and has a kind of come-back effect on the place that I occupy: starting from it, in fact. I find myself absent from the place where I am, in that I see myself in there" (352).

13 Note in this regard, at midcentury, T V was often likened to a mirror, and

during the 1930s and 40s some of the earliest TV sets for home use were designed with mirror projection.

14 Zimmermann, *Reel Families*.

15 Robert E. Smallman, "Sequence Tells the Story," *Popular Photography*, September 1950, 48.

16 John Durniak, "10 Stories around You," *Popular Photography*, June 1959, 73.

17 Durniak, "10 Stories around You," 119.

18 For an oft-cited book that deals especially with television and the "meditization" of live performance, see Auslander, *Liveness*. For his more recent discussion, see Auslander, *Reactivations*.

19 D. Taylor, *Archive and the Repertoire*; Derrida, "Signature Event Context."

20 For hi-fi or hi-fi/TV combination ads in *Ebony*, see, for example, Olympic Radio and Television, *Ebony*, 123; RCA ad, *Ebony*, November 1963, 99; and RCA ad, *Ebony*, December 1963, 51.

21 See Han, *Beyond the Black and White TV*.

22 For example, when Asian and Latinx variety show performers engaged in code switching, viewers who understood those codes likely understood the performances as insider references to their cultural heritage and not just through their stereotyped portrayals. See Han, *Beyond the Black and White TV*.

23 duCille, *Technicolored*, loc. 1431 of 9160, Kindle.

24 Delmont, *Nicest Kids in Town*.

25 Tim Reid and Patricia Turner make these comments in on-camera interviews in Marlon Riggs's 1992 film *Color Adjustment* (New York: Signifyin' Works).

26 See, for example, Sanison, *How to Behave and How to Amuse*, 155.

27 Barthes, *Camera Lucida*, 32.

28 S. C. Gilfillan, "The Future Home Theater," *Independent*, October 17, 1912, 836–91. For more on the home theater, see Spigel, "The Home Theater," in *Make Room for TV*, 99–135.

29 For histories and theories of TV liveness, see Boddy, *Fifties Television*; Feuer, "Concept of Live Television"; Scannell, *Television and the Meaning of Live*; Bourdon, "Live Television Is Still Alive"; and Auslander, *Liveness*.

30 I discuss such ads in *Make Room for TV*, chapter 4. This particular ad recalls early twentieth-century ads for the RCA Victrola with Nipper the dog, who faithfully listened to "his master's voice." Lisa Gitelman claims the advertisement depicted the relationship between the "real" and the "live." Gitelman, *Always Already New*, 80–81.

31 Scannell, *Radio, Television, and Modern Life*, 75–93.

32 Newbold, "'History as It's Made'"; Spigel, "Our TV Heritage," 89.

33 Edward B. Arthur, "Cover the Convention from Your Home," *Popular Photography*, July 1960, 71–73 and 115–16. See also "TV's Images Can Be Photographed," *Popular Science*, August 1950, 184–86; George Gilbert, "Armchair Photography," *Popular Photography*, January 1954, 54–55; R. P. Stevenson, "How You Can Photograph the Fights via Television," *Popular Science*, Feb-

ruary 1951, 214–17; Sussman, *Amateur Photographer's Handbook*, 135; and Ed Corley, "Try Filming TV!" *Popular Photography*, November 1963, 183, 196.

34 D. Taylor, *Archive and the Repertoire*, p. 255 of 279, Kindle.

35 Iversen, "Following Pieces," p. 93 of 470, Kindle.

36 Iversen, "Following Pieces," p. 97 of 470, Kindle.

37 Iversen, "Following Pieces," p. 93 of 470, Kindle.

38 Discussing the "performativity of performance documentation," Auslander considers both performance art and the popular practice of karaoke (which, I think, is closer to the TV screenshots). See *Reactivations*.

39 German cameras were typically more advanced technologically, and the sharp image likely has to do with that.

40 Barthes, *Camera Lucida*, 13–14.

41 Barthes, *Camera Lucida*, 92.

42 Benjamin, remembering his childhood terror in the photography studio, conjures up a hellish death scene, saying it was "like both a boudoir and a torture chamber" whose "screens, cushions, and pedestals . . . craved my image much as the shades of Hades craved the blood of a sacrificial animal"; *Berlin Childhood around 1900*, 131–32. André Bazin writes of the "phantomlike" shadows in family albums and argues, "Photography does not create eternity, as art does, it embalms time, rescuing it simply from its proper corruption." Bazin, "Ontology of the Photographic Image," 14. Susan Sontag claims that the "link between photography and death haunts all photographs of people," and she likens photographs to a "death mask." In Sontag's *On Photography*, p. 70 and 154 of 209, Kindle.

43 When photos are faded, their ghost-like look is likely more pronounced today than in the past.

44 "Christmas Greeting Cards with Your Camera," *Popular Photography*, December 1950, 47.

45 Pringle, "Scampering Sofas," 232.

46 Pringle, "Scampering Sofas," 235–37. Film historians will think of Méliès's trick films, but Pringle argues that Méliès follows the tradition of still trick photography, and she thinks the Chomón example is more apt because of its use of stop motion to make objects appear alive (236). The trope of "entertaining interiors" continues in cinema, for example, in the films of Buster Keaton (particularly those set in houses such as his 1922 film *The Electric House*).

47 When speaking about the mobility of furniture, Pringle relies on the seminal study by Sigfried Giedion, *Mechanization Takes Command*. She also cites stories about furniture gone awry. See "Scampering Sofas," 224–29.

48 Tom Gunning discusses this in "Phantom Images." For more on the history of trick photography, see Fineman, *Faking It*.

49 Westinghouse ad, "No More Tuning," *Saturday Evening Post*, February 8, 1958, 67; RCA TV, "RCA Laboratories—Your 'Magic Carpet,'" *Life*, October 27, 1947, 63; Farnsworth TV, "Tomorrow You'll Broadcast Magic!" (1943); and

Farnsworth TV, "Prince Ali's Magic Tube Comes True!" (1944). Both Farnsworth ads at Ad Access, John W. Hartman Center for Sales Advertising and Marketing History, Duke University, Durham, NC, accessed July 2, 2021, https://repository.duke.edu/dc/adaccess?f%5Bproduct_facet_sim%5D%5B %5D=Television.

50 Freud offers two explanations for the uncanny. The uncanny can be traced to the fear of women, castration, and the return of the repressed. It can also be traced to animistic views of magic. Freud, *Uncanny*.

51 Parks, "Cracking Open the Set." Parks connects the discourses on TV repairmen to gender and sexuality, a point to which I return in chapter 4.

52 Hertzberg, *Handy Man's TV Repair and Maintenance*, 17.

53 Gunning, review of *Photography and Spirit*, 128. For more on spirit photography, see Gunning, "Phantom Images"; Ferris, *Disembodied Spirit*; Gunning, "Uncanny Reflections"; Harvey, *Photography and Spirit*; Chéroux et al., *Perfect Medium*; Gunning, "To Scan a Ghost"; N. West, *Kodak through the Lens of Nostalgia*, 148–53; and Cadwallader, "Spirit Photography."

54 Mason and Mitchell, *Party Games for All*, 89.

55 Eastman Kodak, *How to Make Good Pictures* (1951–52), 186.

56 Sconce, *Haunted Media*.

57 Freud (*Uncanny*) argues that when the animation of inanimate things is comic, it no longer is uncanny.

CHAPTER THREE. TV DRESS-UP

1 "Clothes for TV Watching," *Life*, January 29, 1951, 80–81.

2 Virginia Williams, "At Home Fashions for Christmas," *Cosmopolitan*, December 1951, 23; "At-Home Clothes for Television at Home," *Women's Wear Daily*, April 21, 1949, 3.

3 TV dress-up can be viewed as an extension of women's sartorial displays at early movie theaters. See Stamp, *Movie Struck Girls*, 24–40. Stamp cites a trade ad for "Photo-Machines" for movie theater lobbies. The ad showed women taking pictures of themselves (36). For more on this machine, see Buszek, *Pin-Up Grrrls*, loc. 2992–3022 of 7470, Kindle.

4 I discuss these sorts of ads, jokes, and cartoons in Spigel, *Make Room for TV*, 119–27.

5 Stockton Helffrich cited in Mel Hammer, "What You Can't See on Television: Interview with Stockton Helffrich," *Cosmopolitan*, December 1957, 59. The Continuity Department was in charge of censorship.

6 C. Becker, *It's the Pictures That Got Small*, 69–104. For more on Emerson in relation to her political and feminist contributions, see Mauk, "Politics Is Everybody's Business."

7 Spigel, *Make Room for TV*, 84.

8 Mary Tyler Moore cited in Yohana Desta, "How Mary Tyler Moore Subverted TV Sexism with a Pair of Capris," *Vanity Fair*, January 25, 2017.

9   Madelyn Martin cited in Betty Friedan, "Television and the Feminine Mystique," part 1, *TV Guide*, January 24, 1964, 9–10. Martin was also known as Pugh.

10   C. Becker, *It's the Pictures That Got Small*; Mann, "Spectacularization of Everyday Life"; Doty, "Cabinet of Lucy Ricardo"; Desjardins, *Recycled Stars*. For more contemporary TV and fashion, see Warner, *Fashion on Television*.

11   N. West, *Kodak through the Lens of Nostalgia*, especially 109–35.

12   In 1928, Kodak marketed a "vanity" camera created by industrial designer Walter Dorwin Teague and made to look like a woman's purse.

13   N. West, *Kodak through the Lens of Nostalgia*, 126.

14   E. H. Brown, *Work!*, 201.

15   "Model Mothers," *Life*, May 22, 1944, cited in E. Brown, *Work!*, 201.

16   "Casual Clothes for Suburbia U.S.A.," *Vogue Pattern Book*, October–November 1958, 30–35.

17   "Mrs. Exeter Likes . . . ," *Vogue Pattern Book*, October–November 1958, 36–44.

18   De Certeau, *Practice of Everyday Life*, 29–44.

19   Wissinger, *This Year's Model*, 3.

20   McDowell, "'I Know I Am Posing.'"

21   Thrift, "Understanding the Material Aspects of Glamour," p. 297 of 402, Kindle.

22   Kennedy, *House and the Art of Its Design*, 42.

23   Ads for portable TV sets engaged tropes of sexual liberation, and models in these ads wore clothing that signified "new woman" sexuality—everything from capri pants to go-go boots. See Spigel, "Portable TV."

24   Modern chairs like this one were often used in women's fashion magazines and in men's magazines like *Playboy* as a means of accentuating the female form.

25   Sally Berry and Ruth Murrin, "How to Pose for a Snapshot," *Good Housekeeping*, June 1946, 63.

26   "How to Look Like a *Seventeen* Model," *Seventeen*, June 1958, 42.

27   E. H. Brown, *Work!*, 108.

28   See Eckert, "Carole Lombard in Macy's Window."

29   For an online archive of Hollywood star sewing patterns, see "Movie Stars," Vintage Patterns Wikia, accessed July 2, 2021, https://vintagepatterns.fandom .com/wiki/Category:Movie_Stars. For discussion of such sewing patterns, see Gaines and Herzog, *Fabrications*, 75, 82; and Moseley, "Respectability Sewn Up." For Lucy merchandise, see Landay, "Millions 'Love Lucy.'"

30   Dyer, *Stars*.

31   The plural "everydays" is in the original. *Photoplay*, January 1941, 48–49.

32   "All Dressed Up . . . to Stay Home," *Screenland*, November 1954, 48–50.

33   Gladys Hall, "Bill Cullen: The Man Who Has Everything," *Radio TV Mirror*, December 1956, 36–39; "Link's Silver Jubilee," *Radio TV Mirror*, July 1958, 30–32; Marie Haller, "I'm Glad I Waited," *Radio TV Mirror*, October 1956, 47.

34   During the Depression and through the 1960s, dime stores like Woolworths sold picture frames and wallets that came with signed celebrity headshots

inside. These objects inspired consumers to think about glamour photos as interchangeable (and easy to replace) with their own snapshots. They turned glamour images into tactile things, literally items within an average woman's reach.

35   Stacey, *Star Gazes*, chapter 5; see especially 126–27, 148.
36   Rooks, *Ladies' Pages*. Rooks traces this history from *Ringwood's Afro American Journal of Fashion* (1891–94) through to modern magazines. For "the politics of respectability," see Higginbotham, *Righteous Discontent*.
37   M. E. Williams, "'Crisis' Cover Girl," 206.
38   See, for example, "A Symphony in Fashions," *Ebony*, October 1960, 125–30; "Ebony Fashion Fair Beauties," *Ebony*, October 1961, 119–22; and "Fashion Fair: First Look at New Swimsuits '62," *Ebony*, January 1962, 107–9.
39   For postwar Black modeling agencies , see E. H. Brown, *Work!*, chapter 4, 163–211. For a detailed history of Black marketing in the postwar period, see Chambers, *Madison Avenue and the Color Line*.
40   Exploring *Ebony*'s cover stories of Lena Horne, Megan E. Williams claims they reflected "the magazine's desire to expose an interracial readership to images of a sexy, yet respectable, vision of black upward mobility during the postwar period." M. E. Williams, "'Meet the Real Lena Horne,'" 130.
41   *Jet*, September 71, 1953, cover.
42   For debates on sexuality and race in the magazines, and for readers' letters to the editor on this topic, see M. E. Williams, "'Crisis' Cover Girl"; M. E. Williams, "'Meet the Real Lena Horne'"; and Meyerowitz, "Women, Cheesecake, and Borderline Material," 18–21. Examining letters to the editors of *Ebony* and *Negro Digest* published between 1946 and 1957, Meyerowitz finds that while many readers thought pinups perpetuated racist stereotypes, other readers praised pinups for their ability to demonstrate Black women's beauty in the context of their exclusions from mass media and white beauty culture. For more on African American pinups, see Buszek, *Pin-Up Grrrls*, loc. 4089–4167 of 7470, Kindle.
43   "Backstage," *Ebony*, May 1946, 4.
44   For histories of network TV and African American women, see, for example, Bogle, *Primetime Blues*; Bodroghkozy, *Equal Time*; and Acham, *Revolution Televised*.
45   See Han, *Beyond the Black and White TV*, 96–103.
46   For more on this and other sitcom episodes featuring Asian characters, see Phruksachart, "The Asian American Next Door." For more on Asian women on early TV (especially his discussion of the Korean Kim Sisters' appearances on variety shows), see Han, *Beyond the Black and White TV*, p. 43–73, Kindle.
47   The 1958 Rodgers and Hammerstein Broadway version of *The Flower Drum Song* was based on the 1957 novel of the same name by Chinese American author C. Y. Lee. The 1961 film adaptation was directed by Henry Koster.
48   Kim, "'Serving' American Orientalism."

49 Bodroghkozy, "'Is This What You Mean by Color TV?'"; Acham, *Revolution Televised*, 110–26.

50 Carroll was one among several women of color who found jobs in early television via glamour labor—not only as models but also as makeup artists and costume sewers. Carroll modeled for *Ebony* at the age of fifteen. In 1954, at the age of eighteen, she made her TV debut in the amateur talent show *Chance of a Lifetime* (ABC, 1952–53; DuMont, 1953–55).

51 Cover, *Ebony*, July 1962.

52 Hollywood costume designer William Travilla, when recalling the costumes he created for *Julia*, said, "In the first place, Julia [is] supposed to sew her own clothes. Scenes have been arranged showing her doing so." In other words, the storylines presented Julia's everyday glamour labor as part of the show. William Travilla cited in *"Julia*: Diahann Carroll in Summer of 1968," *50 Years of Film and Fashion Travilla Style* (blog), February 9, 2013, http://travillastyle .blogspot.com/2013/02/julia-diahann-carroll-in-summer-of-1968.html.

53 Diahann Carroll cited in Richard Warren Lewis, "The Importance of Being Julia," *TV Guide*, December 14, 1968, 24–28. For more see Acham, *Revolution Televised*, 110–26.

54 hooks, "In Our Glory," 57, 60.

55 Stacey, *Star Gazing*, 224.

56 Wilson, *Adorned in Dreams*, 260.

57 Butler, *Gender Trouble*. Also see Butler, *Bodies That Matter*.

58 Entwistle, *Fashioned Body*, xxii.

59 I am borrowing Modleski's term in "Rhythms of Reception."

60 Lefebvre discusses the home and women's culture in various places in his first two volumes of *Critique of Everyday Life*. In volume 2, he lashes out at the postwar "re-privatization" of everyday life, and he critiques consumer technologies like "television sets and refrigerators," which he associates with passivity, boredom, and what he calls "empty time" (75). Elsewhere in the same volume, he talks of the "monotonous" and "mind numbing nature of housework" (222) and critiques women's everyday life alongside feminism and the women's press (80–90).

61 Felski, *Doing Time*, p. 85 of 216, Kindle.

62 While I have found some snapshots of men posing alone in stylish clothes (suits, tuxes, trendy casual wear), these are few and far between.

63 McDonough, "Television and the Family," 117, 119. Survey cited in Betty Betz, "Teens and TV," *Variety*, January 7, 1953, 97.

64 For analyses of this film, see, for example, Joyrich, "All That Television Allows"; and Spigel, *Make Room for TV*, 123.

65 Friedan, *Feminine Mystique*.

66 Friedan, "Television and the Feminine Mystique," 8.

67 Lyn Tyrnabene, "How America Lives: The Bored Housewife," *Ladies' Home Journal*, November 1966, 97–98; "City of Single Women," *Ebony*, February 1, 1958, 19–20; H. G. Brown, *Sex and the Single Girl*, 135–36. Although the stories

may have addressed some women's concerns, the figure of the bored or lonely woman is also part of a longer history of psychological (and taste-biased) discourses on women and TV that pathologized women's pleasures in the medium.

68 Ahmed, *Queer Phenomenology*, 40–41.

69 Butler, *Gender Trouble*.

70 Q. Miller, *Camp TV*. Germane to my subject, Miller analyzes *The Bob Cummings Show* (CBS and NBC, 1955–59), which revolves around a pinup photographer.

71 Michele White, "'My Queer eBay'"; Michele White, *Buy It Now*, see especially 110–67.

72 Horak, *Girls Will Be Boys*, chapter 2, loc. 1197–1937 of 9828, Kindle.

73 For analysis of *Johnny Guitar*, see, for example, Robertson, *Guilty Pleasures*, 85–114. For *Calamity Jane* and *Johnny Guitar*, see Halberstam, *Female Masculinity*, 209–10, 194–95.

74 To clarify, my point here is not to engage homophobic stereotypes of military women as lesbians. Such stereotypes circulated in the 1950s and 1960s and were often deployed by men as a way to slander women in the military and keep other women from joining it. I have no idea of the women's sexual orientations. Instead, I am interested in the pose these women assume within the context of the army barracks.

75 This snapshot especially resonates with the history of cross-dressing as well as gender fluid Hollywood and homemade pinups that presented aggressive femininity via the figure of the cigarette-smoking women who sometimes used cigarette holders. Buszek, *Pin-Up Grrrls*, loc. 3722 of 7470, Kindle; Horak, *Girls Will Be Boys*, loc. 2673 of 9828, Kindle. Also see Garber, *Vested Interests*, 152–53, 157, and 174.

76 For the carnivalesque, see Bakhtin, *Rabelais and His World*, 196–277.

77 In this case, the eBay dealer knew the women's profession. In a different snapshot that features one of the same women, there is a toy airplane on the coffee table. See figure 4.17.

78 E. H. Brown, *Work!*, 112.

79 Minow, "Vast Wasteland."

80 During this period, the *Famous Monsters of Filmland Magazine* held photo contests for readers. This poser might have been taking a cue from this.

81 Girard, *My TV Girls* and *The Diary of Tom Wilkins*.

82 Emphasis on "#646-398 Beige" is in original.

83 Barthes, *Camera Lucida*, 34. ("Photography" is capitalized in the original). Speaking of Hollywood glamour, Barthes considers Greta Garbo's face in relation to a mask. Barthes, "Face of Garbo."

84 Hirsch, *Family Frames*, 97–98 and 108–9.

1 "Peggy Corday: Miss Television 1949," *Radio and Television Best*, March 1949, cover and 32.

2 As far as I know, there are three surviving episodes, but Corday is in only two of them. In the credit sequence, Corday appears in an active Kodak Girl role, taking outdoor shots in New York City. Pinup segments depict Corday or other models in sedate clothes or in headshots.

3 Other TV programs featured amateur photography. Notably, in 1952, the Mutual Don Lee television network (a West Coast station group) presented glamour photographer Bruno Bernard (a.k.a. Bernard of Hollywood) as host of "TV Pin-Up School." This aired just once in 1952 as a special episode of *Don Lee Presents*. See *Art Photography*, January 1952, back cover; and "TV Pin-Up School," *Art Photography*, February 1952, n.p.

4 CBS's 1931 newspaper announcement for the opening of its Manhattan radio studio featured a photo of Olive Shea, its CBS Girl and Miss Radio of 1929. For more on radio and television girls, see Spigel, "Made-for-Broadcast Cities."

5 In 1949, the Academy of Television Arts and Sciences gave its Emmy award a female body (as opposed to the Oscar's male form), and in the 1950s and 1960s, the academy promoted the annual event with a live-action Miss Emmy (alternatively dubbed Miss Cinderemmy).

6 For more on this, see Meyerowitz, "Women, Cheesecake, and Borderline Material." Antiobscenity laws were in force in the United States since 1712, and it had been illegal to send obscene materials through the mail since the end of the nineteenth century. But defining obscenity had been left to the states and local authorities. In 1957, the Supreme Court's decision in *Roth v. the United States* defined obscenity more specifically: Congress could ban material "utterly without redeeming social importance" and whose "dominant theme . . . taken as a whole" would appear to the "average person, applying contemporary community standards," to "appeal to the prurient interest." The ruling led to what was known as the Roth test, which state and local authorities could apply to what they deemed to be obscene materials. Because the Court's ruling was broad and open to interpretation, however, the Roth test had the paradoxical effect of opening the door to more court battles. In 1973, the Court revised its previous rulings, effectively granting states greater freedom in obscenity rulings and setting up a new Miller test (named for *Miller vs. California*). See Strub, *Obscenity Rules*; Heins, *Not in Front of the Children*, 58–66, 85–87; and Stone, *Sex and the Constitution*, 263–87.

7 Meyerowitz, "Women, Cheesecake, and Borderline Material"; Buszek, *Pin-Up Grrrls*; M. E. Williams, "'Crisis' Cover Girl"; M. E. Williams, "'Meet the Real Lena Horne.'"

8 Despite Vargas's aesthete orientation, in 1943 the US Post Office declined to grant second-class (discount) status to *Esquire* on the grounds of obscenity,

especially targeting the Vargas Girls. The ensuing court battle was decided in favor of the magazine, which (paradoxically) helped open the door for more men's magazines and pinups in the years to come.

9 For images and discussion, see, for example, Martingnette and Meisel, *Great American Pinup*.

10 "Strategic support material" also included the distribution of nude photographs that would later be considered pornographic.

11 According to Elaine Tyler May, during and after World War II the use of pinups as military mascots was part of a more general cultural association between the bomb and "explosive femininity." The "bikini" (one of the most popular postwar pinup costumes) was christened as such in 1947 by its French designer Louis Réard, who named it after the US government's 1946 atomic bomb tests over the Pacific islands of the Bikini Atoll. See Tyler May, *Homeward Bound*, 110–12.

12 *Ebony* featured illustrated pinups by African American artist E. Simms Campbell, who also created *Esquire*'s Esky mascot.

13 For more on Grable as pinup, see Gaines, "Popular Icon as Commodity and Sign."

14 After 1957, Vargas worked exclusively for *Playboy*. Before starting *Playboy*, Hefner worked as a journalist for *Esquire* and as a selling agent for wholesalers of some of the more salacious girlie magazines. Hefner combined the two pinup modes (tasteful sophistication and sleaze).

15 At that point, *Playboy* referred to Monroe as the "Sweetheart of the Month." The term *Playmate* made its debut in the second issue.

16 Hugh Hefner quoted in "Hugh Hefner Playboy Enterprises," *Fortune Small Business Magazine*, September 1, 2003, n.p. Maintaining the concept, in 2005, Hefner debuted his E! Entertainment cable TV show *The Girls Next Door*. For more on the "girl next door" concept, see Preciado, *Pornotopia*.

17 For more on the centerfold and *Playboy*'s status as "media architecture," see Preciado, *Pornotopia*, 58.

18 Consistent with this ambivalence and contradiction, some actresses who played iconic sitcom moms also posed for cheesecake pinups, including Donna Reed (who posed for wartime pinups), Mary Tyler Moore, Lucille Ball, and Diahann Carroll. In that sense, viewers aware of the cheesecake pinups might have interpreted the sitcom housewives through the lens of this more explicitly sexualized gender performance.

19 The House hearings indulged the McCarthy era's homophobic *lavender scare* tactics, suggesting that the magazines would lead to homosexuality and sexual "perversions" among boys. The General Federation of Women's Clubs also protested the magazines' effects on children, but their concern lay especially with protecting young girls.

20 Meyerowitz, "Women, Cheesecake, and Borderline Material," 21.

21 Letter from Betty Gay Swan, *Playboy*, December 1954, 3, quoted in Meyerowitz, "Women, Cheesecake, and Borderline Material," 22.

22 Letter from Alice Soriano, *Playboy*, September 1954, 4, quoted in Meyerowitz, "Women, Cheesecake, and Borderline Material," 14.

23 Buszek, *Pin-Up Grrrls*, loc. 3658 of 7470, Kindle.

24 M. E. Williams, "'Crisis' Cover Girl"; M. E. Williams, "'Meet the Real Lena Horne'"; Buszek, *Pin-Up Grrrls*, loc. 4089–4167 of 7470, Kindle; Meyerowitz, "Women, Cheesecake, and Borderline Material," 18–21.

25 Nishikawa, "Race, Respectability, and the Short Life of *Duke* Magazine." Nishikawa argues that *Duke* tapped into some readers' desire to see images of beautiful Black women in print. Nevertheless, *Duke* tried to contain Black sexuality within older "settler" concepts of respectability, hoping to reach more conservative, upper-class Black male readers. The strategy backfired. Readers and critics were disappointed by *Duke*'s upper-crust respectability and its failure to represent a more modern concept of Black sexuality.

26 Other prominent women in the midcentury pinup trade include Alice Gowland, the major business brains behind Peter Gowland's glamour photography studio, and Irving Klaw's sister Paula Klaw, who co-owned their shop and helped produce their pinups and striptease films.

27 For the phone in early cinema, see Gunning, "Heard over the Phone."

28 For Robida, see Hopkins, "Albert Robida's Visions of Future Time"; and Huhtamo, "Elements of Screenology," 77. Robida is now hailed as the father of steampunk.

29 Uricchio, "Television's First 75 Years," 298–300.

30 *Esquire*, November 1950, cover. Moore's pinup is also featured in a pullout centerfold and other illustrations in the issue.

31 In a different pinup in 1948, Monroe appeared in a two-piece bathing suit posing on the sound stage of the newly built Don Lee Television Studio in Hollywood.

32 "Love on a Late Night Show," *Life*, February 1955, 55–56, 58; "TV Gets a Love Goddess," *Playboy*, February 1955, 41.

33 Ehrenreich, *Hearts of Men*, loc. 826 of 3484, Kindle. See also Preciado, *Pornotopia*.

34 Hefner, editorial, *Playboy*, December 1953.

35 Thompson, "Parodic Sensibility," 298.

36 In 1969–70, Hefner briefly revived the show in a somewhat revised format as *Playboy after Dark*.

37 This ad was published in 1966 as part of Hefner's "What Sort of Man Reads Playboy?" advertising campaign, which ran from 1958 to 1974.

38 On the stereo, masculinity, and the bachelor pad, see Ehrenreich, *Hearts of Men*, loc. 927 and 938 of 3484, Kindle; Keightley, "'Turn It Down!'"; Taylor, *Strange Sounds*, 78–80; Preciado, *Pornotopia*, 83–106; Wojcik, *Apartment Plot*, 88–138.

39 *Playboy*, March 1956, centerfold.

40 For the racism embedded in color film technology, see Dyer, *White*, 92–94.

For the same regarding TV, see Mulvin and Sterne, "Scenes from an Imaginary Country," 33; and Murray, *Bright Signals*, 107–12.

41 Ruth Sondak was an army photographer during World War II and photographed politicians and celebrities after the war, freelancing for numerous magazines. The *Playboy* centerfold photo is uncredited in the issue, and Playboy Enterprises could not verify the photographer, but several sources attribute it to Sondak. See, for example, Drew Harwell, "How Women's Voices Are Shifting Playboy from Topless to Thoughtful," *Washington Post*, February 4, 2016.

42 The bookshelf is a mix of "high" and "low," featuring a biography of Albert Einstein and an issue of *TV Guide*.

43 Readers' letters joked about the centerfold's depiction of the Playmate and the TV set as competing sites of visual attraction. One reader wrote, "The one thing in your picture that puzzles us is the fact that there seems to be a girl blocking the TV set. What brand is it? (The TV set.)" Cited in Thompson, "Parodic Sensibility," 297.

44 Photographed by Lawrence Schiller and Ron Vogel, Staley is dressed in peekaboo slippers, and hides her nudity by pulling a dressing room curtain over her body and using a script to hide but also call attention to her censorable body parts. Promoting the CBS studios, the photo features a large CBS camera decorated with the CBS eye, which adds to the Peeping Tom scenario. *Playboy*, November 1958, centerfold.

45 I looked through 1950s and 1960s issues of *Bachelor, Modern Man, Topper, Spree, Caper, Tab, Frolic, TV Gals and Gags, Gent, Dude, Wink, Rogue*, and *Escapade* at the Kinsey Institute Library at Indiana University, Bloomington. I found TV pinups (often multiple examples) in the first eight of these, but all the magazines referenced TV in either cartoons or articles (for example, about television's effects on sex, or about TV programs and stars).

46 "Bachelorette of the Month," *Bachelor*, December 1964, 32–33.

47 *Spree* 2, no. 14 (1960): 9.

48 "New Way to Bring Out the Old," *Modern Man*, Summer 1965, 14.

49 See, for example, Parks, "Cracking Open the Set," especially 266–73.

50 It is possible the bikini was painted on the photo after the fact, which was a typical practice to get around obscenity laws when sending photos through the mail. Photos were sometimes made in two versions, one for the legal borderline and one for the underground pornography market.

51 TV pinups even took the form of a popular adult joke book, *TV Girls and Gags*, which began publication in 1954. The magazine had previously appeared under the name *Hollywood Girls and Gags*, so the switch to TV was likely a merchandizing tactic to revamp the older version with the novelty of television.

52 Schaefer, *Bold! Daring! Shocking! True!*.

53 Joseph Folds, "Portrait of a Home," *Popular Photography*, May 1948, 56–58;

"How to Photograph Your Aquarium," *Popular Photography*, December 1950, 48–49; "Filming the Family Candidly," *U.S. Camera*, March 1948, 52–61; "Better Living Beautiful Baby," *Popular Photography*, October 1956, 140.

54 Peter Gowland, "You and Your Model," *Popular Photography*, October 1953, 142.

55 Bernard Davis, "How to Shoot Your Wife," *Popular Photography*, November 1953, 46–47.

56 The news segment aired on the Miami CBS affiliate station WTVJ. See Reel #S8A (cans 3063–66) TVNO881, Florida Moving Image Archives, Wolfson Archives, Miami Dade College, Miami, accessed July 3, 2021, https://www.mdc.edu/archives/wolfson-archives/. The segment is at "Bunny Yeager, 1929–2014," Wolfson Archive, video, 2:23, May 27, 2014, https://www.youtube.com/watch?v=Uh36RM7gWWk.

57 For analysis of Yeager's self-portraits that considers their importance for feminism, see Wright, "Having Her Cheesecake and Eating It."

58 Yeager also appeared in a 1958 episode of the CBS panel quiz show *To Tell the Truth*, where the celebrity panel had to guess which of the three constants was the female pinup photographer.

59 Yeager, *Bunny Yeager's Art of Glamour Photography*, 10.

60 Yeager, *Bunny Yeager's Art of Glamour Photography*, 25.

61 Mason, *Bunny Yeager's Darkroom*, 131. Yeager also posed models with hi-fi cabinets and radios. See Yeager, *Photographing the Female Figure*, 104, 90, 103, 106; Yeager, *Bunny Yeager's Art of Glamour Photography*, 43.

62 Yeager, *Bunny's Honeys*, 16.

63 For early films with dressing screens and undressing scenes, see *Le Coucher de la Mariée* (Albert Kirchner, dir., 1899); and *From Show Girl to Burlesque Queen* (A. E. Weed, dir., 1903). For a gender fluid example, see *Photographie d'une étoile* (Pathé brothers, dirs., 1906). For later examples, see *The Affairs of Anatol* (Cecil B. DeMille, dir., 1921); *Betty Boop's Rise to Fame* (Max Fleischer, dir., 1934); and *Blackmail* (Alfred Hitchcock, dir., 1929). For related issues, see Strauven, "Early Cinema's Touch(able) Screens." Although Huhtamo does not consider dressing screens' erotic implications, he discusses them in "Elements of Screenology," 49.

64 Buszek, *Pin-Up Grrrls*, loc. 3609 of 7470, Kindle. Buszek takes issue with Robert Westbrook, who sees the World War II–era homemade pinups as "icons of obligation," in which women fulfilled their patriotic duties by sending their pinups to soldiers. Westbrook, "I Want a Girl Just Like the Girl."

65 Buszek, *Pin-Up Grrrls*, loc. 3704–14 of 7470, Kindle.

66 Buszek, *Pin-Up Grrrls*, loc. 3714 of 7470, Kindle.

67 Kodak responded in kind with youth culture party scene ads for its Instamatic camera.

68 D'Emilio and Freedman, *Intimate Matters*, 130–32.

69 The Kinsey Report found that modern women were more likely than their Victorian ancestors to have intercourse before marriage. Kinsey et al., *Sex-*

ual Behavior in the Human Female; Masters and Johnson, *Human Sexual Response*. Masters and Johnson began their research in 1957.

70 Neuhaus, "The Importance of Being Orgasmic."

71 Buszek, *Pin-Up Grrrls*, loc. 3658 of 7470, Kindle.

72 For the record album, see "Ann Corio, Sonny Lester and His Orchestra— How to Strip for Your Husband," Discogs, accessed July 3, 2021, https://www .discogs.com/Ann-Corio-Sonny-Lester-His-Orchestra-How-To-Strip-For -Your-Husband/release/2456207.

73 Friedan, "Television and the Feminine Mystique," 8.

74 Although Polaroid cameras allowed people to bypass developers, I have not found any Polaroid TV pinups.

75 For the history of midcentury photographers, physique magazines, and companies that made and distributed these photos, see Waugh, *Hard to Imagine*, especially 215–52; and Johnson, *Buying Gay*. Waugh and Johnson both discuss Alfred Kinsey's close relationship with the photographers and the vast collection at the Kinsey Institute.

76 Michele White, "'My Queer eBay'"; Michele White, *Buy It Now*, especially 110–42.

77 Thank you to David Chapman, who gave me this photograph.

78 Chapman and Waugh, *Comin' at Ya!*, 144.

79 Waugh, "Foreword," 10.

80 L. Williams, *Hard Core*.

81 For pornography on early cable, see Stadel, "Cable, Pornography, and the Reinvention of Television."

82 Inside cover, *Bachelor*, August 1966.

CHAPTER FIVE. TV MEMORIES

1 Acland, *Residual Media*.

2 Raymond Williams discusses the concept of "dominant, residual, and emergent" cultures in *Marxism and Literature* and in "Base and Superstructure in Marxist Cultural Theory."

3 Bolter and Grusin, *Remediation*.

4 Benjamin, "Paris, the Capital of the Nineteenth Century," especially 13.

5 For scholarship on photo sharing and digital photography, see Hand, *Ubiquitous Photography*; Larsen and Sandbye, *Digital Snapshots*; Jurgenson, *Social Photo*; van Dijck, *Culture of Connectivity*; Leaver, Highfield, and Abidin, *Instagram*; Frosh, *Poetics of Digital Media*; Lister, *Photographic Image in Digital Culture*; and Manovich, *Instagram and Contemporary Image*.

6 Van Dijck, *Mediated Memories in the Digital Age*, 116.

7 See van Dijck's chapter "Flickr between Participatory and Connective Culture" in *Culture of Connectivity*, 89–109.

8 Seth Fiegerman, "Pinterest Hits 300 Million Monthly Users and Its Stock Is Soaring," *CNN Business*, August 1, 2019, https://www.cnn.com/2019/08/01

/tech/pinterest-earnings/index.html. In 2019, Pew estimated that 37 percent of American adults used Instagram and 28 percent used Pinterest, making these photo-share sites even more popular than other niche social media sites like Snapchat (24 percent) and LinkedIn (27 percent). Flickr was not on this list. "Social Media Fact Sheet," Pew Research Center, June 12, 2019, https://www.pewresearch.org/internet/fact-sheet/social-media/.

9   Hand, *Ubiquitous Photography*, 164.

10 Kevan Gilbert, *Christmas—Aunty Carol with Doll by Tree and TV*, Flickr, uploaded December 14, 2007, https://www.flickr.com/photos/kevangilbert/2109284625/in/photolist-4doCQi.

11 Sandy, *My Brother Gregg and I—Easter 1950s—Houston, Texas*, Flickr, uploaded March 2, 2008, https://www.flickr.com/photos/nbklx17/2305562579/in/dateposted/.

12 Roadsidepictures, found photo, 1957, uploaded August 5, 2010, Flickr, https://www.flickr.com/photos/roadsidepictures/4864290070/in/dateposted/.

13 Michael Daddino, *Dad by the TV at 60 Turner Place*, Flickr, photo dated May 1962, https://www.flickr.com/photos/epicharmus/4652224921/in/dateposted/.

14 Hirsch (*Family Frames*, 22–23) develops the concept of "postmemory" in relation to Holocaust photos shared among generations in families. Postmemory can serve a critical function in thinking about—and feeling the pain of—others and in forming political resistance in the present. While I find the concept useful, I note that TV snapshots are very different from photos of Holocaust survivors. I do not mean to equivocate between the two, nor do I think TV snapshots are sites of political engagement in the same sense.

15 Barthes, *Camera Lucida*, 15.

16 See, for example, Ernst, *Digital Memory and the Archive*; Parikka, *What Is Media Archaeology?*; and Hoskins, *Digital Memory Studies*.

17 Ernst, "Tempor(e)alities and Archive-Textures of Media-Connected Memory," p. 144 of 313, Kindle.

18 Murray, "New Media and Vernacular Photography," loc. 4391 of 7330, Kindle.

19 Murray, "New Media and Vernacular Photography," loc. 4589 of 7330, Kindle.

20 Bazin, "Ontology of the Photographic Image," 14.

21 Hoskins, "Memory of the Multitude," p. 86 of 313, Kindle. Although I find the memory of the multitudes a useful concept for explaining the anonymous routes of digital culture, it seems to me that digital memory still contains niche sorts of memory cultures that gather around, for example, issues of national heritage, diasporic memory and community formations, as well as forms of collective belonging.

22 John Atherton, email message to author, November 29, 2020. For the Flickr commentary, see John Atherton, *Early 1950s Television Set*, ca. 1953, Flickr, https://www.flickr.com/photos/gbaku/2513320483/in/dateposted/. For the NRK TV post, see Lars Karelius Noer, "Blindtest av tv-skjermer—en god eller dårlig ide?," NRK Beta, February 4, 2010, https://nrkbeta.no/2010/02/04

/blindtest/?utm_source=feedburner&utm_medium=feed&utm_campaign
=Feed:+nrkbeta+(NRKbeta).

23 Kuhn, *Family Secrets*, 5, 10.

24 Boym, *Future of Nostalgia*, 5.

25 Jurgenson, *Social Photo*, p. 4 and 5 of 136, Kindle.

26 Appadurai, *Modernity at Large*, 78.

27 Boym, "Nostalgia and Its Discontents."

28 N. West, *Kodak through the Lens of Nostalgia*, 10.

29 Holdsworth, *Television, Memory and Nostalgia*; Cook, *Screening the Past*;
    Grainge, *Monochrome Memories*; Landsberg, *Prosthetic Memory*; Darian-
    Smith and Turnbull, *Remembering Television*; Bevan, *Aesthetics of Nostalgia TV*.

30 Holdsworth, *Television, Memory and Nostalgia*, 103.

31 Holdsworth, *Television, Memory and Nostalgia*, 98.

32 I am borrowing this phrase from Keats, *Crack in the Picture Window*.

33 Lynne's Lens, *Family Portrait*, Flickr, uploaded on December 21, 2012, https://
    www.flickr.com/photos/25726169@N03/8294607732/in/dateposted/.

34 Cardboard America, *A Woman at Her Zenith*, Flickr, uploaded August 11,
    2011, https://www.flickr.com/photos/hollywoodplace/4594094246/in/pool
    -57256543@N00/.

35 Rick Hebenstreit, *Retro Christmas*, Flickr, uploaded February 23, 2008, https://
    www.flickr.com/photos/rick019/2286483040/in/album-72157603900219227/;
    Easttexchem, Img_0042 (Typical 1960s television in the living room scene),
    Flickr, uploaded April 16, 2012, https://www.flickr.com/photos/oxforddevon22
    /6937971934/in/pool-27636970@N00/.

36 For cable nostalgia networks, see Kompare, *Rerun Nation*, 169–96; Spi-
    gel, "From the Dark Ages to the Golden Age"; and Spigel, "Our Television
    Heritage."

37 Wilson and Yochim, "Pinning Happiness." For "happy objects," see Ahmed,
    Promise of Happiness.

38 Good, "From Scrapbook to Facebook."

39 I have previously discussed this with respect to cable TV nostalgia networks.
    See Spigel, "From the Dark Ages to the Golden Age."

40 For the original post and comments on this and related photos, see Timeless
    Photoworks (a.k.a. John Gonzales), *Vivian*, Flickr, uploaded May 21, 2012,
    https://www.flickr.com/photos/topog/7265803550/in/photostream/.

41 For these and other contemporary pinup artists, see Buszek, *Pin-Up Grrrls*,
    chapter 8, loc. 5109–5817 of 7470, Kindle.

42 Kurpaska, "Nostalgia and Retro-Femininity."

43 Natalia Quiroz, *TV . . . o No TV*, Flickr, December 13, 2006, https://www.flickr
    .com/photos/nataliaquiros/with/321573621/.

44 Chip York, untitled pinups of Anna-Marie (album), 2010, https://www.flickr
    .com/photos/37435081@N03/albums/72157623430794767.

45 Theresa Thompson, untitled, caption: "June, don't you think this Bench

Monday group of yours is setting a bad example for the Beaver?," Flickr, uploaded August 24, 2009, https://www.flickr.com/photos/theresasthompson /3853280387/in/photostream/.

46 Kelly McCarthy, *TV Land II*, Flickr, uploaded February 18, 2017, https://www .flickr.com/photos/kelly_mccarthy/33285020061/in/dateposted/. McCarthy made a series of these.

47 Eva Mañez, *Pola TV*, Flickr, August 7, 2009, https://www.flickr.com/photos /evamanez/4011628584/in/dateposted/.

48 Christine Von Diepenbroek, *The Show Must Go On* (no original production date), Fine Art America, uploaded September 5, 2019, https://fineartamerica .com/featured/the-show-must-go-on-christine-von-diepenbroek.html.

49 Gill, "Postfeminist Media Culture." In *Pin-up Grrrls*, Buszek explicitly critiques and avoids the term *postfeminism*; instead, she refers to contemporary pinups as "postmodern feminist" pinups (loc. 5439 of 7470, Kindle). Writing in 2006, Buszek was responding to debates regarding postfeminism's lack of political engagement and the idea (as the prefix *post* suggests) that feminist struggle was somehow over. Instead, she argues, contemporary pinup artists continue to engage feminist issues and politics. I agree, but it should be noted that there are many debates and points of view regarding the politics of postfeminism and the shifting landscape of feminism(s) since the time Buszek and Gill wrote their texts. In 2016 Gill updated her ideas but still sees value in the concept. See Gill, "Post-postfeminism?" In any case, I am reluctant to use the term *postfeminist* as a catchall for the online pinups and artists, who produce different kinds of affective engagement with the form, and with feminism(s).

50 S. Stewart, *On Longing*, 151–52.

51 For a trick shot that recalls the woman "trapped" in TV scenario, see 2eyes _photos, *The Corner*, Flickr, uploaded by December 28, 2008, https://www .flickr.com/photos/2eyes_photos/3265789293/in/dateposted/.

52 Connolly, *TV Museum*; For other histories of artists' renderings of TV, see Farmer, *New Frontier*; and Holdsworth, *Television, Memory and Nostalgia*.

53 Sara-Lusa Menina, untitled, Flickr, uploaded August 16, 2009, https://www .flickr.com/photos/lusachica/3826368658/in/dateposted/.

54 Chrissie White, *A Peculiar Sort of Thing*, Flickr, February 26, 2008, https:// www.flickr.com/photos/prettypony/2294930417/in/dateposted/dateposted.

55 Darkman (a.k.a. Darko), *Imagine If You Will . . .* , Flickr, uploaded April 4, 2014, https://www.flickr.com/photos/120201892@N02/with/14715426193/.

56 Riddim Ryder, *As If You Never Existed*, uploaded November 2014, https:// www.flickr.com/photos/riddimryder/15787073895/in/photolist/.

57 De Kosnik, *Rogue Archives*.

58 Saidiya Hartman, "Venus in Two Acts." In this essay, Hartman promotes her method of "critical fabulation" as a means of redressing the violence not just of slavery but also of the archive formed through white violence and power. See also Hartman's more recent study, *Wayward Lives, Beautiful Experiments*,

which uses extant sources, including photographs, to speculate on the lives of young Black women in early twentieth-century urban America.

59 To respect Mamie Till's original purpose, I won't reprint the photograph here. See DeNeen L. Brown, "Emmett Till's Mother Opened His Casket and Sparked the Civil Rights Movement," *Washington Post*, July 12, 2018.

60 Derrida and Stiegler, *Echographies of Television*, 62–63.

61 Derrida, *Archive Fever*, 20.

62 Foucault, *Archaeology of Knowledge*, 118–31.

63 Chun, "Enduring Ephemeral," 160.

64 Vestberg, "Photographic Image in Digital Archives," loc. 3304 of 7330, Kindle.

65 I am borrowing a term from George Lipsitz's book *Possessive Investment in Whiteness*.

66 Garvey, *Writing with Scissors*, p. 131 of 304, Kindle.

67 duCille, *Technicolored*, loc. 1181 of 9160, Kindle.

68 duCille, *Technicolored*, loc. 509–10 of 9160, Kindle.

69 duCille, *Technicolored*, loc. 514 and 539 of 9160, Kindle.

70 Lin, *Insomnia and the Aunt*, 18.

71 Lin, *Insomnia and the Aunt*, 19.

72 Lin, *Insomnia and the Aunt*, 45.

73 Lin, *Insomnia and the Aunt*, 42.

74 Kittler, *Discourse Networks*; Ernst, *Digital Memory and the Archive*.

75 Ernst, "Let There Be Irony," 592.

76 Ernst, *Digital Memory and the Archive*, 46. While I find much of the work in media archaeology to be insightful and important, obviously I don't agree with Ernst's cold nonhuman conclusions. In *Rogue Archives*, De Kosnik forcefully critiques Ernst's perspective, instead arguing (more in tune with actor-network theory) for a middle ground where human and nonhuman actors (like computers) produce social practices together, and where people still have agency in the creation and preservation of the past. De Kosnik, *Rogue Archives*, loc. 1284–1306 of 9138, Kindle.

CONCLUSION

1 Amy Holdsworth has recently made a similar case for the return to studies of everydayness by discussing her own encounters with television over her lifecycle. In her "autoethnography," *On Living with Television*, she especially highlights how everyday experience, memory, anticipation, and ordinary affects are intertwined as "loops" of experience with the temporal flows and textuality of programming.

2 Ouellette, "Will the Revolution Be Televised?"; Moran, *There's No Place Like Home Video*.

3 Jenkins, *Convergence Culture*.

4 Hilderbrand, *Inherent Vice*.

5   See, for example, "30th Anniversary of the Video Camera, 1984–2014—90's VHS Memories Nostalgia," Weird Paul (a.k.a. Paul Petroskey), video, 3:42, September 1, 2014, https://www.youtube.com/watch?v=If5tcMVtijo.

6   Gazzard, "Between Pixels and Play."

7   Found at a flea market in Beijing, the snapshots initially appeared in Sauvin and Kessels, *Me TV*. The snapshots also appeared in Erik Kessels, "The People's Republic of Television: Portraits from 1980s China," *Time*, January 14, 2015.

8   Gitelman, *Always Already New*.

9   Barthes, *Camera Lucida*, 115.

10   Freud, *Interpretation of Dreams*.

11   Steedman, "Intimacy in Research."

12   Campt, *Listening to Images*.

BIBLIOGRAPHY

Acham, Christine. *Revolution Televised: Prime Time and the Struggle for Black Power*. Minneapolis: University of Minnesota Press, 2004.

Acland, Charles R., ed. *Residual Media*. Minneapolis: University of Minnesota Press, 2007.

Ahmed, Sara. *The Promise of Happiness*. Durham, NC: Duke University Press, 2010.

Ahmed, Sara. *Queer Phenomenology: Orientations, Objects, Others*. Durham, NC: Duke University Press, 2006.

Appadurai, Arjun. *Modernity at Large: Cultural Dimensions of Globalization*. Minneapolis: University of Minnesota Press, 1996.

Auslander, Philip. *Liveness: Performance in a Mediatized Culture*. London: Routledge, 2008.

Auslander, Philip. *Reactivations: Essays on Performance and Its Documentation*. Ann Arbor: University of Michigan Press, 2018.

Bailey, Hillary G. *Indoor Photography*. Chicago: Ziff-Davis, 1940.

Bakhtin, Mikhail. *Rabelais and His World*. Translated by Hélène Iswolsky. Bloomington: Indiana University Press, 1984.

Barthes, Roland, *Camera Lucida: Reflections on Photography*. Translated by Richard Howard. New York: Hill and Wang, 1981.

Barthes, Roland. "The Face of Garbo." In *Mythologies*, translated by Annette Lavers, 56–57. 1957. Reprint, New York: Farrar, Straus and Giroux, 1972.

Barthes, Roland. "The Great Family of Man." In *Mythologies*, translated by Annette Lavers, 100–102. 1957. Reprint, New York: Farrar, Straus and Giroux, 1972.

Barthes, Roland. *Mythologies*. Translated by Annette Lavers. 1957. Reprint, New York: Farrar, Straus and Giroux, 1972.

Bateson, Gregory. "A Theory of Play and Fantasy." In *Steps to an Ecology of Mind: Collected Essays in Anthropology, Psychiatry, Evolution, and Epistemology*, 183–98. 1955. Reprint, Northvale, NJ: Jason Aronson, 1972.

Bazin, André. "The Ontology of the Photographic Image." In *What Is Cinema?* vol. 1, translated by Hugh Gray, 9–16. 1967. Reprint, Berkeley: University of California Press, 2005.

Becker, Christine. *It's the Pictures That Got Small: Hollywood Film Stars on 1950s Television*. Middletown, CT: Wesleyan University Press, 2009.

Becker, Ron. *Gay TV and Straight America*. New Brunswick, NJ: Rutgers University Press, 2006.

Benjamin, Walter. *Berlin Childhood around 1900*. Translated by Howard Eiland. Cambridge, MA: Harvard University Press, 2006.

Benjamin, Walter. "Paris, the Capital of the Nineteenth Century." In *The Arcades Project*, edited by Rolf Tiedman, translated by Howard Eiland and Kevin McLaughlin, 3–13. Cambridge, MA: Harvard University Press, 1999.

Berger, John. *Understanding a Photograph*. New York: Aperture, 2013.

Bevan, Alex. *The Aesthetics of Nostalgia TV: Production Design and the Boomer Era*. New York: Bloomsbury, 2019.

Bird, William. "From Fair to Family." In *From Receiver to Remote Control: The TV Set*, edited by Matthew Geller and Reese Williams, 63–84. New York: New Museum of Contemporary Art, 1990. Exhibition catalog.

Boddy, William. *Fifties Television: The Industry and Its Critics*. Urbana: University of Illinois Press, 1992.

Bodroghkozy, Aniko. *Equal Time: Television and the Civil Rights Movement*. Urbana: University of Illinois Press, 2012.

Bodroghkozy, Aniko. "'Is This What You Mean by Color TV?' Race, Gender, and Contested Meanings in NBC's *Julia*." In *Private Screenings: Television and the Female Consumer*, edited by Lynn Spigel and Denise Mann, 143–69. Minneapolis: University of Minnesota Press, 1992.

Bogle, Donald. *Primetime Blues: African Americans on Network TV*. New York: Farrar, Straus and Giroux, 2001.

Bolter, Jay David, and Richard Grusin. *Remediation: Understanding New Media*. Cambridge, MA: MIT Press, 1999.

Bonner, Frances. *Ordinary Television: Analyzing Popular TV*. London: Sage, 2003.

Bourdieu, Pierre. *Distinction: A Social Critique of the Judgement of Taste*. Translated by Richard Nice. London: Routledge, 1986.

Bourdieu, Pierre. *Photography: A Middlebrow Art*. Translated by Shawn Whiteside. 1965. Reprint, Stanford, CA: Stanford University Press, 1990.

Bourdon, Jérôme. "Live Television Is Still Alive: Television as an Unfulfilled Promise." *Media, Culture, and Society* 22, no. 5 (2000): 531–56.

Boym, Svetlana. *The Future of Nostalgia*. New York: Basic, 2002.

Boym, Svetlana. "Nostalgia and Its Discontents." *Hedgehog Review* 9, no. 2 (2007): 7–18.

Brown, Elspeth H. *Work! A Queer History of Modeling*. Durham, NC: Duke University Press, 2019.

Brown, Elspeth H., and Sara Davidmann. "'Queering the Trans* Family Album': Elspeth H. Brown and Sara Davidmann, in Conversation." *Radical History Review*, no. 122 (2015): 188–200.

Brown, Helen Gurley. *Sex and the Single Girl*. New York: Geis Associates, 1962.

Browne, Simone. *Dark Matters: On the Surveillance of Blackness*. Durham, NC: Duke University Press, 2015.

Brunsdon, Charlotte. *The Feminist, the Housewife, and the Soap Opera*. Oxford: Oxford University Press, 2000.

Bryson, Norman. *Looking at the Overlooked: Four Essays on Still Life Painting*. London: Reaktion, 1990. Kindle.

Buse, Peter. *The Camera Does the Rest: How Polaroid Changed Photography*. Chicago: University of Chicago Press, 2016. Kindle.

Buszek, Maria Elena. *Pin-Up Grrrls: Feminism, Sexuality, Popular Culture*. Durham, NC: Duke University Press, 2006. Kindle.

Butler, Judith. *Bodies That Matter: The Discursive Limits of Sex*. London, Routledge, 1993.

Butler, Judith. *Gender Trouble: Feminism and the Subversion of Identity*. New York: Routledge, 1990.

Cadwallader, Jen. "Spirit Photography and the Victorian Culture of Mourning." *Modern Language Studies* 37, no. 2 (2008): 8–31.

Campt, Tina M. *Image Matters: Archive, Photography, and the African Diaspora in Europe*. Durham, NC: Duke University Press, 2012. Kindle.

Campt, Tina M. *Listening to Images*. Durham, NC: Duke University Press, 2017.

Campt, Tina M., Marianne Hirsch, Gil Hochberg, and Brian Wallis, eds. *Imagining Everyday Life: Engagements with Vernacular Photography*. New York: Steidl/Walther Collection, 2020.

Cassidy, Marsha. *What Women Watched: Daytime Television in the 1950s*. Austin: University of Texas Press, 2005.

Chalfen, Richard. *Snapshot Versions of Life*. Madison, WI: Popular Press, 2008.

Chambers, Jason. *Madison Avenue and the Color Line: African Americans in the Advertising Industry*. Philadelphia: University of Pennsylvania Press, 2008.

Chapman, David, and Thomas Waugh. *Comin' at Ya!: The Homoerotic 3-D Photographs of Denny Denfield*. Vancouver, BC: Arsenal Pulp Press, 2007.

Chéroux, Clément, Andreas Fischer, Pierre Apraxine, Denis Canguilhem, and Sophie Schmit, eds. *The Perfect Medium: Photography and the Occult*. New Haven, CT: Yale University Press, 2005.

Chun, Wendy Hui Kyong. "The Enduring Ephemeral, or the Future Is a Memory." *Critical Inquiry* 35, no. 1 (2008): 148–71.

Classen, Steven. *Watching Jim Crow: The Struggle over Mississippi TV, 1955–1969*. Durham, NC: Duke University Press, 2004.

Connolly, Maeve. *TV Museum: Contemporary Art and the Age of Television*. Chicago: University of Chicago Press, 2014.

Cook, Pam. *Screening the Past: Memory and Nostalgia in Cinema*. London: Routledge, 2005.

Cowan, Ruth Schwartz. *More Work for Mother: The Ironies of Household Technology from the Open Hearth to the Microwave*. New York: Basic, 1985.

Cripps, Thomas. "*Amos 'n' Andy* and the Debate over American Racial Integration." In *Critiquing the Sitcom: A Reader*, edited by Joanne Morreale, 25–40. Syracuse, NY: Syracuse University Press, 2002.

Cvetkovich, Ann. *An Archive of Feelings: Trauma, Sexuality, and Lesbian Public Culture*. Durham, NC: Duke University Press, 2003.

Cvetkovich, Ann. "Photographing Objects as Queer Archival Practice." In *Feeling Photography*, edited by Elspeth H. Brown and Thy Phu, loc. 5712–6220 of 9316. Durham, NC: Duke University Press, 2014. Kindle.

Darian-Smith, Kate, and Paula Hamilton. "Part of the Family: Australian Histories of Television, Migration and Memory." In *Remembering Television: Histories, Technologies, Memories*, edited by Kate Darien-Smith and Sue Turnbull, 30–51. Newcastle upon Tyne: Cambridge Scholars, 2012.

Darian-Smith, Kate, and Sue Turnbull, eds. *Remembering Television: Histories, Technologies, Memories*. Newcastle upon Tyne: Cambridge Scholars, 2012.

DeCarava, Roy, and Langston Hughes. *The Sweet Flypaper of Life*. 1955. Reprint, Brooklyn: First Print, 2018.

de Certeau, Michel. *The Practice of Everyday Life*. Translated by Steven Rendall. Berkeley: University of California Press, 1984.

de Certeau, Michel. "Spatial Stories." In *The Practice of Everyday Life*, translated by Steven Rendall, 115–30. Berkeley: University of California Press, 1984.

De Kosnik, Abigail. *Rogue Archives: Digital Cultural Memory and Media Fandom*. Cambridge, MA: MIT Press, 2016.

Delmont, Matthew F. *The Nicest Kids in Town: American Bandstand, Rock 'n' Roll, and the Struggle for Civil Rights in 1950s Philadelphia*. Berkeley: University of California Press, 2012.

D'Emilio, John, and Estelle B. Freedman. *Intimate Matters: A History of Sexuality in America*. New York: Harper and Row, 1988.

Derrida, Jacques. *Archive Fever: A Freudian Impression*. Translated by Eric Prenowitz. Chicago: University of Chicago Press, 1996.

Derrida, Jacques. "Signature Event Context." In *Margins of Philosophy*, translated by Alan Bass, 307–30. Chicago: University of Chicago Press, 1982.

Derrida, Jacques, and Bernard Stiegler. *Echographies of Television: Filmed Interviews*. Translated by Jennifer Bajorek. Cambridge: Polity, 2002.

Desjardins, Mary. *Recycled Stars: Female Film Stardom in the Age of Hollywood and Video*. Durham, NC: Duke University Press, 2015.

Doty, Alex. "The Cabinet of Lucy Ricardo: Lucille Ball's Star Image." *Cinema Journal* 29, no. 4 (1990): 3–22.

Douglas, Mary. *Purity and Danger*. 1966. Reprint, New York: Routledge, 2002.

Douglas, Susan J. *Inventing American Broadcasting, 1899–1922*. Baltimore, MD: Johns Hopkins University Press, 1989.

duCille, Ann. *Technicolored: Reflections on Race in the Time of TV*. Durham, NC: Duke University Press, 2018. Kindle.

Dyer, Richard. *Stars*. 1980. Reprint, London: BFI, 2008.

Dyer, Richard. *White: Essays on Race and Culture*. New York: Routledge, 1997.

Eastman Kodak. *How to Make Good Pictures: A Book for the Amateur Photographer*. Rochester, NY: Eastman Kodak, 1922.

Eastman Kodak. *How to Make Good Pictures: A Guide for the Amateur Photographer*. 29th ed. Rochester, NY: Eastman Kodak, 1951–52.

Eckert, Charles. "The Carole Lombard in Macy's Window." In *Fabrications: Costume and the Female Body*, edited by Jane Gaines and Charlotte Herzog, 100–121. New York: Routledge, 1990.

Edwards, Elizabeth, and Janice Hart, eds. *Photographs, Objects, Histories: On the Materiality of Images*. New York: Routledge, 2004.

Ehrenreich, Barbara. *The Hearts of Men: American Dreams and the Flight from Commitment*. New York: Anchor Books, 1983. Kindle.

Entwistle, Joanne. *The Fashioned Body: Fashion, Dress, and Social Theory*. 2nd ed. Cambridge: Polity, 2015.

Ernst, Wolfgang. *Digital Memory and the Archive*. Edited by Jussi Parikka. Minneapolis: University of Minnesota Press, 2012.

Ernst, Wolfgang. "Let There Be Irony: Cultural History and Media Archaeology." *Art History* 28, no. 5 (2005): 582–603.

Ernst, Wolfgang. "Tempor(e)alities and Archive-Textures of Media-Connected Memory." In *Digital Memory Studies: Media Pasts in Transition*, edited by Andrew Hoskins, p. 144 of 313. New York: Routledge, 2018. Kindle.

Farmer, John Alan, ed. *The New Frontier: Art and Television, 1960–65*. Austin, TX: Austin Museum of Art, 2000. Exhibition catalog.

Felski, Rita. *Doing Time: Feminist Theory and Postmodern Culture*. New York: New York University Press, 2000. Kindle.

Ferris, Alison, ed. *The Disembodied Spirit*. Brunswick, ME: Bowdoin College Museum of Art, 2003. Exhibition catalog.

Feuer, Jane. "The Concept of Live Television: Ontology as Ideology." In *Regarding Television*, edited by E. Ann Kaplan, 12–22. Los Angeles: American Film Institute, 1983.

Fineman, Mia. *Faking It: Manipulated Photography before Photoshop*. New York: Met Publications, 2013. Exhibition catalog.

Foote, Nelson. "Family Living as Play." *Marriage and Family Living* 1, no. 4 (1955): 296–301.

Forman, Murray. *One Night on TV Is Worth Weeks at the Paramount: Popular Music on Early Television*. Durham, NC: Duke University Press, 2012.

Foucault, Michel. *The Archaeology of Knowledge and the Discourse on Language*. Translated by A. M. Sheridan Smith. New York: Pantheon, 1972.

Foucault, Michel. "Of Other Spaces: Utopias and Heterotopias." In *Rethinking Architecture: A Reader in Cultural Theory*, edited by Neil Leach, 350–56. London: Routledge, 1997.

Freud, Sigmund. *The Interpretation of Dreams*. Translated by James Strachey. 1899. Reprint, New York: Avon, 1998.

Freud, Sigmund. *The Uncanny*. Translated by David McLintock. 1919. Reprint, New York, Penguin, 2003.

Friedan, Betty. *The Feminine Mystique*. New York: Norton, 1963.

Friedberg, Anne. *Window Shopping: Cinema and the Postmodern*. Berkeley: University of California Press, 1993.

Frith, Simon. "The Pleasures of the Hearth: The Making of BBC Light Entertainment." In *Music for Pleasure: Essays in the Sociology of Pop*, 24–44. New York: Routledge, 1988.

Frosh, Paul. *The Poetics of Digital Media*. Cambridge: Polity, 2019.

Gaines, Jane. "The Popular Icon as Commodity and Sign: The Circulation of Betty Grable, 1941–45." PhD diss., Northwestern University, 1982.

Gaines, Jane, and Charlotte Herzog, eds. *Fabrications: Costume and the Female Body*. New York: Routledge, 1990.

Garber, Marjorie. *Vested Interests: Cross Dressing and Cultural Anxiety*. New York: Routledge, 1991.

Garvey, Ellen Gruber. *Writing with Scissors: American Scrapbooks from the Civil War to the Harlem Renaissance*. New York: Oxford University Press, 2012. Kindle.

Gates, Racquel. "Activating the Negative Image." *Television and New Media* 16, no. 7 (2015): 616–30.

Gauntlett, David, and Annette Hill. *TV Living: Television, Culture and Everyday Life*. London: Routledge, 1999.

Gazzard, Alison. "Between Pixels and Play: The Role of the Photograph in *Videogame Nostalgias*." *Photography and Culture* 9, no. 2 (2016): 154–62.

Geller, Matthew, and Reese Williams. *From Receiver to Remote Control: The TV Set*. New York: New Museum of Contemporary Art, 1990. Exhibition catalog.

Geraghty, Christine. *Women and Soap Opera: A Study of Prime Time Soaps*. Cambridge: Polity, 1991.

Giedion, Sigfried. *Mechanization Takes Command: A Contribution to Anonymous History*. 1948. Reprint, Minneapolis: University of Minnesota Press, 2014.

Gill, Rosalind. "Postfeminist Media Culture: Elements of a Sensibility." *European Journal of Cultural Studies* 10, no. 2 (2007): 147–66.

Gill, Rosalind, "Post-Postfeminism? New Feminist Visibilities in Postfeminist Times." *Feminist Media Studies* 16, no, 4 (2016): 610–30.

Gillespie, Marie. *Television, Ethnicity, and Cultural Change*. London: Routledge, 1995.

Girard, Sébastien. *The Diary of Tom Wilkins*. Self-published in the studio of Sébastien Girard, 2017. https://www.sebastiengirard.com/#.

Girard, Sébastien. *My TV Girls*. Self-published in the studio of Sébastien Girard, 2017. https://www.sebastiengirard.com/#.

Gitelman, Lisa. *Always Already New: Media, History, and the Data of Culture*. Cambridge, MA: MIT Press, 2008.

Goc, Nicola. "Snapshot Photography, Women's Domestic Work, and the 'Kodak Moment.'" In *Home Sweat Home: Perspectives on Housework and Modern Relationships*, edited by Elizabeth Patton and Mimi Choi, 27–47. Lanham, MD: Rowman and Littlefield, 2014.

Goffman, Erving. *The Presentation of Self in Everyday Life*. New York: Doubleday, 1959.

Good, Katie Day. "From Scrapbook to Facebook: A History of Personal Media Assemblage and Archives." *New Media and Society* 15, no. 4 (2013): 557–73.

Gottschalk, Simon, and Jennifer Whitmer. "Hypermodern Dramaturgy in Online Encounters." In *The Drama of Social Life: A Dramaturgical Handbook*, edited by Charles Edgley, 306–34. Little Rock: University of Arkansas Press, 2013.

Grainge, Paul. *Monochrome Memories: Nostalgia and Style in Retro America*. London: Praeger, 2002.

Gray, Ann. *Video Playtime: The Gendering of a Leisure Technology*. London: Routledge, 1992.

Gray, Herman. *Reading Race: Television and the Struggle for Blackness*. Minneapolis: University of Minnesota Press, 1995.

Gregg, Melissa, and Gregory J. Seigworth, eds. *The Affect Theory Reader*. Durham, NC: Duke University Press, 2010.

Gunning, Tom. "Heard over the Phone: *The Lonely Villa* and the de Lorde Tradition of the Terrors of Technology." *Screen* 32, no. 2 (1991): 184–96.

Gunning, Tom. "Phantom Images and Modern Manifestations: Spirit Photography, Magic Theater, Trick Films, and Photography's Uncanny." In *Fugitive Images: From Photography to Video*, edited by Patrice Petro, 42–71. Bloomington: Indiana University Press, 1995.

Gunning, Tom. Review of *Photography and Spirit*, by John Harvey. *Magic, Ritual, and Witchcraft* 5, no. 1 (2010): 127–29.

Gunning, Tom. "To Scan a Ghost: The Ontology of Mediated Vision." *Grey Room* 26 (Winter 2007): 94–127.

Gunning, Tom. "Uncanny Reflections, Modern Illusions: Sighting the Modern Optical Uncanny." In *Uncanny Modernity: Cultural Theories, Modern Anxieties*, edited by Jo Collins and John Jervis, 68–90. London: Palgrave, 2008.

Halberstam, Jack. *Female Masculinity*. Durham, NC: Duke University Press, 1998.

Hall, Stuart. "Reconstruction Work: Images of Post-War Black Settlement." In *Family Snaps: The Meanings of Domestic Photography*, edited by Jo Spence and Patricia Holland, 152–64. London: Virago, 1991.

Hall, Stuart, Dorothy Hobson, Andrew Lowe, and Paul Willis, eds. *Culture, Media, Language: Working Papers in Cultural Studies, 1972–79*. London: Routledge, 2003.

Han, Benjamin, M. *Beyond the Black and White TV: Asian and Latin American Spectacle in Cold War America*. New Brunswick, NJ: Rutgers University Press, 2020.

Hand, Martin. *Ubiquitous Photography*. Cambridge: Polity, 2012.

Hartman, Saidiya. "Venus in Two Acts." *Small Axe* 12, no. 2 (2008): 1–14.

Hartman, Saidiya. *Wayward Lives, Beautiful Experiments: Intimate Histories of Riotous Black Girls, Troublesome Women, and Queer Radicals*. New York: Norton, 2019.

Harvey, John. *Photography and Spirit*. London: Reaktion, 2007.

Heins, Marjorie. *Not in Front of the Children: "Indecency," Censorship, and the Innocence of Youth*. New Brunswick, NJ: Rutgers University Press, 2007.

Heitner, Devorah. *Black Power TV*. Durham, NC: Duke University Press, 2013.

Hertzberg, Robert. *Handy Man's TV Repair and Maintenance*. New York: Fawcett, 1955.

Higginbotham, Evelyn Brooks. *Righteous Discontent: The Women's Movement in the Black Baptist Church, 1880–1920*. Cambridge, MA: Harvard University Press, 1993.

Highmore, Ben. *The Everyday Life Reader*. London: Routledge, 2002.

Hilderbrand, Lucas. *Inherent Vice: Bootleg Histories of Video Tape and Copyright*. Durham, NC: Duke University Press, 2009.

Hillis, Ken, and Michael Petit with Nathan Scott Epley, eds. *Everyday eBay: Culture, Collecting, and Desire*. New York: Routledge, 2006.

Hirsch, Marianne, ed. *The Familial Gaze*. Hanover, NH: University Press of New England, 1999.

Hirsch, Marianne. *Family Frames: Photography, Narrative, and Postmemory*. Cambridge, MA: Harvard University Press, 2012.

Hirsch, Marianne. "Introduction: Familial Looking." In *The Familial Gaze*, edited by Marianne Hirsch, xi–xxv. Hanover, NH: University Press of New England, 1999.

Hobson, Dorothy. *Soap Opera*. Cambridge: Polity, 2003.

Holdsworth, Amy. *On Living with Television*. Durham, NC: Duke University Press, 2021.

Holdsworth, Amy. *Television, Memory and Nostalgia*. London: Palgrave Macmillan, 2011.

Holdsworth, Amy, and Karen Lury, "Growing Up and Growing Old with Television: Peripheral Viewers and the Centrality of Care." *Screen* 57, no. 2 (2016): 184–96.

hooks, bell. "In Our Glory: Photography and Black Life." In *Art on My Mind: Visual Politics*, 54–64. New York: New Press, 1995.

Hopkins, Fleur. "Albert Robida's Visions of Future Time: The Magic Lantern Turned into a Magic Mirror." *Magic Lantern Gazette* 28, no. 1 (2016): 3–19.

Horak, Laura. *Girls Will Be Boys: Cross-Dressed Women, Lesbians, and American Cinema, 1908–1934*. New Brunswick, NJ: Rutgers University Press, 2016. Kindle.

Hoskins, Andrew, ed. *Digital Memory Studies: Media Pasts in Transition*. New York: Routledge, 2018. Kindle.

Hoskins, Andrew. "Memory of the Multitude: The End of Collective Memory." In *Digital Memory Studies: Media Pasts in Transition*, edited by Andrew Hoskins, loc. 86 of 313. New York: Routledge, 2018. Kindle.

Huhtamo, Erkki. "Elements of Screenology: Toward an Archaeology of the Screen." *ICONICS: International Studies of the Modern Image* 7 (2004): 31–82.

Huizinga, Johan. *Homo Ludens: A Study of the Play-Element in Culture*. 1949. Reprint, Kettering, OH: Angelica, 2016.

Hurm, Gerd, Anke Reitz, and Shamoon Zamir, eds. *The Family of Man Revisited: Photography in a Global Age*. London: I. B. Tauris, 2017.

Iversen, Margaret. "Following Pieces: On Performative Photography." In *Photography Theory*, edited by James Elkins, loc. 93 of 470. New York: Routledge, 2007. Kindle.

Jenkins, Henry. *Convergence Culture: Where Old and New Media Collide*. New York: New York University Press, 2006.

Jenkins, Henry. *Textual Poachers: Television Fans and Participatory Culture*. New York: Routledge, 1992.

Johnson, David. *Buying Gay: How Physique Entrepreneurs Sparked a Movement*. New York: Columbia University Press, 2021.

Joyrich, Lynne. "All That Television Allows: TV Melodrama, Postmodernism, and Consumer Culture." In *Private Screenings: Television and the Female Consumer*, edited by Lynn Spigel and Denise Mann, 227–52. Minneapolis: University of Minnesota Press, 1992.

Joyrich, Lynne. "Epistemology of the Console." *Critical Inquiry* 27, no. 3 (2001): 439–67.

Joyrich, Lynne. "Queer Television Studies: Currents, Flows, and (Main) Streams." *Cinema Journal* 53, no. 2 (2014): 133–39.

Jurgenson, Nathan. *The Social Photo: On Photography and Social Media*. London: Verso, 2019.

Kavka, Misha. *Reality Television, Affect, and Intimacy: Reality Matters*. London: Palgrave Macmillan, 2008.

Keats, John. *The Crack in the Picture Window*. New York: Houghton Mifflin Harcourt, 1956.

Keightley, Keir. "'Turn It Down!' She Shrieked: Gender, Domestic Space, and High Fidelity." *Popular Music* 15, no. 2 (1996): 149–77.

Kennedy, Robert Woods. *The House and the Art of Its Design*. Huntington, NY: Krieger, 1953.

Kim, L. S. "'Serving' American Orientalism: Negotiating Identities in *The Courtship of Eddie's Father*." *Journal of Film and Video* 56, no. 4 (2004): 21–33.

Kinsey, Alfred C., Wardell B. Pomeroy, Clyde E. Martin, and Paul H. Gebhard. *Sexual Behavior in the Human Female*. 1953. Reprint, Bloomington: Indiana University Press, 1998.

Kittler, Friedrich. *Discourse Networks: 1800/1900*. Translated by Michael Metteer, with Chris Cullens. Stanford, CA: Stanford University Press, 1992.

Kompare, Derek. *Rerun Nation: How Repeats Invented American Television*. New York: Routledge, 2004.

Kuhn, Annette. *Family Secrets: Acts of Memory and Imagination*. London: Verso, 1995.

Kumar, Shanti. *Gandhi Meets Primetime: Globalization and Nationalism in Indian Television*. Urbana: University of Illinois Press, 2006.

Kurpaska, Anna. "Nostalgia and Retro-Femininity in Self-Presentations of 50+ Women on Flickr." *Photography and Culture* 9, no. 2 (2016): 135–49.

Landay, Lori. "Millions 'Love Lucy': Commodification and the Lucy Phenomenon." *NWSA Journal* 11, no. 2 (1999): 25–47.

Landsberg, Alison. *Prosthetic Memory: The Transformation of American Remembrance in the Age of Mass Culture*. New York: Columbia University Press, 2004.

Larsen, Jonas, and Mette Sandbye, eds. *Digital Snapshots: The New Face of Photography*. London: I. B. Tauris, 2014.

Latour, Bruno. *Reassembling the Social: An Introduction to Actor-Network Theory*. London: Oxford University Press, 2005.

Lavin, Maude. "TV Design." In *From Receiver to Remote Control: The TV Set*, edited by Matthew Geller and Reese Williams, 86–87. New York: New Museum of Contemporary Art, 1990. Exhibition catalog.

Leal, Ondina Fachel. "Popular Taste and Erudite Repertoire: The Place and Space of TV in Brazil." *Cultural Studies* 4, no. 1 (1990): 19–29.

Leaver, Tama, Tim Highfield, and Crystal Abidin, eds. *Instagram: Visual Social Media Cultures*. Cambridge: Polity, 2020.

Lefebvre, Henri. *Critique of Everyday Life*. Vol. 1, *Introduction*. Translated by John Moore. 1947. Reprint, London: Verso, 2008.

Lefebvre, Henri. *Critique of Everyday Life*. Vol. 2, *Foundations for a Sociology of the Everyday*. Translated by John Moore. 1961. Reprint, London: Verso, 2008.

Lefebvre, Henri. *The Production of Space*. Translated by Donald Nicholson-Smith. 1974. Reprint, London: Blackwell, 1991.

Leslie, Esther, ed. and trans. *Walter Benjamin: On Photography*. Glasgow: Reaktion, 2015. Kindle.

Levine, Elana. *Her Stories: Daytime Soap Opera and US Television History*. Durham, NC: Duke University Press, 2020.

Lin, Tan. *Insomnia and the Aunt*. Chicago: Kenning Editions, 2011.

Lipsitz, George. *The Possessive Investment in Whiteness: How White People Profit from Identity Politics*. Philadelphia: Temple University Press, 2006.

Lister, Martin, ed. *The Photographic Image in Digital Culture*. 2nd ed. London: Comedia, 2014.

Lull, James. *Inside Family Viewing: Ethnographic Research on Television*. London: Routledge, 1999.

Mankekar, Purnima. *Screening Culture, Viewing Politics: An Ethnography of Television, Womanhood, and Nation in Postcolonial India*. Durham, NC: Duke University Press, 1999.

Mann, Denise. "The Spectacularization of Everyday Life: Recycling Hollywood Stars and Fans in Early Variety Shows." In *Private Screenings: Television and the Female Consumer*, edited by Lynn Spigel and Denise Mann, 41–70. Minneapolis: University of Minnesota Press, 1992.

Manovich, Lev. *Instagram and Contemporary Image*. Self-published, PDF, 2017. http://manovich.net/index.php/projects/instagram-and-contemporary-image.

Markham, Annette, "The Dramaturgy of Digital Experience." In *The Drama of Social Life: A Dramaturgical Handbook*, edited by Charles Edgley, 279–94. Farnham, UK: Ashgate, 2013.

Martingnette, Charles, and Louis K. Meisel. *The Great American Pinup*. Los Angeles: Taschen, 2011.

Marvin, Carolyn. *When Old Technologies Were New: Thinking about Electric Technologies in the Late Nineteenth Century*. Oxford: Oxford University Press, 1988.

Mason, Bernard S., and Elmer D. Mitchell. *Party Games for All: Social Mixers, Games and Contests, Stunts and Tricks*. New York: Barnes and Noble, 1946.

Mason, Petra, ed. *Bunny Yeager's Darkroom: Pinup Photography's Golden Era*. New York: Rizzoli, 2012.

Masters, William H., and Virginia E. Johnson. *Human Sexual Response*. New York: Bantam, 1996.

Mauk, Maureen. "Politics Is Everybody's Business: Resurrecting Faye Emerson, America's Forgotten First Lady of Television." *Journal of Cinema and Media Studies* 59, no 4 (2020): 129–52.

McCarthy, Anna. *Ambient Television: Visual Culture and Public Space*. Durham, NC: Duke University Press, 2001.

McCarthy, Anna. "*Ellen*: Making Queer Television History." GLQ 7, no. 4 (2001): 593–620.

McCarthy, Anna. "From Screen to Site: Television's Material Culture, and Its Place." *October* 98 (Fall 2001): 93–111.

McDonald, J. Fred. *Blacks and White TV: African Americans in Television since 1948*. Chicago: Nelson-Hall, 1992.

McDonough, E. C. "Television and the Family." *Sociology and Social Research* 40, no. 4 (1956): 117–19.

McDowell, Felice. "'I Know I Am Posing' . . . Feeling the Post in Postwar Fashion Modeling." *Fashion Theory* 21, no. 2 (2017): 157–73.

Meyerowitz, Joanne. "Women, Cheesecake, and Borderline Material: Responses to Girlie Pictures in the Mid-Twentieth Century U.S." *Journal of Women's History* 8, no. 3 (1996): 9–35.

Miller, Daniel. *The Comfort of Things*. Cambridge: Polity, 2008.

Miller, Daniel. *Stuff*. Cambridge: Polity, 2010.

Miller, Quinlan. *Camp TV: Queer Sitcom History*. Durham, NC: Duke University Press, 2019.

Minow, Newton. "The Vast Wasteland." Address to the Thirty-ninth Annual Convention of the National Association of Broadcasters, Washington, DC, May 9, 1961. In *Equal Time: The Private Broadcaster and the Public Interest*, 45–69. New York: Atheneum, 1964.

Modleski, Tania. "The Rhythms of Reception: Daytime Television and Women's Work." In *Regarding Television*, edited by E. Ann Kaplan, 67–75. Los Angeles: American Film Institute, 1983.

Moores, Shaun. *Satellite Television and Everyday Life*. Luton: University of Luton Press, 1997.

Moran, James M. *There's No Place Like Home Video*. Minneapolis: University of Minnesota Press, 2002.

Morley, David. *Family Television: Cultural Power and Domestic Leisure*. London: Routledge, 1985.

Moseley, Rachel. "Respectability Sewn Up: Dressmaking and Film Star Style in the Fifties and Sixties." *European Journal of Cultural Studies* 4, no. 4 (2001): 473–90.

Mulvin, Dylan, and Jonathan Sterne. "Scenes from an Imaginary Country: Test Images and the American Color Television Standard." *Television and New Media* 17, no. 1 (2016): 21–43.

Murray, Susan. *Bright Signals: A History of Color TV*. Durham, NC: Duke University Press, 2018.

Murray, Susan. "New Media and Vernacular Photography: Revisiting Flickr." In *The Photographic Image in Digital Culture*, edited by Martin Lister, loc. 4391 of 7330. 2nd ed. London: Comedia, 2014. Kindle.

Needham, Gary. "Scheduling Normativity: Television, the Family, and Queer Temporality." In *Queer TV: Theories, Histories, Politics*, edited by Glyn Davis and Gary Needham, 143–58. New York: Routledge, 2009.

Nelson, George, and Henry Wright, *Tomorrow's House: How to Plan Your Post-War Home Now*. New York: Simon and Schuster, 1945.

Neuhaus, Jessamyn. "The Importance of Being Orgasmic: Sexuality, Gender, and Marital Sex Manuals in the United States, 1920–1963." *Journal of the History of Sexuality* 10, no, 4 (2000): 447–73.

Newbold, Kate. "'History as It's Made': The Popular Practice of TV Photography in the Postwar Era." *Velvet Light Trap*, no. 71 (2013): 59–69.

Newman, Michael. *Atari Age: The Emergence of Video Games in America*. Cambridge, MA: MIT Press, 2018.

Nishikawa, Kinohi. "Race, Respectability, and the Short Life of *Duke* Magazine." *Book History* 15: 152–82.

Noriega, Chon. *Shot in America: Television, the State, and the Rise of Chicano Cinema*. Minneapolis: University of Minnesota Press, 2000.

Olin, Margaret. *Touching Photographs*. Chicago: University of Chicago Press, 2012.

Olofsson, Jennie. "Revisiting the TV Object: On the Site-Specific Location and Objecthood of Swedish Television during Its Inception." *Television and New Media* 20, no. 10 (2012): 1–6.

O'Sullivan, Tim. "Television Memories and Cultures of Viewing, 1950–65." In *Popular Television in Britain: Studies in Cultural History*, edited by John Corner, 159–81. London: BFI, 1991.

Ouellette, Laurie. *Lifestyle TV*. New York: Routledge, 2016.

Ouellette, Laurie. "Will the Revolution Be Televised? Camcorders, Activism, and Alternative Television in the 1990s." In *Transmission 2*, edited by Peter d'Agostino and David Rafler, 165–87. Thousand Oaks, CA: Sage, 1990.

Parikka, Jussi. *What Is Media Archaeology?* Cambridge: Polity, 2012.

Parks, Lisa. "Cracking Open the Set: Television Repair and Tinkering with Gender." *Television and New Media* 1, no. 3 (2000): 257–78.

Pascucci, Ernest. "Intimate Televisions." In *Architecture of the Everyday*, edited by Steven Harris and Deborah Berke, 39–54. Princeton, NJ: Princeton Architectural Press, 1997.

Penati, Cecilia. "'Remembering Our First TV Set': Personal Memories as a Source for Television Audience History." *View* 2, no. 3 (2013): 4–12. https://www.viewjournal.eu/16/volume/2/issue/3/.

Perich, Shannon. *The Changing Face of Portrait Photography: From Daguerreotype to Digital*. Washington, DC: Smithsonian Books, 2011.

Perlman, Allison. *Public Interests: Media Advocacy and Struggles Over U.S. Television*. New Brunswick, NJ: Rutgers University Press, 2016.

Perry, Joe. "Healthy for Family Life: Television, Masculinity, and Domestic Modernity during West Germany's Miracle Years." *German History* 24, no. 4 (2007): 560–95.

Phurksachart, Melissa. "The Asian American Next Door: Enfiguring the Model Minority on the Domestic Melodrama." *Amerasia Journal* 42, no. 2 (2016): 96–117.

Pinney, Christopher. *Camera Indica: The Social Life of Indian Photographs*. Chicago: University of Chicago Press, 1998.

The Practical Encyclopedia of Good Decorating and Home Improvement. Vol. 3. New York: Greystone, 1970.

Preciado, Paul. *Pornotopia: An Essay on Playboy's Architecture and Biopolitics*. Brooklyn, NY: Zone, 2014.

Pringle, Patricia. "Scampering Sofas and 'Skuttling' Tables: The Entertaining Interior." *Interiors* 1, no. 3 (2010): 219–43

Riesman, David. *The Lonely Crowd*. New Haven, CT: Yale University Press, 1950.

Rivero, Yeidy. *Broadcasting Modernity: Cuban Commercial Television, 1950–60*. Durham, NC: Duke University Press, 2015.

Robertson [Wojcik], Pamela. *Guilty Pleasures: Feminist Camp from Mae West to Madonna*. Durham, NC: Duke University Press, 1996.

Rooks, Noliwe. *Ladies' Pages: African American Women's Magazines and the Culture That Made Them*. New Brunswick, NJ: Rutgers University Press, 2004.

Rose, Gillian. *Doing Family Photography: The Domestic, the Public, and the Politics of Sentiment*. Farnham, UK: Ashgate, 2010.

Rose, Gillian. "Family Photographs and Domestic Spacings: A Case Study." *Transactions of the Institute of British Geographers*, n.s., 28, no. 1 (2003): 5–18.

Roth-Ey, Kristin. "Finding a Home for Television in the USSR, 1950–1970." *Slavic Review* 66, no. 2 (2007): 278–306.

Sanison, G. H. *How to Behave and How to Amuse: A Handy Manual of Etiquette and Parlor Games*. New York: Christian Herald, 1895.

Sauvin, Thomas, and Erik Kessels, eds. *Me TV*. Self-published, 2014. http:// kesselskramerpublishing.com/catalogue/me-tv/.

Scannell, Paddy. *Radio, Television, and Modern Life*. London: Wiley Blackwell, 1996.

Scannell, Paddy. *Television and the Meaning of Live: An Enquiry into the Human Situation*. Cambridge: Polity, 2014.

Schaefer, Eric. *Bold! Daring! Shocking! True! A History of Exploitation Films, 1919–1959*. Durham, NC: Duke University Press, 1999.

Sconce, Jeffrey. *Haunted Media: Electronic Presence from Telegraphy to Television*. Durham, NC: Duke University Press, 2000.

Sekula, Allan. "The Traffic in Photographs." *Art Journal* 41, no. 1 (1981): 15–25.

Silverstone, Roger. *Television and Everyday Life*. London: Taylor and Francis, 1994.

Slack, Jennifer Daryl. "The Theory and Method of Articulation in Cultural Studies: First Encounters." In *Critical Dialogues in Cultural Studies*, edited by David Morley and Kuan-Hsing Chen, 112–30. London: Routledge, 1996.

Smith, Kathryn M. "Domesticating Television: Changing Attitudes in Postwar Britain." *Interiors* 3, no. 1–2 (2012): 23–42.

Smith, Shawn Michelle. *Photography on the Color Line: W. E. B. Du Bois, Race, and Visual Culture*. Durham, NC: Duke University Press, 2004.

Sontag, Susan. "Notes on 'Camp.'" In *Against Interpretation and Other Essays*, 275–92. 1964. Reprint, New York: Farrar, Straus and Giroux, 2001.

Sontag, Susan. *On Photography*. New York: Farrar, Straus and Giroux, 1973. Kindle.

Spark, Penny. *As Long as It's Pink: The Sexual Politics of Taste*. London: Pandora, 1995.

Spence, Jo, and Patricia Holland, eds. *Family Snaps: The Meanings of Domestic Photography*. London: Virago, 1991.

Spigel, Lynn. "From the Dark Ages to the Golden Age: Women's Memories and Television Reruns." *Screen* 36, no. 1 (1995): 16–33.

Spigel, Lynn. "Made-for-Broadcast Cities." In *The Studio Book*, edited by Brian Jacobson, 213–41. Berkeley: University of California Press, 2020.

Spigel, Lynn. *Make Room for TV: Television and the Family Ideal in Postwar America*. Chicago: University of Chicago Press, 1992.

Spigel, Lynn. "Object Lessons for the Media Home: From Storagewall to Invisible Design." *Public Culture* 24, no. 3 (2012): 535–76.

Spigel, Lynn. "Our Television Heritage: Television, the Archive, and the Reasons for Preservation." In *A Companion to Television*, edited by Janet Wasko, 67–102. London: Blackwell, 2005.

Spigel, Lynn. "Portable TV: Studies in Domestic Space Travel." In *Welcome to the Dreamhouse: Popular Media and Postwar Suburbs*, 60–103. Durham, NC: Duke University Press, 2001.

Spigel, Lynn, and Denise Mann, eds. *Private Screenings: Television and the Female Consumer*. Minneapolis: University of Minnesota Press, 1992.

Stacey, Jackie. *Star Gazing: Hollywood Cinema and Female Spectatorship*. London: Routledge, 1994.

Stadel, Luke. "Cable, Pornography, and the Reinvention of Television, 1982–89." *Cinema Journal* 53, no. 3 (2014): 52–75.

Stamp, Shelley. *Movie-Struck Girls: Women and Motion Picture Culture after the Nickelodeon*. Princeton, NJ: Princeton University Press, 2000.

Steedman, Carolyn. "Intimacy in Research: Accounting for It." *History of the Human Sciences* 21, no. 4 (2008): 17–33.

Steichen, Edward. *The Family of Man*. 1955. Reprint, New York: Museum of Modern Art, 2002.

Stewart, Kathleen. *Ordinary Affects*. Durham, NC: Duke University Press, 2007. Kindle.

Stewart, Susan. *On Longing: Narratives of the Miniature, the Gigantic, the Souvenir, the Collection*. Durham, NC: Duke University Press, 1993.

Stone, Geoffrey R. *Sex and the Constitution: Sex, Religion, and Law from America's Origins to the Twenty-First Century*. New York: Norton, 2017.

Strauven, Wanda. "Early Cinema's Touch(able) Screens: From Uncle Josh to Ali Barbouyou." *NECSUS*, Autumn 2012, 1–48.

Strub, Whitney. *Obscenity Rules: "Roth v. United States" and the Long Struggle over Sexual Expression*. Lawrence: University of Kansas Press, 2013.

Sussman, Aaron. *The Amateur Photographer's Handbook*. 3rd ed. New York: Crowell, 1948.

Swaim, Ginalie. "'Our Ticket to 1950s Culture': Accounts of Early Television in Our Readers' Households." *Palimpsest* 75, no. 4 (1994): 150–61.

Swaim, Ginalie. "When Television Entered the Iowa Household." *Palimpsest* 75, no. 2 (Summer 1994): 50–66.

Tahmahkera, Dustin. *Tribal Television: Viewing Native People in Sitcoms*. Chapel Hill: University of North Carolina Press, 2014.

Taylor, Diana. *The Archive and the Repertoire: Performing Cultural Memory in the Americas*. Durham, NC: Duke University Press, 2003.

Taylor, Timothy D. *Strange Sounds: Music, Technology and Culture*. New York: Routledge, 2001.

Thompson, Ethan. "The Parodic Sensibility and the Sophisticated Gaze: Masculinity and Taste in Playboy's *Penthouse*." *Television and New Media* 9, no. 4 (Fall, 2008): 284–304.

Thompson, Ethan, Jeffrey Jones, and Lucas Hatlen, eds. *Television History, the Peabody Archive, and Cultural Memory.* Athens: University of Georgia Press, 2019.

Thrift, Nigel. "Understanding the Material Aspects of Glamour." In *The Affect Theory Reader,* edited by Melissa Gregg and Gregory J. Seigworth, 297 of 402. Durham, NC: Duke University Press, 2010. Kindle.

Tichi, Cecelia. *Electronic Hearth: Creating an American Television Culture.* New York: Oxford University Press, 1991.

Tinkler, Penny. "'Picture Me as a Young Woman': Researching Girls' Photo Collections from the 1950s and 1960s." *Photography and Culture* 3, no. 3 (2010): 261–81.

Torres, Sasha. *Black, White, and in Color: Television and Black Civil Rights.* Princeton, NJ: Princeton University Press, 2003.

Turner, Fred. *The Democratic Surround: Multimedia and American Liberalism from World War II to the Psychedelic Sixties.* Chicago: University of Chicago Press, 2015.

Tyler May, Elaine. *Homeward Bound: American Families in the Cold War Era.* New York: Basic Books, 1988.

Ureta, Sebastián. "'There Is One in Every Home': Finding the Place of Television in New Homes among a Low-Income Population in Santiago, Chile." *International Journal of Cultural Studies,* 11, no. 4 (2008): 477–97.

Uricchio, William. "Television's First 75 Years: The Interpretive Flexibility of a Medium in Transition." In *The Oxford Handbook of Film and Media Studies,* edited by Robert Kolker, 286–305. Oxford: Oxford University Press, 2008.

Vanderbilt, Amy. *The Complete Book of Etiquette.* Garden City, NY: Doubleday, 1957.

VanderBurgh, Jennifer. "Grounding TV's Material Heritage: Place-Based Projects That Value or Vilify Amateur Videocassette Recordings of Television." *View* 8, no, 15 (2019): 1–20.

van Dijck, José. *The Culture of Connectivity: A Critical History of Social Media.* New York: Oxford University Press, 2013.

van Dijck, José. *Mediated Memories in the Digital Age.* Stanford, CA: Stanford University Press, 2007.

Varela, Mirta. *La televisión criolla: Desde sus inicios hasta la llegada del hombre a la Luna, 1951–1969.* Buenos Aires: EDHASA, 2005.

Veblen, Thorstein. *Theory of the Leisure Class.* 1899. Reprint, Oxford: Oxford University Press, 2007.

Vestberg, Nina Lager. "The Photographic Image in Digital Archives." In *The Photographic Image in Digital Culture,* 2nd ed., edited by Martin Lister, loc. 3304 of 7330. London: Comedia, 2014. Kindle.

Villarejo, Amy. *Ethereal Queer: Television, Historicity, Desire.* Durham, NC: Duke University Press, 2014.

Wald, Gayle. *It's Been Beautiful: Soul! and Black Power Television.* Durham, NC: Duke University Press, 2015.

Warner, Helen. *Fashion on Television: Identity and Celebrity Culture*. London: Bloomsbury, 2014.

Waugh, Thomas. "Foreword: On First Looking into Chapman's Homos." In *Comin' at Ya!: The Homoerotic 3-D Photographs of Denny Denfield*, edited by David Chapman and Thomas Waugh, 7–22. Vancouver: Arsenal Pulp Press, 2007.

Waugh, Thomas. *Hard to Imagine: Gay Male Eroticism in Photography and Film from Their Beginnings to Stonewall*. New York: Columbia University Press, 1996.

Weber, Anne-Katrin. "Television before TV: A Transnational History of an Experimental Medium on Display, 1928–39." PhD diss., University of Lausanne, 2015.

Weber, Brenda R. *Makeover TV: Selfhood, Citizenship, and Celebrity*. Durham, NC: Duke University Press, 2009.

Weber, Samuel. "Television Set and Screen." In *Mass Mediauras: Form, Technics, Media*, 108–28. Stanford, CA: Stanford University Press, 1996.

West, Amy. "Reality Television and the Power of Dirt." *Screen* 52, no. 1 (2011): 63–77.

West, Nancy. *Kodak through the Lens of Nostalgia*. Charlottesville: University Press of Virginia, 2000.

Westbrook, Robert. "'I Want a Girl Just Like the Girl That Married Harry James': American Women and the Problem of Political Obligation in World War II." *American Quarterly* 2, no. 3 (1990): 587–614.

Wheatley, Helen. *Spectacular Television: Exploring Televisual Pleasure*. London: I. B. Tauris, 2016.

White, Michele. *Buy It Now: Lessons from eBay*. Durham, NC: Duke University Press, 2012.

White, Michele. "'My Queer eBay': 'Gay Interest' Photographs and the Visual Culture of Buying." In *Everyday eBay: Culture, Collecting, and Desire*, edited by Ken Hillis and Michael Petit with Nathan Scott Epley, 245–67. New York: Routledge, 2006.

White, Mimi. "'A House Divided.'" *European Journal of Cultural Studies* 20, no. 5 (2017): 575–91.

Whyte, William H., Jr. *The Organization Man*. New York: Simon and Schuster, 1956.

Williams, Linda. *Hard Core: Power, Pleasure, and the Frenzy of the Visible*. Berkeley: University of California Press, 1999.

Williams, Mark. "Strains of Orientalism in Early Los Angeles Television." In *Living Color: Race and Television in the United States*, edited by Sasha Torres, 12–34. Durham, NC: Duke University Press, 1998.

Williams, Megan E. "The 'Crisis' Cover Girl: Lena Horne, the NAACP, and Representations of African American Femininity, 1941–1945." *American Periodicals* 16, no. 2 (2006): 200–218.

Williams, Megan E. "'Meet the Real Lena Horne': Representations of Lena Horne in 'Ebony' Magazine." *Journal of American Studies* 43, no. 1 (2009): 117–30.

Williams, Raymond. "Base and Superstructure in Marxist Cultural Theory." In *Problems in Materialism and Culture*, 31–49. London: Verso, 1980.

Williams, Raymond. *Marxism and Literature*. New York: Oxford University Press, 1977.

Williams, Raymond. *Problems in Materialism and Culture*. New York: Verso, 1980.

Williams, Raymond. *Television: Technology and Cultural Form*. New York: Schocken, 1975.

Willis, Deborah, ed. *Picturing Us: African American Identity in Photography*. New York: New Press, 1994.

Willis, Deborah. "A Search for Self: The Photograph in Black Family Life." In *The Familial Gaze*, edited by Marianne Hirsch, 107–23. Hanover, NH: University Press of New England, 1999.

Wilson, Elizabeth. *Adorned in Dreams: Fashion and Modernity*. 1985. Reprint, London: I. B. Tauris, 2003.

Wilson, Julie, and Emily Chivers Yochim. "Pinning Happiness: Affect, Social Media, and the Work of Mothers." In *Cupcakes, Pinterest, and Ladyporn: Feminized Popular Culture in the Early Twenty-First Century*, edited by Elana Levine, loc. 5065–5433 of 7073. Urbana: University of Illinois Press, 2015. Kindle.

Wissinger, Elizabeth. *This Year's Model: Fashion, Media, and the Making of Glamour*. New York: New York University Press, 2015.

Wojcik, Pamela Robertson. *The Apartment Plot: Urban Living in American Film and Popular Culture, 1945–1975*. Durham, NC: Duke University Press, 2010.

Wright, Ellen. "Having Her Cheesecake and Eating It: Performance, Professionalism, and the Politics of the Gaze in the Pin-Up Self-Portraiture and Celebrity of Bunny Yeager." *Feminist Media Histories* 2, no. 4 (2016): 116–42.

Yeager, Bunny. *Bunny's Honeys: Bunny Yeager, Queen of Pinup Photography*. New York: Taschen, 1995.

Yeager, Bunny. *Bunny Yeager's Art of Glamour Photography*. New York: American Photographic, 1962.

Yeager, Bunny. *Photographing the Female Figure*. New York: Fawcett, 1957.

Yoshimi, Shunya. "'Made in Japan': The Cultural Politics of Home Electrification in Postwar Japan." *Media, Culture and Society* 21, no. 2 (1999): 149–71.

Zimmermann, Patricia. "Hollywood, Home Movies, and Common Sense: Amateur Film as Aesthetic Dissemination and Social Control, 1950–62." *Cinema Journal* 27, no. 4 (1988): 23–44.

Zimmermann, Patricia. *Reel Families: A Social History of Amateur Film*. Bloomington: Indiana University Press, 1995.

INDEX

Page locators in italics indicate figures

fashion: African American, 142–44; designed for TV viewing, 121–24; history and theory, 131–32, 139–142, 146–47, 165; magazines, 87, 131, 136; midcentury women's, 132; models, 131–32, 133, 134, 136, 137, 142, 144, 158, 167, 170; photography, 131, 133; tie-ins with Hollywood industry, 137; western wear, 163–64, 166, 167. See also everyday glamour; glamour; glamour labor
Federation of Women's Clubs, 184, 279n19
Felski, Rita, 148, 150
Feminine Mystique, The (Friedan), 157, 203, 217
feminism, second-wave, 147, 184, 203, 217–18
fireplaces, as background for poses, 76–77
Flickr, 224–28, 232–33, 246; FlickrPro, 249
Foote, Nelson, 74–75
Foucault, Michel, 82, 248, 270n12
found objects/photos, 14, 16, 171, 223, 226, 262
Freedman, Estelle, 216–17
Freud, Sigmund, 104, 118, 248, 261, 273n50
Friedan, Betty, 157–58, 203, 217–18
Friedlander, Lee, 58–59, 59, 114, 115, 241, 242

Garvey, Ellen Gruber, 250
gaze: domestic, 55, 123, 148; familial, 8–9
Gazzard, Alison, 259
gender: roles, 4, 6, 8, 10, 34, 36, 49, 94, 118, 131, 139, 142, 205, 206, 220, 231, 257; destabilized by drag, 163; fluid, 165; performance of, 6, 22, 79, 89, 131, 133, 146–47, 163, 168, 171–74, 256
ghosts, TV, 102–4, 114, 116–18, 242, 246
Girard, Sébastien, 171
girlie magazines, 131, 178, 183–84, 191, 202
Gitelman, Lisa, 259, 271n30
glamour, 22, 44, 121–23, 122, 126, 129–31; African American, 142–45, 145; ambivalent values of, 137–38; Asian, on TV 143–44; "antiglamour," 160, 161; Hollywood, 131, 137–45, 140, 141, 145; Latin American, on TV, 143; photography, 137; "world building" dimensions of, 133. See

also dress-up poses; everyday glamour; fashion; glamour labor
"glamour girl," on TV, 129–30
glamour labor, 133–37, 134, 135, 143, 145, 148, 168, 174, 208, 276n50
Goc, Nicola, 44, 269n37
Goffman, Erving, 21, 75–76, 79
Good, Katie Day, 234
Gowland, Peter, 179, 202
Grable, Betty, 183, 206
"grrrl power," 182, 235
Grusin, Richard, 224
Gunning, Tom, 116

Halberstam, Jack, 165
Hall, Stuart, 12, 16
Hand, Martin, 225–26
Hart, Janice, 18, 20
Hartman, Saidiya, 247, 286n58
Haunted Media (Sconce), 116, 118
Hayworth, Rita, 183
Helffrich, Stockton, 129
Hefner, Hugh, 183–84, 191, 193, 279n14
Hepburn, Audrey, 130, 137
heterotopia, 270n12
Hirsch, Marianne, 8–9, 173, 227
hobby art, TV, 10, 21, 97, 104, 105, 106
Holdsworth, Amy, 21, 232, 287n1
Hollywood: star profiles in fanzines, 137–38; stars and women's aspirations, 139; tie-ins with fashion industry, 137; TV production site, 72, 74. See also celebrity photographs
Home (NBC, 1954–57), 129
home movies, 37, 86
home theater, 71, 74, 82–83, 93–97
hooks, bell, 11–12, 13, 145
Horak, Laura, 165
Horne, Lena, 142, 143, 275n40
Hoskins, Andrew, 229
How to Make Good Pictures (Kodak), 29, 56, 116
Hughes, Langston, 12–13

I Love Lucy (CBS, 1951–57), 74, 108, 130; merchandise tie-ins, 137

prop: photographic, 28, 32, 76, 60, 136–37, 163, 166, 183; erotic, in pinups, 185, 186, 194, 196, 202; sitcom, 74; TV set used as, 4, 71, 76, 79, 93, 145, 178

Pugh, Madelyn. *See* Martin, Madelyn

punctum, 7–8, 18, 51, 65, 247, 261–62; "low punctum," 46, 132, 139, 216, 229–30, 257, 260

queer orientation, 48, 76, 161–62

Queer Phenomenology (Ahmed), 48

racism: counter-narratives to, 142–45; Emmett Till murder, 246–49; fashion and movie industry, 142–45; internet, 251; Jim Crow era, 11–13; "Shirley card" tests for color photography, 14; skin tone tests for color TV, 194; television industry, 13, 35–36, 90–93, 143

Radio, Television, and Modern Life (Scannell), 96–97

Radio Television Best (magazine), *176, 177,* 176–78, 179

Reid, Tim, 92

Reiner, Carl, 130

remakes, TV snapshot, 224, 232–46

remediation, 224, 227

residual media, 224, 257–58

respectability politics, 142–43

retro aesthetics, 22, 182, 233–37, 241

retro TV pinups, 235–40, *236–40*

Riggs, Marlon, 249–51

ritual: family, 79, 258; object, 68; national and public, 95, 99; performance, 75; play, 74–75; posing place in the TV setting, 77, 79, 126, 136, 148, 158, 227, 256, 259; snapshots as 6, 19, 87, 100, 150, 256; time, 26

Robert-Houdin, Jean-Eugène, 113

Robida, Albert, 186–88, *187,* 220

Rooks, Noliwe, 142

Rose, Gillian, 9, 69–70

Ryder, Riddim, 242, 245, *245*

Scannell, Paddy, 96–97

Schaefer, Eric, 201

Sconce, Jeffrey, 116, 118

Scott, Grenville Michael, 219

scrapbooking, 233–35, 241; by African Americans, 250–51

screenshots, 5, 21, *96,* 96–100, *100,* 171, *172, 173,* 175

selfies, 4, 224, 259–60

self-reflexive, 71, 73–74, 76, 104–5

Sex and the Single Girl (Brown), 158, 217, 276–77n67

sexuality, 8, 10, 21, 132, 196; censored or sanitized, 132, 182, 218; exoticized, 143; midcentury focus on, 184, 216–18; performance, of, 8, 142–43, 146–44, 166, 185; women's agency and pleasure in, 142, 183, 216–17. *See also* drag and masquerade; pinups; queer orientation

Sherman, Cindy, 173, 235

sitcom, 35, 72–74, *73,* 76, 108, 129, 130, 131, 144, 160, 163, 182, 233, 249, 250, 251, 252

Smith, Shawn Michelle, 14

snapshot photography: cameras, 2–7, 13–14, 274n12; histories and theories of, 5–11, 13–17, 15, 18, 28–29, 66. *See also* family photography; photography

Snapshot Versions of Life (Chalfen), 28–29

Soirées Fantastiques (Robert-Houdin), 113

Sondak, Ruth, 194, 281n41

Sontag, Susan, 102, 169, 228, 272n42

space: as "complex of mobilities," 39, 42; doubling of, 96–98, 105; heterotopic, 82; orientation toward, 21, 48, 116, 161; play, 42, *43;* spatial practices, 42, *43,* 44; "spatial stories," 36

Spark, Penny, 37

Spree (magazine), 183, 196

Stacey, Jackie, 139, 146

Stafford, Marian, *Playboy* TV Playmate, 194–96, *195,* 219

Staley, Joan, *Playboy* TV Playmate, 196, 281n44

Steedman, Carolyn, 261

Steichen, Edward, 11

Stewart, Kathleen, 19

Stewart, Susan, 241